T0343126

BRITISH & COMMONWEALTH FIGHTER AIRCRAFT OF WORLD WAR II

1939–45

BRITISH & COMMONWEALTH FIGHTER AIRCRAFT OF WORLD WAR II 1939–45

EDWARD WARD

amber
BOOKS

First published in 2025

Published by Amber Books Ltd
United House
London N7 9DP
United Kingdom
www.amberbooks.co.uk
Facebook: amberbooks
YouTube: amberbooksltd
Instagram: amberbooksltd
X(Twitter): @amberbooks

ISBN: 978-1-83886-562-7

Editor: Michael Spilling
Designer: Keren Harragan
Picture research: Terry Forshaw

Printed in China

Contents

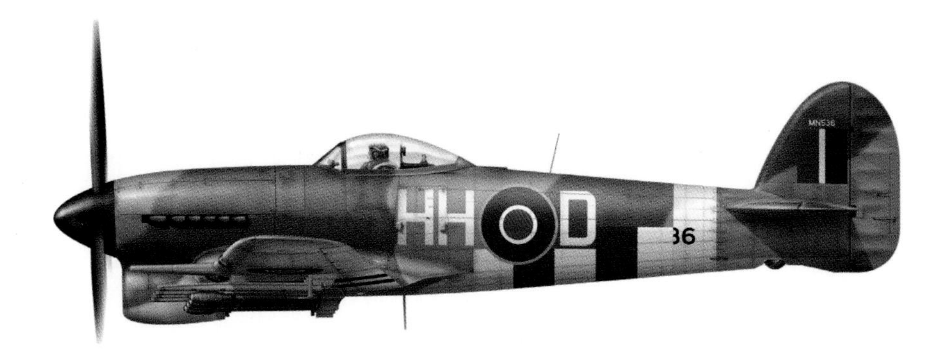

Introduction

Both during and after World War II, the Battle of Britain came to become the defining moment of the British wartime experience, when 'the Few' battled the might of the Luftwaffe and won the world's first decisive battle fought solely in the air. As a result the fighter aircraft, and the Supermarine Spitfire in particular (despite the greater contribution to the battle of the less aesthetically pleasing Hawker Hurricane), continues to hold a unique place in the popular national identity.

The RAF entered World War II in a position of technological if not numerical strength, particularly in the field of fighter design, which it would maintain for the entire conflict. In September 1939 the Hurricane and Spitfire were amongst the finest fighter aircraft in the world, and both were available in considerable numbers. It had been a close run thing however – three quarters of the Hurricanes, and virtually all of the Spitfires available to Fighter Command in 1939 had been delivered in the last 12 months of peace and without the breathing room bought by the Munich agreement of September 1938, the RAF would have been in a far weaker position at the outbreak of war.

From biplane to jet fighter

Nonetheless, the modernisation and expansion plan was far from complete and the RAF was compelled to use the last of its biplane fighters during the initial stages of the conflict. However, the remarkable pace of development of the war years resulted in the same service introducing the Meteor, its first jet fighter, into widespread service before the end of hostilities, coincidentally built by Gloster, the very company responsible for the last British biplane fighter, the Gladiator. Technology, in the form of another British invention, radar, revolutionised night fighting and the larger twin engine fighters

The Gladiator prototype, K5200, differed from production aircraft in having an open cockpit. In this view, the starboard underwing 0.303in (7.7mm) Lewis machine-gun blister may be seen.

These No. 56 Sqn aircraft are seen around the time that the Typhoon was shown to the press for the first time – in April 1943. The nearest pair are from the small batch of Hawker-built Mk IBs; almost all production Typhoons were built by Gloster Aircraft.

developed to carry the first airborne radar sets became the scourge of the night Blitz over London and later of German night fighters over the very heart of the Third Reich. The two most successful night fighters, the Bristol Beaufighter and de Havilland Mosquito, were also both remarkably capable multi-role aircraft and flew by day in a variety of roles, including anti-shipping strikes and ground attack. Curiously, the premier fighter bomber of the latter stages of the war was the Hawker Typhoon, which had not proved an unequivocal success as an interceptor but became a fearsome close support asset.

Naval aviation

In contrast to its land-based counterparts, British naval aviation was in a state of transition at the start of the war. The Fleet Air Arm had been a branch of the RAF formed in 1924 and had arguably been somewhat neglected over the following years as the Air Force's primary focus had centred on land-based aircraft. This all changed in May 1939 when the Fleet Air Arm was placed under direct Admiralty control, and although modern designs such as the Skua and Fulmar were either in service or under development, they were few in number and inferior to their shore-based counterparts. At the outbreak of war, the Royal Navy had a mere 232 frontline aircraft on strength, precious few of which were fighters. Though both the Hurricane and Spitfire were adapted for naval use and widely deployed, neither was an unqualified success as a carrier aircraft. The Navy's fighter requirements relied on the products of the US aircraft industry much more heavily than those of the RAF, culminating in the use of the potent Vought F4U Corsair and Grumman F6F Hellcat in the last two years of the conflict. Eventually British industry produced the superlative Sea Fury, which was on the verge of becoming operational as the war ended.

UF N
UF P
UF W
UF Y
UF D

SINGLE-ENGINE FIGHTERS

The development of British fighter aircraft during World War II was dominated by the Supermarine Spitfire, an aircraft that transcended its function as a weapon of war to become a symbol of the British and Commonwealth war effort. Nonetheless, many other domestically produced and imported single-engined fighters were used by the RAF with varying degrees of success over the course of the conflict. The following aircraft are featured in this chapter:

- Hawker Fury
- Grumman Goblin
- Gloster Gauntlet
- Gloster Gladiator & Sea Gladiator
- Hawker Hurricane
- Supermarine Spitfire
- Boulton Paul Defiant
- Brewster Buffalo
- Bell Airacobra
- Curtiss Mohawk
- Curtiss Tomahawk
- Curtiss Kittyhawk
- Hawker Typhoon
- Hawker Tempest
- North American Mustang
- Republic Thunderbolt
- Commonwealth Boomerang

Hurricane Mk IIBs of 601 Squadron based at Duxford airfield cruise over the farmland of Essex.

Hawker Fury

One of the oldest fighter designs to engage in combat in World War II, the elegant Hawker Fury was the first Royal Air Force (RAF) fighter to exceed 322km/h (200mph) in level flight and remained in limited frontline service in the opening stages of World War II.

The Fury first flew in March 1931, one of the earliest designs to be produced by the prolific Sydney Camm (1893–1966). Popular with peacetime RAF pilots, it was noted for its highly sensitive controls and excellent handling, as well as being terrifically fast for its day and possessing an outstanding climb rate. The economic situation of the early 1930s resulted in only two squadrons being equipped with Furies (as opposed to 10 squadrons of the slower but cheaper Bristol Bulldog). An improved Hawker Fury Mk II was flown in 1936 with a more powerful Kestrel engine but all RAF Furies were withdrawn from frontline use in January 1939, though the aircraft served on for a time as a trainer.

Export success

The Fury enjoyed modest success on the export market with small numbers being sold to Spain, Portugal, Iran and Yugoslavia as well as South Africa and it was with the latter two nations that the aircraft would see active combat service in World War II. South Africa purchased seven Furies in 1935, the first single seat fighters to be acquired by the nation since it received 22 SE.5as in 1920, and subsequently a further 22 Furies were supplied to the South African Air Force (SAAF), the last as late as January 1941. In May 1940 a detachment of SAAF Furies was shipped to Kenya for action in the East African campaign where they undertook army co-operation and ground attack duties as well as airfield defence. Italian aircraft were encountered on several occasions and three Caproni Ca.133s were shot down by Furies though their by now rather pedestrian performance saw several enemy aircraft escape. Returning to South Africa in April 1941, the Fury remained in frontline SAAF service until August 1943.

Balkans war

Yugoslavia acquired 13 Furies during 1936 and 1937 before building a further 40 under licence. All of these featured a more powerful Kestrel engine of 556kW (745hp), a low drag radiator and a cantilever undercarriage with internally sprung wheels. Despite their manifest obsolescence, Furies shot down five enemy aircraft during the invasion of Yugoslavia, including two Bf 109s and two Bf 110s. Although most surviving aircraft were destroyed to prevent them falling into enemy hands, at least two Furies remained airworthy when the country surrendered on 17 April 1941, and these aircraft were later evaluated by Italian pilots.

Hawker Fury Mk I

Weight (maximum take-off): 1583kg (3490lb)
Dimensions: Length 8.15m (26ft 9in), Wingspan 9.14m (30ft), Height 3.1m (10ft 2in)
Powerplant: One 391kW (525hp) Rolls-Royce Kestrel IIS V-12 liquid-cooled piston engine
Maximum speed: 333km/h (207mph)
Range: 408km (305 miles)
Ceiling: 8990m (29,500ft)
Crew: 1
Armament: Two synchronised 7.7mm (0.303in) Vickers machine guns, fixed forward firing in fuselage top decking

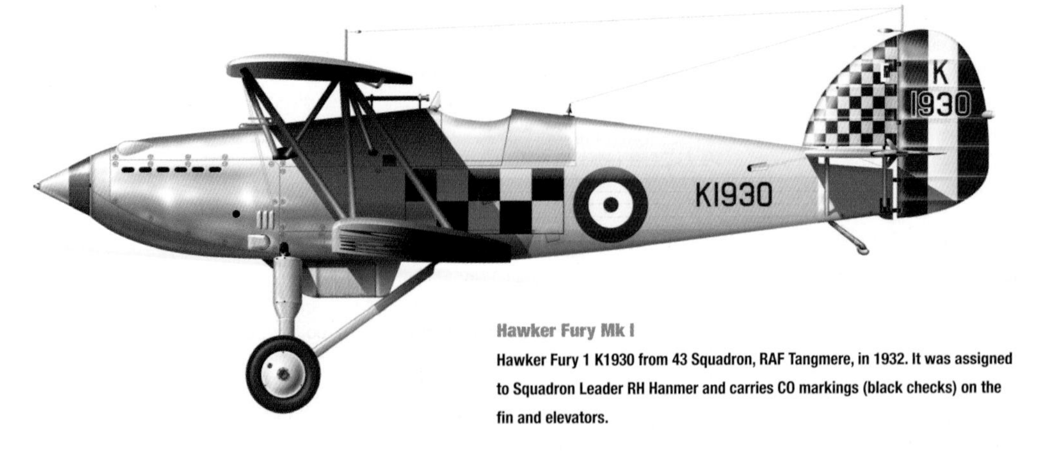

Hawker Fury Mk I

Hawker Fury 1 K1930 from 43 Squadron, RAF Tangmere, in 1932. It was assigned to Squadron Leader RH Hanmer and carries CO markings (black checks) on the fin and elevators.

Grumman Goblin

Grumman's first aircraft design, the two-seat FF was notably fast when it entered service but such was the pace of aeronautical progress in the 1930s that the aircraft was effectively obsolete when it was taken on strength with the Royal Canadian Air Force (RCAF) in 1940.

Grumman Goblin Mk I

Goblin 344 is pictured as it appeared when based at Dartmouth, Nova Scotia in 1941, by which time the aircraft was obsolete. The fact that the Goblin was used in a frontline role at all by this date reflected the severe shortage of modern fighter aircraft in Canada.

Grumman Goblin Mk I

Weight (Maximum take-off): 2256kg (4973lb)

Dimensions: Length: 8m (24ft 10in), Wingspan: 10.6m (34ft 6in), Height: 2.9m (9ft 6in)

Powerplant: One 597kW (800hp) Wright R-1820-F52 Cyclone nine-cylinder air-cooled radial engine

Speed: 560km/h (216mph)

Range: 1014km (630 miles)

Ceiling: 7,255m (23,800ft)

Crew: 2

Armament: Two fixed forward firing 7.62mm (0.3in) Browning machine guns and two flexibly mounted 7.62mm (0.3in) Browning machine guns in rear cockpit

When Grumman, an aircraft component manufacturer, flew their first complete aircraft, the XFF-1, for the first time on 29 December 1931, it was the world's first carrier aircraft with a retractable undercarriage. When fitted with its definitive Wright Cyclone engine, the XFF-1 was capable of 201mph (323km/h), which was faster than any other US Navy fighter. Production aircraft entered service with VF-5B on USS Lexington in June 1933 and the aircraft remained in frontline US service until late 1940.

Canadian production

The Canadian Car and Foundry Company acquired a manufacturing licence for an improved FF-1, designated the G-23, and subsequently built 52 examples. In 1937, 34 of the G-23 were purchased by the Spanish Republican government, thus bypassing the US embargo placed on arms sales to either side during the Spanish Civil War. Referred to as the GE-23 Delfin (Dolphin) by the Spanish Republican Air Force (SRAF), the aircraft was outclassed by opposing fighters though a solitary victory against a Heinkel He 59 became the only recorded kill by a Grumman designed biplane. Eleven GE-23s survived the conflict to serve in the Ejército del Aire Español.

The RCAF had initially rejected the aircraft due to its comparatively slow speed but the outbreak of war resulted in an urgent need to shore up Canadian fighter strength and the G-23s were, at least, immediately available. The RCAF took 15 of the G23s on strength and named them the Goblin I. 'A' Flight of No. 118 RCAF Squadron was equipped with Goblins at Rockcliffe in Ottawa, subsequently becoming No. 118 Fighter Squadron and moving to Dartmouth, Nova Scotia, where the Goblins flew on anti-submarine patrols and maritime reconnaissance. Amazingly, given their obvious obsolescence by this time, the 15 Grumman Goblins represented the sole fighter defence of the east coast of Canada until the aircraft were supplemented by Curtiss Kittyhawks late in 1941 and the last was withdrawn in April 1942.

Gloster Gauntlet

During 1937, the Gauntlet was the most numerous fighter in service with the Royal Air Force (RAF) but by December 1939, the type had disappeared from Fighter Command. Gauntlets served on however in the Middle East and Africa.

Gloster Gauntlet Mk II

Operating with No. 3 Squadron RAAF in November 1940, K7843 wears the standard RAF temperate camouflage scheme.

The SS.18, the prototype of what became the Gauntlet, had flown as early as 1929 but there followed an unusually long development process. This period saw the prototype fitted with six different engines and various different armament fits in response to changing Air Ministry requirements before eventually coalescing into the SS.19B of 1933. This possessed a performance sufficiently good to prompt an order for 24 aircraft, enough to replace the Bristol Bulldogs of one squadron, and the name 'Gauntlet' was selected for the new aircraft.

The first Gauntlets were delivered to No. 19 Squadron in May 1935, becoming immediately popular with aircrew due to the aircraft's excellent handling and stellar performance. The Gloster fighter was 56mph (90km/h) faster than the Bulldog it replaced, and until early 1937 was the fastest aircraft in the RAF. Further orders followed and eventually the Gauntlet would equip 14 UK-based squadrons. The late 1930s were, however, a period of exceptionally rapid development and the Gauntlet was no match for modern monoplane fighters such as the Bf 109. All Gauntlets had been replaced, initially with Gladiators, later with Hurricane and Spitfires, before any could see action in Europe.

East African campaign

Re-equipment of squadrons in the Middle East proceeded with less urgency however, and Gauntlets saw action with several squadrons well into 1940 in British, Australian and South African service. In Sudan, between August and December 1940, No. 430 Flight, an RAF Army Cooperation unit flying a mixture of Gauntlets and Vickers Vincents engaged in ground attack missions during the East African campaign. During an attack on an Italian airfield on 7 September 1941 one of the Gauntlets shot down a Caproni Ca.133 to record the type's only confirmed victory. Later the same year the Royal Australian Air Force's (RAAF) No. 3 Squadron flew a few Gauntlets on close support missions in the opening stages of General Wavell's (1883–1950) first Libyan campaign in the Western Desert. However, despite suffering no losses, the Gauntlets were withdrawn after only four days due to the difficulty of obtaining spares. The Gauntlet also served in action with both the South African Air Force's (SAAF) Nos 1 and 2 Squadron in the East African campaign. The latter squadron still retained three of the elderly biplanes on strength in early 1941, by which time they were the last Gauntlets in frontline service anywhere.

Gloster Gauntlet Mk II

Weight (Maximum take-o ff): 1801kg (3970lb)
Dimensions: Length 8.05m (26ft 5in), Wingspan 10m (32ft 10in), Height 3.12m (10ft 3in)
Powerplant: One 481kW (645hp) Bristol Mercury VI S2 nine-cylinder air-cooled radial piston engine
Maximum speed: 370km/h (230mph)
Range: 740km (460 miles)
Ceiling: 10,200m (33,500ft)
Crew: 1
Armament: Two synchronised 7.7mm (0.303in) Vickers machine guns, fixed forward firing in fuselage top decking

Gloster Gladiator & Sea Gladiator

The last British biplane fighter, the Gladiator was conceptually obsolete at the start of World War II but saw a considerable amount of service during the early years of the conflict.

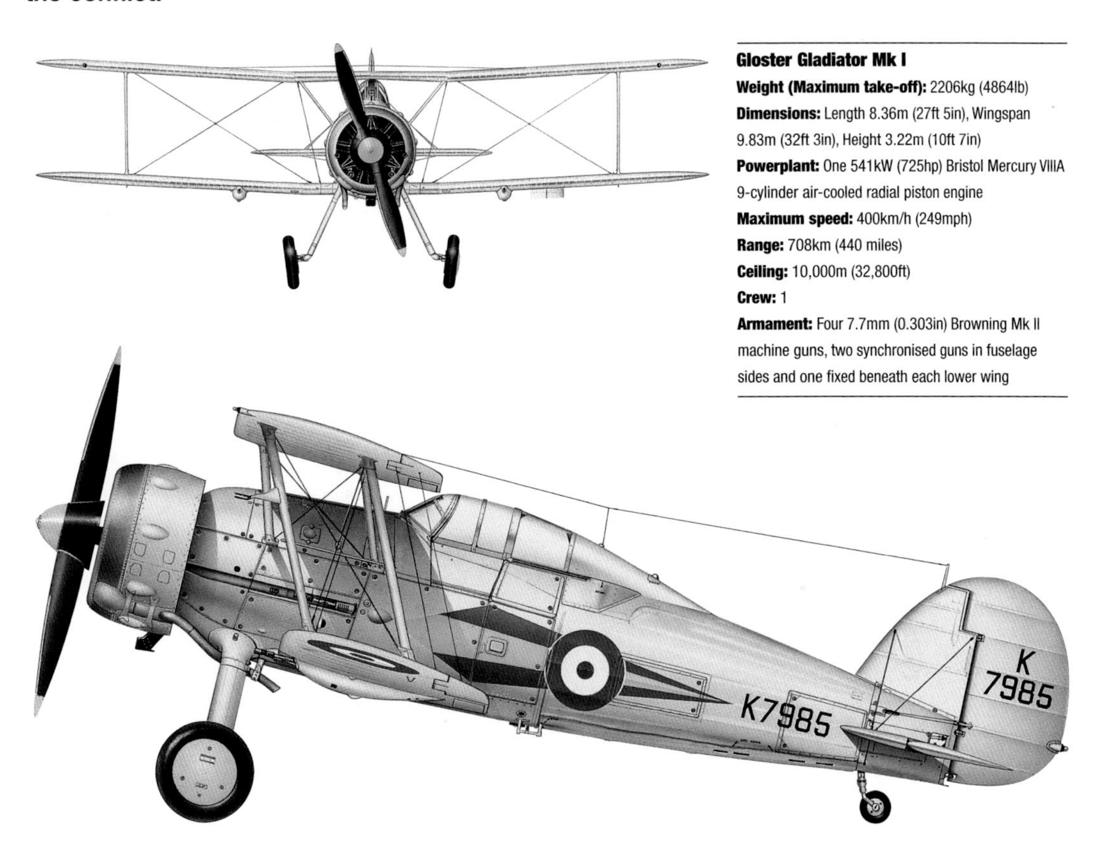

Gloster Gladiator Mk I

Weight (Maximum take-off): 2206kg (4864lb)

Dimensions: Length 8.36m (27ft 5in), Wingspan 9.83m (32ft 3in), Height 3.22m (10ft 7in)

Powerplant: One 541kW (725hp) Bristol Mercury VIIIA 9-cylinder air-cooled radial piston engine

Maximum speed: 400km/h (249mph)

Range: 708km (440 miles)

Ceiling: 10,000m (32,800ft)

Crew: 1

Armament: Four 7.7mm (0.303in) Browning Mk II machine guns, two synchronised guns in fuselage sides and one fixed beneath each lower wing

Gloster Gladiator Mk I

This Gladiator Mk I, K7986, bears the pre-war colours of No 79 Squadron, which was based at Biggin Hill, Kent, in 1937.

The Gladiator began life as a response to Air Ministry specification F.7/30 calling for a four gun fighter capable of 404km/h (250mph). At the time this specification was issued, the Gauntlet was in development and designer Henry Folland (1889–1954) believed that a “refined Gauntlet” could meet the requirements of F.7/30. The first Gladiator, then known by the internal designation SS.37 consisted of a Gauntlet modified by removing one set of interplane struts from the wings, necessitating some localised strengthening of the wing structure, replacing the vee strut undercarriage with cantilever legs and Dowty internally sprung wheels, and adding two more machine guns in fairings under the lower wings.

Bristol expected to have an 588kW (800hp) Mercury engine in production by the time the aircraft was in production but the first prototype flew with a Mercury IV on 12 September 1934. By the time the

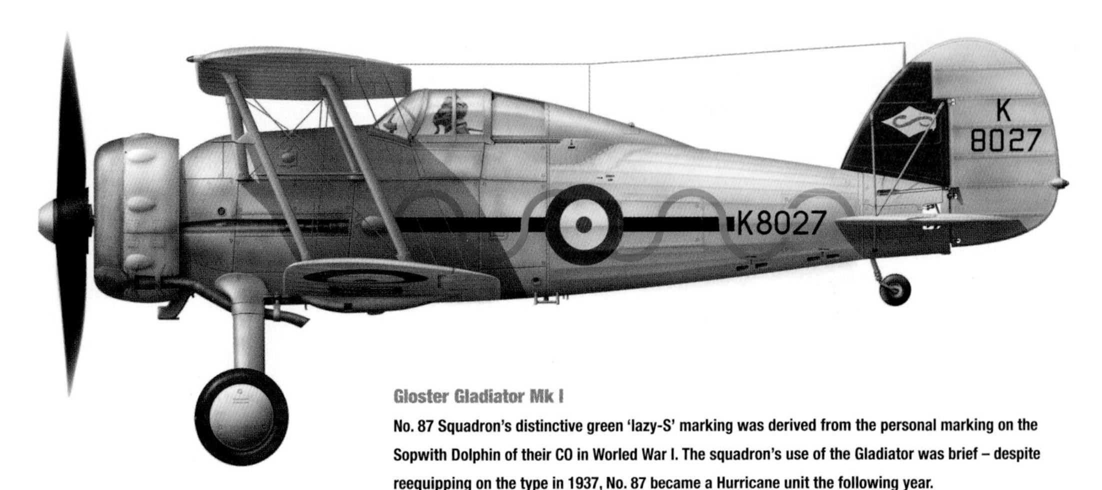

Gloster Gladiator Mk I

No. 87 Squadron's distinctive green 'lazy-S' marking was derived from the personal marking on the Sopwith Dolphin of their CO in Worled War I. The squadron's use of the Gladiator was brief – despite reequipping on the type in 1937, No. 87 became a Hurricane unit the following year.

Gloster Gladiator Mk I

Before 1938 RAF fighter squadrons displayed a variety of quite flamboyant colour schemes. No. 72 Squadron flew the Gladiator from May 1937 to May 1939, initially with the simple but arresting red-and-blue stripe squadron marking. The blue fin denotes the flight commander's aircraft of 'B' flight.

Gloster Gladiator Mk I

Weight (Maximum take-off): 2206kg (4864lb)

Dimensions: Length 8.36m (27ft 5in), Wingspan 9.83m (32ft 3in), Height 3.22m (10ft 7in)

Powerplant: One 541kW (725hp) Bristol Mercury VIIIA 9-cylinder air-cooled radial piston engine

Maximum speed: 400km/h (249mph)

Range: 708km (440 miles)

Ceiling: 10,000m (32,800ft)

Crew: 1

Armament: Four 7.7mm (0.303in) Browning Mk II machine guns, two synchronised guns in fuselage sides and one fixed beneath each lower wing

---

SS.37 was undergoing Air Ministry trials at Martlesham Heath, a 474kW (645hp) Mercury VIS had been fitted and production machines would be built with the 610kW (830hp) Mercury IX. The ready availability of the SS.37, as a relatively modest update to the Gauntlet, was seen as a simple means to modernise the Royal Air Force (RAF) quickly whilst awaiting the appearance of the first monoplane fighters, and the aircraft was ordered into production in June 1935 adopting the name 'Gladiator'. Production aircraft were fitted with a fully enclosed cockpit, the first RAF fighter to be so equipped.

Middle East service

Deliveries to the RAF began in February 1937 with No. 72 Squadron at Tangmere becoming the first Gladiator unit, quickly followed by eight other squadrons before the end of the year. Of these, most remained based in the UK until re-equipped with eight gun monoplane fighters but No. 80 Squadron moved to the Middle East in 1938 and was in action against Arab insurgents in Palestine during the same year. Further squadrons would subsequently operate the Gladiator in the Middle East as well as North Africa, and a tropical filter and desert equipment were developed for these theatres. At home, delays to the Hurricane and Spitfire resulted in the development of the Gladiator Mk II with a three-blade metal propeller and further contracts for Gladiators were issued, production eventually reaching 747 aircraft, all of which were delivered to the RAF by the end of August 1939. Part of Mk II production was of a navalised variant, the Sea Gladiator, the first 38 of which were produced in interim form with an arrestor hook and naval radio, followed by 60 built to full Sea Gladiator standard with a dinghy pack carried between the undercarriage legs and various internal modifications.

Following the outbreak of war, two Gladiator units, Nos 607 and 615 squadrons, moved to France as part of the Advanced Air Striking Force (AASF), ultimately proving to be totally outclassed by modern German aircraft. The first Gladiators to see heavy fighting, however, were those of No. 264 Squadron in Norway, operating initially from a frozen lake near Lesjaskog. Despite losing all but four of their aircraft within 24 hours due to Luftwaffe attacks, managed to shoot down six confirmed and eight

Gloster Gladiator Mk II

Weight (Maximum take-off): 2084kg (4594lb)
Dimensions: Length 8.36m (27ft 5in), Wingspan 9.83m (32ft 3in), Height 3.58m (10ft 7in)
Powerplant: One 620kW (830hp) Bristol Mercury IX 9-cylinder air-cooled radial piston engine
Maximum speed: 413km/h (257mph)
Range: 714km (444 miles)
Ceiling: 10,210m (33,500ft)
Crew: 1
Armament: Four 7.7mm (0.303in) Browning Mk II machine guns, two synchronised guns in fuselage sides and one fixed beneath each lower wing

Gloster Gladiator Mk II

N2312 of No. 615 Squadron was based at Merville, France in late 1939 and features the camouflage introduced during the Munich Crisis. The serial has been overpainted, and the undersides painted half night and white to provide a quick visual friend or foe identification measure.

probable enemy aircraft. Brought back to strength with 16 new aircraft, the squadron operated from the arctic base of Bardufoss until their evacuation in early June 1940.

In the East African campaign and the early stages of the fighting in the Western Desert, the Gladiator saw considerable action against Italian aircraft, its primary fighter opposition during this period being the Fiat CR.42 biplane of similar performance. As well as forming the equipment of four RAF squadrons, South African units also received ex-RAF Gladiators in East Africa, using them to form part of both Nos 1 and 2 Fighter Squadrons.

RAAF service

The Royal Australian Air Force (RAAF) also operated the type, with No. 3 Squadron receiving aircraft transferred from No. 33 Squadron RAF. The Gladiators of No. 3 Squadron became the first Australian aircraft to be involved in combat during World War II when, on 19 November 1940, four RAAF aircraft encountered a formation of 18 CR.42s, shooting down six for the loss of one of their own.

Gladiator operations continued in the Middle East until September 1941 but RAF Gladiators also fought in Greece, with these aircraft later passed to the Royal Hellenic Air Force (RHAF), which continued to use them until April 1941.

Sea Gladiators

No account of the Gladiator would be complete without mentioning the remarkable career of the handful of Sea Gladiators on Malta, which for a time represented the entire fighter defence of the island. With never more than four aircraft airworthy at any one time, the Gladiators intercepted formations of Italian bombers attacking the island until the first Hurricanes were delivered to Malta in early July 1940. The slightly inaccurate belief that the defence of the entire island rested on a trio of these aircraft led to the names 'Faith', 'Hope' and 'Charity' being retrospectively bestowed upon them by the press though these names were never carried by any of the Gladiators in action.

The Gladiator also did well on the export market with Belgium, China, Greece, Latvia, Lithuania, Sweden and the Republic of Ireland all placing orders for the type, many of which saw action. In addition, Finland, Portugal and Norway bought second-hand RAF Gladiators.

Sea Gladiator Mk II

The only surviving Sea Gladiator of Malta's Hal Far Flight, N5520 was presented to the people of Malta in 1943 and is preserved today at the National War Museum in Valetta.

Gloster Sea Gladiator Mk II

Weight (Maximum takeoff): 2277kg (50,19lb)
Dimensions: Length: 8.36m (27ft 5in), Wingspan: 9.83m (32ft 3in), Height: 3.58m (11ft 9in)
Powerplant: One 630kW (840hp) Bristol Mercury VIIIAS 9-cylinder air-cooled radial piston engine
Speed: 407km/h (253mph)
Range: 670km (415 miles)
Ceiling: 10,210m (33,500ft)
Crew: 1
Armament: Two 7.62mm (0.303in) Browning machine guns fixed forward-firing in forward fuselage, two 7.62mm (0.303in) Browning machine guns fixed forward-firing under wings

Hawker Hurricane

The first monoplane fighter to enter RAF service and the first British combat aircraft to exceed 300mph (483kph), the Hurricane was built in enormous numbers and served with many nations throughout World War II.

In contrast to its great rival, the Spitfire, which was the Supermarine company's first fighter design, the Hurricane was just one of an evolutionary line of Hawker fighters that had begun with the Woodcock in 1919 and would progress to the Harrier of the late 1960s. The specific origin of the Hurricane can be traced to August 1933 when Sydney Camm (1893–1966), chief designer of the Hawker company, entered into discussions with the Director of Technical Development at the Air Ministry. They wanted to develop a single-seat four-gun monoplane fighter derived from the Fury biplane which had recently entered the Royal Air Force's (RAF) service.

Camm's team duly drew up plans for a monoplane aircraft utilising a very similar fuselage to the Fury, although equipped with an enclosed cockpit with a rearward sliding canopy. The engine was to be a Rolls-Royce Goshawk of 485kW (660hp) and the fabric covered cantilever monoplane wing was of a relatively thick section. A fixed undercarriage was to be fitted with spats covering the mainwheels.

Fury monoplane

This early iteration of the 'Fury Monoplane' was to remain on the drawing board for in 1934 Rolls-Royce made details known of its P.V.12 engine which offered 40 per cent more power at take-off than the Kestrel V as fitted to the Fury and 60 per cent more at medium altitude as opposed to the relatively modest 10–15 per cent improvement offered by the Goshawk. Perhaps more importantly, the P.V.12 was a conventional engine, a straightforward development of the dependable Kestrel, and not reliant, like the Goshawk, on an untried evaporative cooling system which required large condensing surfaces and would likely have proved vulnerable in combat. The Fury Monoplane was redesigned to take the new engine and was now internally referred to as the 'Interceptor Monoplane' at Hawker and further development saw the addition of retractable undercarriage. Hawker had built a mock-up of the new fighter by January 1935 and on the basis of this the Air Ministry ordered a single prototype, work up to this point having

Hawker Hurricane Mk I

Weight (Maximum take-off): 3024kg (6661lb)
Dimensions: Length 9.58m (31ft 5in), Wingspan 12.19m (40ft), Height 3.95m (12ft 11.5in)
Powerplant: One 770kW (1030hp) Rolls-Royce Merlin III V-12 liquid-cooled piston engine
Maximum speed: 508km/h (316mph)
Range: 445km (716 miles)
Ceiling: 10,120m (33,200ft)
Crew: 1
Armament: Eight 7.7mm (0.303in) Browning machine guns fixed, firing forward in wings

Hawker Hurricane Mk I
Serving with 73 Squadron as part of the RAF's Advanced Air Striking Force at Norrent Fontes in France, N2587 wears the rudder stripes adopted as an ID aid which matched those typically painted on French aircraft (though with the colours reversed).

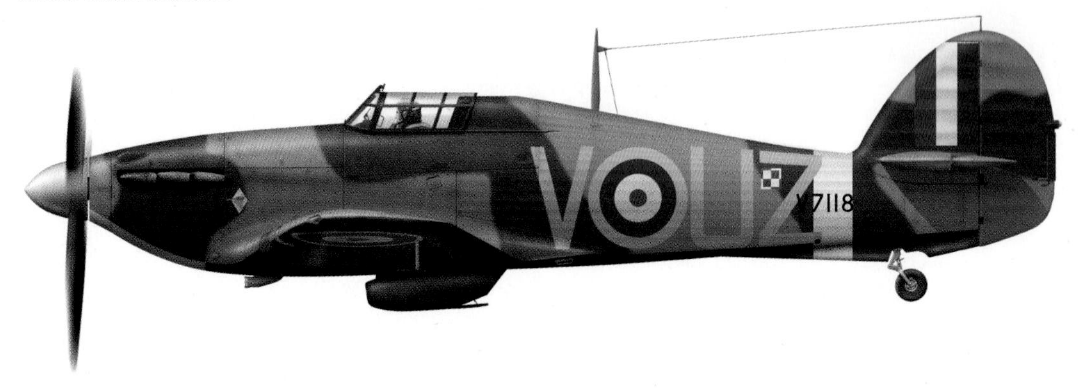

Hawker Hurricane Mk I

No. 306 'Torun' Squadron was a Polish-manned unit formed on the Hurricane in August 1940. Hurricane V7118 was on the strength of the unit when it was based at Church Fenton in Yorkshire.

Hawker Hurricane Mk I

Weight (Maximum take-off): 3024kg (6661lb)
Dimensions: Length 9.58m (31ft 5in), Wingspan 12.19m (40ft), Height 3.95m (12ft 11.5in)
Powerplant: One 770kW (1030hp) Rolls-Royce Merlin III V-12 liquid-cooled piston engine
Maximum speed: 508km/h (316mph)
Range: 445km (716 miles)
Ceiling: 10,120m (33,200ft)
Crew: 1
Armament: Eight 7.7mm (0.303in) Browning machine guns fixed, firing forward in wings

---

been as a private venture by Hawker, and specified that the armament should be increased to eight 7.7mm (0.303in) machine guns, all mounted in the wings.

The prototype fighter, as yet unnamed and referred to by its Air Ministry Specification F36/34, made its first flight on 6 November 1935. It was powered by one of the earliest Merlin engines, a Merlin C rated at 990hp and much of the early trials flying was beset with engine problems, the Merlin being at a very early stage of development. By the time the prototype had been submitted for service trials at the Aeroplane and Armament Experimental Establishment (A & AEE) at Martlesham Heath, the canopy had received extra frames, the radiator bath had been enlarged and the tailplane struts had been removed.

Testing proved satisfactory and a contract for 600 production aircraft was placed on 20 July 1936, the name 'Hurricane' having been officially adopted the previous month.

Rapid production

Hawker, cognisant of the worsening international situation and convinced war was imminent, had begun plans for the construction of 1,000 Hurricanes three months before the contract was issued and as such production of the new fighter was able to proceed rapidly. A new factory was built to produce the aircraft and the first Hurricane Mk I off the assembly line flew on 12 October 1937. Deliveries to the RAF began before the end of the year and the first Hurricane squadron, No. 111, had a full complement of aircraft by February 1938. In the same month the Squadron Leader of No. 111 Squadron, John Gillan, gave the Hurricane a brief moment of pre-war fame when, assisted by a strong tail wind, he flew from Edinburgh to Northolt in 48 minutes. This equated to the unprecedented average ground speed of around 658km/h (409mph) and comfortably exceeded the then absolute speed record for landplanes of 610km/h (379mph) set the previous year by a prototype Messerschmitt Bf 109.

Further squadrons followed swiftly and the rate at which Hurricane squadrons were formed exceeded the rate of any previous peacetime programme. Teething issues were minimal and the introduction of the aircraft to squadron service was remarkably trouble free, especially given the technological leap the Hurricane represented over the open cockpit biplanes many of these squadrons were then flying. By the outbreak of war, 18 squadrons were equipped with the Hurricane.

Shortly after the first production aircraft appeared, spinning trials revealed that slightly more fin and rudder area would be beneficial, leading to the distinctive ventral fin being added under the tailplane of the Hurricane and conferring upon it its characteristic drooped tail profile. Other experimental work before the outbreak of war saw variable pitch and then constant speed propellers fitted, which despite a considerable weight penalty conferred a marked improvement in climb rate, and the latter would become a standard fit during 1940. The armament was also looked at: as early as April 1936 a four 20mm (0.79in) cannon wing was studied but at the time the weight of these guns and ammunition was considered too great for a single engined aircraft. A single Hurricane was, however, fitted with two 20mm (0.79in) Oerlikon cannon under the wings for test purposes and remarkably this experimental aircraft was flown operationally during the Battle of Britain, scoring one victory.

Less visibly obvious but of higher immediate importance was the switch from a fabric covered to a metal skinned wing, conferring greater strength, and the first Hurricane so equipped flew on 28 April 1939. Tooling was produced to allow metal skinned wings to be introduced onto the production line in March 1940. Protection for the pilot was also progressively increased in the form of an armour plate behind the seat and a bulletproof glass windscreen. On 17 May 1939, the first Hurricane fitted with a Vokes filter for operations in sandy and dusty environments was flown, a precursor to the many aircraft so fitted that would soon be serving in North Africa.

From BEF to Battle of Britain

Following the outbreak of war, the Hurricane was the most modern fighter to be sent to France as part of Britain's Advanced Air Striking Force (AASF). A Hurricane of No. 1 Squadron became the first British fighter based in France to score an air-to-air victory, destroying a Do 17 near Toul on 30 October 1939. Sporadic action was fought for the following few months followed by the heavy and continuous fighting of the Battle for France during May 1940. More than 200 Hurricanes were lost in France but production levels accelerated to remarkable heights, from an average monthly production of 64 Hurricanes at the end of 1939, to 236 per month during the first three months of 1940, and Hurricane output remained above or higher than this figure until mid-1943. Hurricanes were also sent to Norway and Malta during the early war period, engaging in intense action in both locations.

Following the fall of France, the Hurricane experienced its finest hour, the Battle of Britain. As the most numerous of British fighters, the brunt of the fighting fell on the Hurricane's shoulders and it famously destroyed more enemy aircraft than all other defences combined during the battle. Nevertheless, this action also demonstrated that the Spitfire was the better air superiority fighter and as such the Hurricane was utilised in a greater variety of roles, exported more widely (initially at least), and sent overseas in large numbers earlier than the precious Spitfires, which were primarily reserved for UK based squadrons until later in the war. In fact, the Hurricane's availability in quantity was sufficient to allow stocks of the fighter to be exported even as the UK was hurriedly rearming before the outbreak of war.

Hawker Hurricane Mk I

Another Polish Hurricane, V7339 was on the strength of No. 317 'City of Wilno' Squadron, one of 15 Polish manned squadrons in the RAF. This unit was based at RAF Fairwood Common, near Swansea in Wales in mid 1941.

Hawker Hurricane Mk I

Weight (Maximum take-off): 3024kg (6661lb)
Dimensions: Length 9.58m (31ft 5in), Wingspan 12.19m (40ft), Height 3.95m (12ft 11.5in)
Powerplant: One 770kW (1030hp) Rolls-Royce Merlin III V-12 liquid-cooled piston engine
Maximum speed: 508km/h (316mph)
Range: 445km (716 miles)
Ceiling: 10,120m (33,200ft)
Crew: 1
Armament: Eight 7.7mm (0.303in) Browning machine guns fixed, firing forward in wings

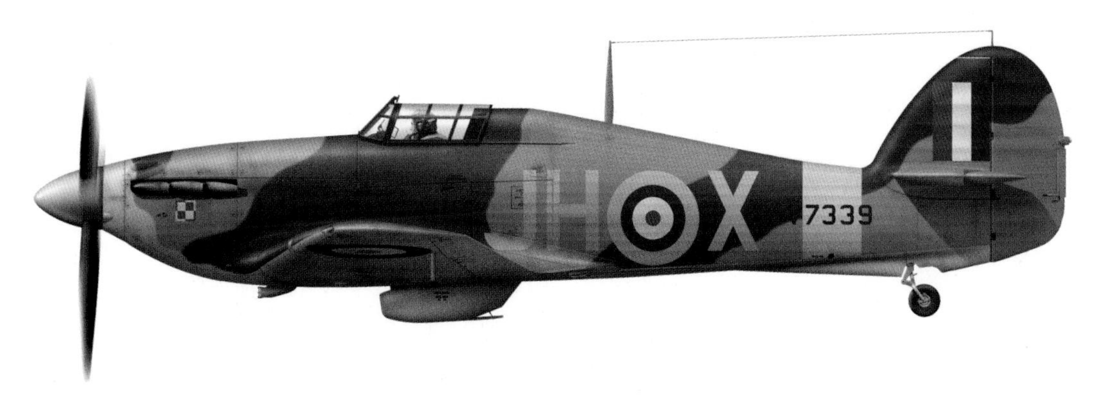

Canadian Hurricanes

As one might expect, Commonwealth nations were early users and both Canada and South Africa placed orders for Hurricanes in 1938 with the first 20 Royal Canadian Air Force (RCAF) Hurricanes delivered by August 1939. They were used to equip No. 1(F) Squadron at Sea Island, though the squadron and its Hurricanes were shipped back to the UK in June 1940 to strengthen British defences. Further RCAF Hurricane units were subsequently formed in Britain. Canada also became a source of production for the Hurricane after the British Government sought a new location for fighter aircraft production that could not be disrupted by enemy bombing. The Canadian Car & Foundry Company (CC&F) in Montreal was selected as the prime contractor and flew their first Hurricane I on 10 January 1940.

Initially identical to the British Mk I, after the first 60 were built Canadian Hurricanes switched to the US licence-built Packard Merlin 28 engine and were designated Hurricane Mk X. A switch to more Canadian-sourced equipment resulted in the Mk XI and an engine change to the Merlin 29 resulted in the Hurricane XII with 12 guns and XIIA with eight. In total 1,448 Hurricanes were completed in Canada, most of which were shipped to the RAF in Europe.

SAAF service

South Africa meanwhile received its first seven Hurricanes in early 1939 with 24 more following after the outbreak of war, enough to equip two units. South African Air Force (SAAF) Hurricane squadrons saw service against the Italians in East Africa. At the same time, in Europe, the Hurricane had been ordered by Romania, Yugoslavia, and Belgium, with the latter two nations also obtaining a manufacturing licence. All three received aircraft during 1939 and whilst the Belgian and Yugoslav aircraft fought brief but intense actions against invading German forces, the 50 Romanian aircraft were utilised against the Union of Soviet Socialist Republics (USSR) during Operation Barbarossa, with two Romanian pilots achieving 'ace' status on the type. Finland also fought the USSR with the Hurricane after obtaining 12 aircraft in 1940, and as such the type became one of very few aircraft procured and used by both Axis and Allied nations – indeed, Finnish and Soviet Hurricanes occasionally clashed in battle. In addition to the aircraft utilised by combatant countries, the neutral nations of Persia, Turkey, Ireland, Portugal and Egypt all operated Hurricanes during the war.

The Hurricane saw its first significant combat in the defence of France in 1940. No. 87 Squadron was among the units committed to the Advanced Air Striking Force during the Battle of France. This photograph shows the squadron's Hurricanes 'somewhere in France' in March 1940.

Hurricane Mk II

The end of the Battle of Britain coincided with the entry into service of the Hurricane Mk II, which was to become the most-produced production variant, differing primarily in its use of the Merlin XX engine, and was built in several sub-variants. The Mk IIA was essentially the same as the Mk I but for the engine, while the Mk IIB introduced a wing armament of 12 7.7mm (0.30in) machine guns. The Mk IIC had four 20mm (0.79in) cannon armament, and in later production form featured wings with hardpoints for 230 or 110kg (500 or 250lb) bombs or fuel tanks. The Mk IID carried two 40mm (1.57in) Vickers S guns specifically for anti-tank duties.

'Hurribombers'

The most important of these was the Mk IIC and during 1941, as the Hurricane found itself gradually outclassed by enemy aircraft. The Mk IIC would find wider employment as a night-fighter and intruder, and as the 'Hurribomber' utilised in ground attack missions, often flying with Spitfires as top cover. The Mk IIC aircraft maintained its air-superiority

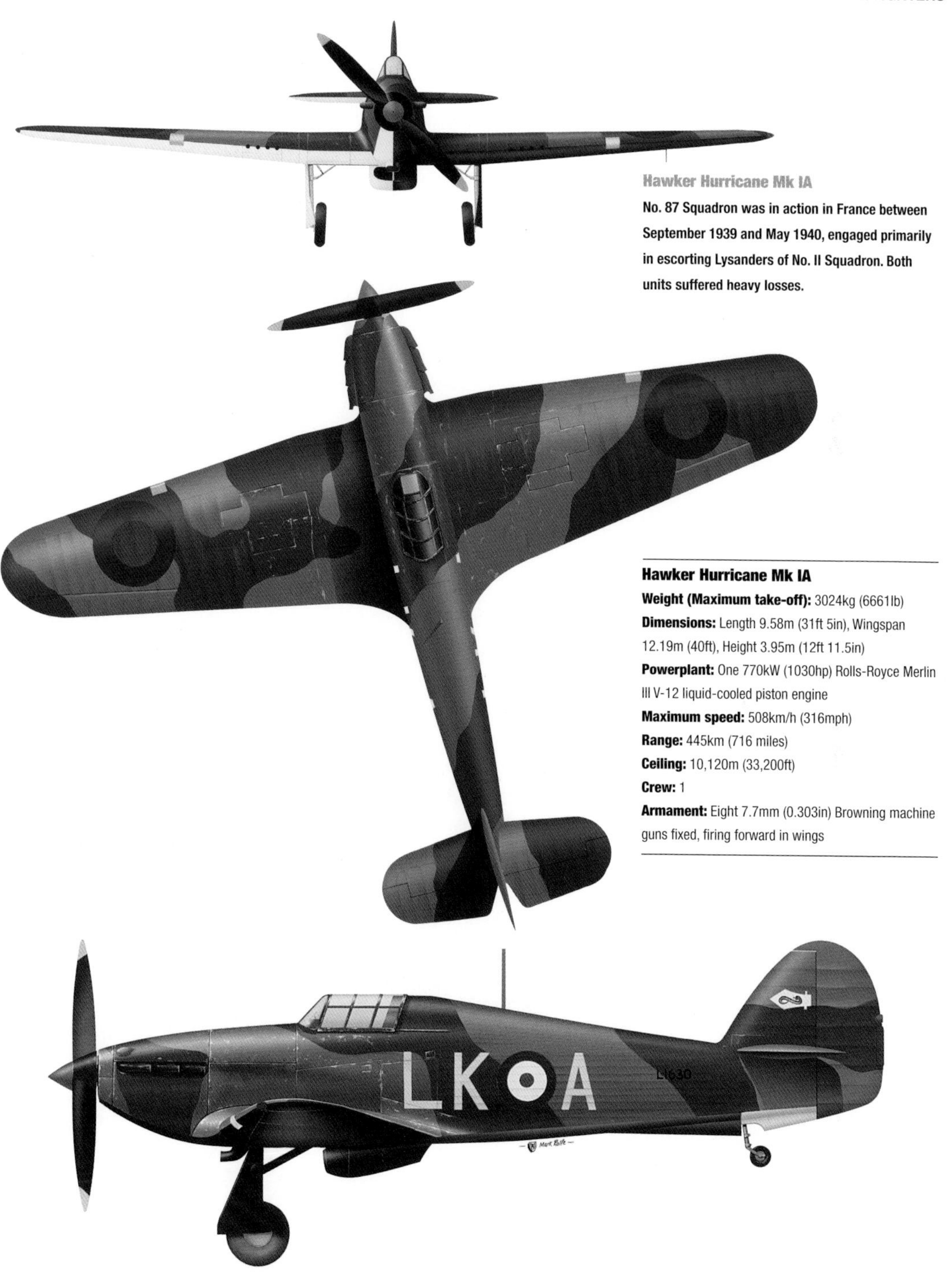

Hawker Hurricane Mk IA

No. 87 Squadron was in action in France between September 1939 and May 1940, engaged primarily in escorting Lysanders of No. II Squadron. Both units suffered heavy losses.

Hawker Hurricane Mk IA

Weight (Maximum take-off): 3024kg (6661lb)

Dimensions: Length 9.58m (31ft 5in), Wingspan 12.19m (40ft), Height 3.95m (12ft 11.5in)

Powerplant: One 770kW (1030hp) Rolls-Royce Merlin III V-12 liquid-cooled piston engine

Maximum speed: 508km/h (316mph)

Range: 445km (716 miles)

Ceiling: 10,120m (33,200ft)

Crew: 1

Armament: Eight 7.7mm (0.303in) Browning machine guns fixed, firing forward in wings

role overseas, becoming the most numerous fighter type during most of the campaign in the Western Desert, Egypt. The Hurricane also became the first Allied aircraft to be supplied to the Soviet Union, and around 3,000 would eventually be shipped there to become the most numerous British aircraft in Soviet service. Though appreciated for its easy flying characteristics and reliability, the Hurricane was generally unpopular with Soviet pilots due to its inferior speed, some 25–31mph (40–50km/h) slower than the Bf 109E at the low and medium altitudes at which combat generally occurred in Russia. Several Hurricanes were modified by the Soviets as open cockpit two-seaters for artillery spotting duties, with a second crewmember seated in a second cockpit, complete with a rear gun, behind the pilot's seat.

Ground-attack asset

The last large-scale use of the Hurricane as a pure air-superiority fighter was against the Japanese over the Arakan front in the first half of 1943 and close support missions became the aircraft's primary role for the latter half of its operational career. Ground attack duties with the Hurricane had begun in late 1940, with aircraft involved in anti-shipping patrols along the French coast and by the start of 1942, some 30 UK-based squadrons were flying the Hurricane against targets of opportunity in occupied France.

The use of air to ground rockets was pioneered by Hurricanes, experiments at the A & AEE leading to the adoption of the 27kg (60lb) RP-3 rocket with four carried under each wing. The rockets were regularly used in combat in both Europe and the Far East after their first employment during the latter stages of the campaign in the Western Desert, Egypt.

The increasing use of the Hurricane as a ground attack asset also drove the development of a variant optimised for close support duties, and initially referred to as the 'low attack' version, becoming the Mk IV by the time the prototype flew (the Mk III was to be a variant powered by the Merlin 28 that was never built).

Production Mk IVs were externally distinguishable by the deeper ventral radiator bath and featured a Merlin 24 or 27, increased armour protection, and the 'universal wing' which could be armed with two 110 or 230kg (250 or 500lb) bombs, two 40mm (1.57in) Vickers S guns or two 40mm (1.57in) Rolls-Royce B.H. type guns, two SBC (small bomb containers) or SCI (smoke curtain installation), two 45 or 90 gallon drop tanks, or up to eight RP-3 rockets. All were fitted with the tropical filter and were usually operated with 40mm (1.57in) guns or rocket armament.

Arakan Front

Mk IVs were heavily committed, alongside Mk IICs, to close support operations during the fighting on the Arakan front in Burma (modern-day Myanmar) and fought until the end of the war in Europe as part of the RAF's Balkan Air Force (BAF). The final

Hawker Hurricane Mk IIB

Weight (Maximum take-off): 3742kg (8249lb)
Dimensions: Length 9.83m (32ft 3in) Wingspan 12.19m (40ft) Height 4m (13ft 2in)
Powerplant: One 1089kW (1460hp) Rolls-Royce Merlin XX V-12 liquid-cooled piston engine
Maximum speed: 528km/h (328mph) or 499km/h (310mph) when fitted with tropical filter
Range (internal fuel only): 740km (460 miles)
Ceiling: 10,850m (35,600ft)
Crew: 1
Armament: Twelve 7.7mm (0.303in) Browning machine guns fixed, firing forward in wings

Hawker Hurricane Mk IIB

The standard grey and green camouflage scheme was adopted because aircraft were spending a greater time flying over the sea during Fighter Command's "lean into France". BD707 was operated by No. 402 Squadron RCAF, based at Southend in Essex in 1941.

Hawker Hurricane Mk IIB

Hurricanes saw widespread service overseas. BE171 was based at Mingaladon in Burma during early 1942, where it was used by No. 17 Squadron RAF.

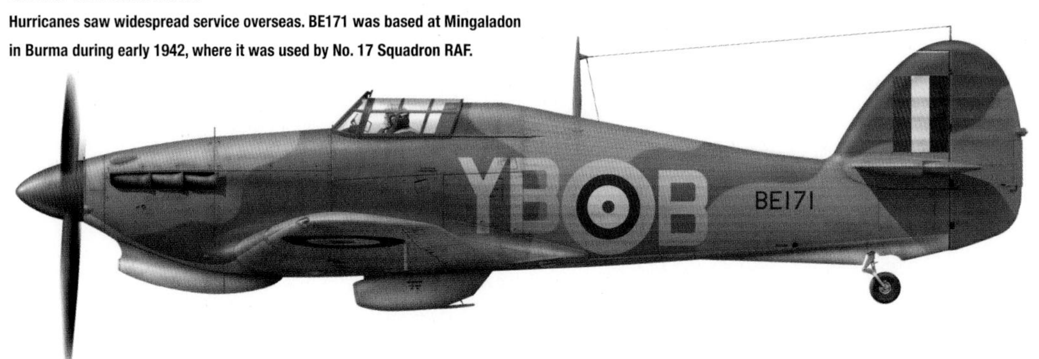

Hawker Hurricane Mk IIb

Hawker Hurricane IIb, serial no. Z3230, flew with 402 (RCAF) Sqn, from Digby in Lincolnshire, May 1941. At this time, G – 'George' – was flown by Squadron Leader 'Bob' Morrow (later DFC).

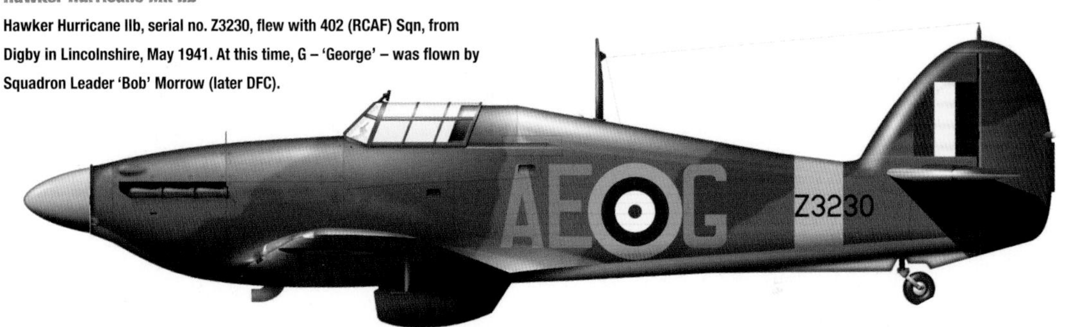

Hurricane variant, the Mk V, was fitted with a low-altitude Merlin 32 and four-bladed propeller but insuperable cooling problems resulted in this variant never progressing beyond the prototype stage. The final Hurricane, a Mk IIC, rolled off the production line in August 1944, becoming the last of 14,487 Hurricanes to be built.

Naval fighter

The availability, relatively high performance and docile flying characteristics of the Hurricane saw it adapted into a naval fighter (described separately) as well as seeing it much utilised on trials work. Particularly noteworthy experimental use included the Hillson 'Slip-wing', a second wing mounted above the fuselage to convert the Hurricane into a biplane and allow it to take off at greatly overloaded weights. The second wing was intended to be jettisoned in flight but although a prototype was built, an attempt to release the wing whilst aloft was never attempted.
The Hurricane was also used in an impressive experiment wherein a bomber aircraft towed a single engine fighter behind it, primarily as a means of deploying fighters overseas at high speed. Utilising a Wellington towing a Hurricane with a hemp rope attached to a steel cable and towing shackle, flight trials proved that the scheme was technically possible but the Merlin engine could not be restarted after a prolonged tow due to the oil and cooling systems icing up and the scheme was abandoned.

Hawker Hurricane Mk IIB

Weight (Maximum take-off): 3742kg (8249lb)
Dimensions: Length 9.83m (32ft 3in) Wingspan 12.19m (40ft) Height 4m (13ft 2in)
Powerplant: One 1089kW (1460hp) Rolls-Royce Merlin XX V-12 liquid-cooled piston engine
Maximum speed: 528km/h (328mph) or 499km/h (310mph) when fitted with tropical filter
Range (internal fuel only): 740km (460 miles)
Ceiling: 10,850m (35,600ft)
Crew: 1
Armament: Twelve 7.7mm (0.303in) Browning machine guns fixed, firing forward in wings

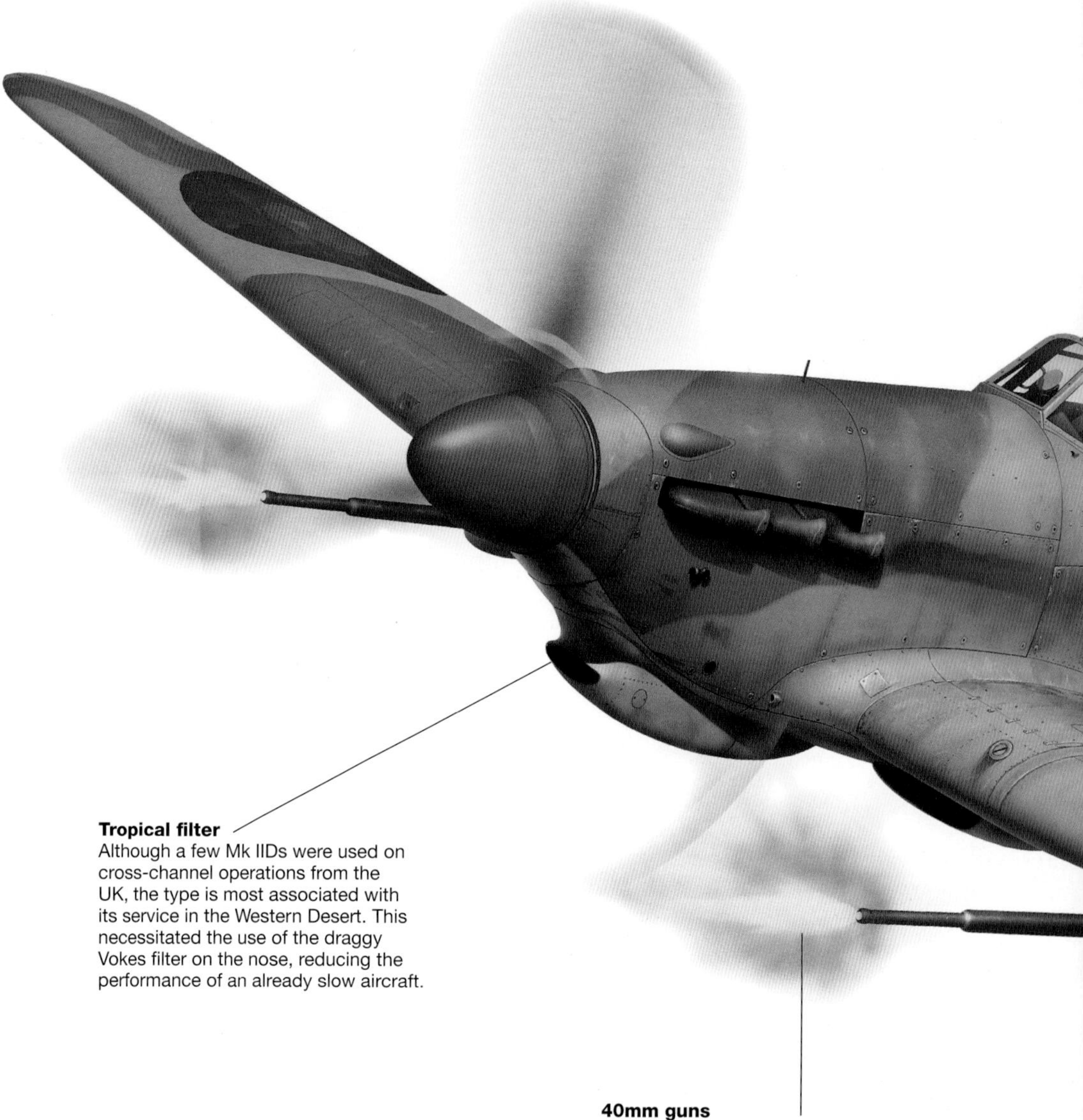

Tropical filter
Although a few Mk IIDs were used on cross-channel operations from the UK, the type is most associated with its service in the Western Desert. This necessitated the use of the draggy Vokes filter on the nose, reducing the performance of an already slow aircraft.

40mm guns
The Vickers 'S' cannon utilised by the Mk IID had been developed as a defensive weapon for bombers during the 1930s, utilising the ammunition of the Navy's QF 2-pounder anti-aircraft gun. Although studied for use in other aircraft, only the Hurricane ever used the 'S' gun in action.

Hawker Hurricane Mk IID

The most specialised Hurricane variant to enter production, the anti-tank Mk IID utilised a pair of 40mm (1.57in) cannon to engage armoured vehicles. Making its debut in 1942 with No. 6 Squadron in North Africa, the Mk IID proved effective in its intended role, but vulnerable to enemy fighter aircraft, resulting in the addition of extra armour.

Overseas use
Initial use of the Mk IID was in North Africa, and this example of No. 6 Squadron, operating in Tunisia in April 1943, wears typical desert camouflage. The Mk IID later undertook intense operations in the close support role in Burma.

Hawker Hurricane Mk IID

Weight (Maximum take-off): 3951kg (8710lb)
Dimensions: Length 9.83m (32ft 3in) Wingspan 12.19m (40ft) Height 4m (13ft 2in)
Powerplant: One 1089kW (1460hp) Rolls-Royce Merlin XX V-12 liquid-cooled piston engine
Maximum speed: 460km/h (286mph)
Range: 740km (460 miles)
Ceiling: 10,365m (34,000ft)
Crew: 1
Armament: Two 40mm (1.57in) Vickers S guns mounted under wings and two 7.7mm (0.303in) Browning machine guns fixed, firing forward in wings

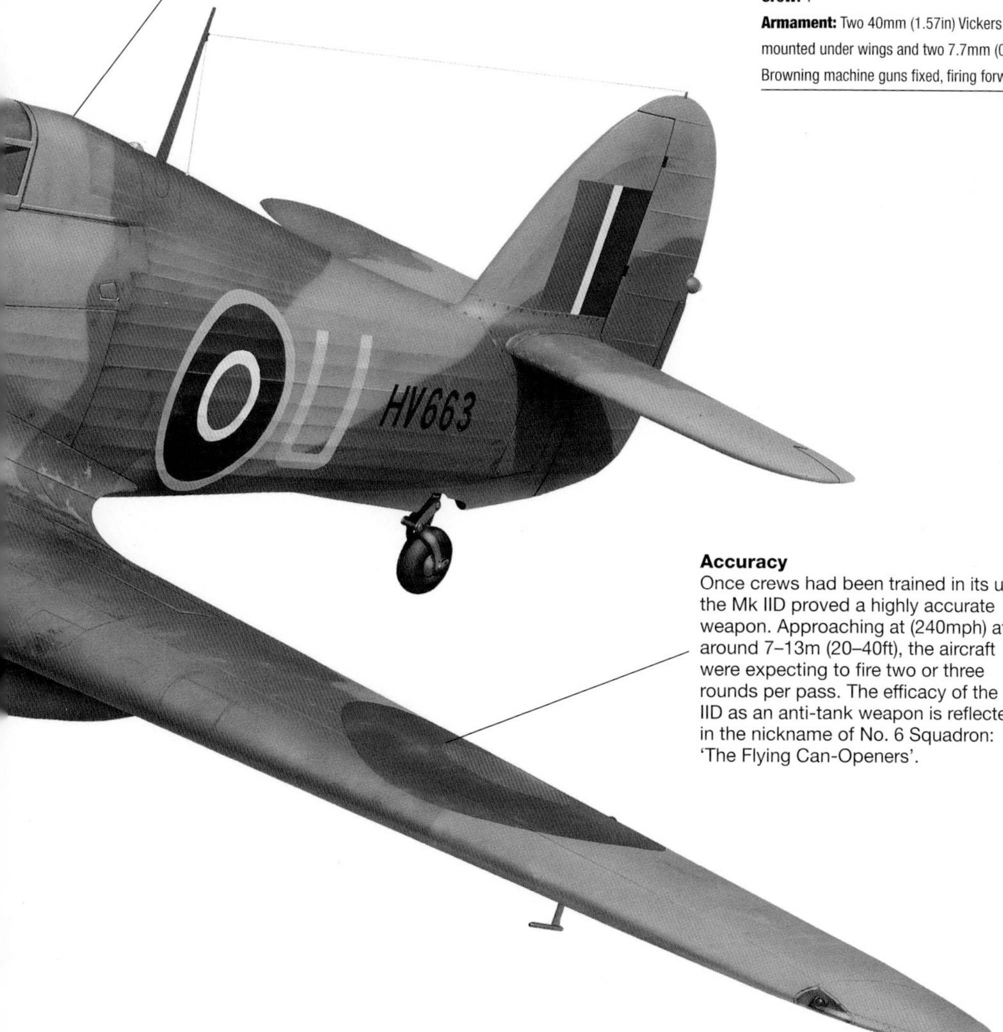

HV663

Accuracy
Once crews had been trained in its use, the Mk IID proved a highly accurate weapon. Approaching at (240mph) at around 7–13m (20–40ft), the aircraft were expecting to fire two or three rounds per pass. The efficacy of the Mk IID as an anti-tank weapon is reflected in the nickname of No. 6 Squadron: 'The Flying Can-Openers'.

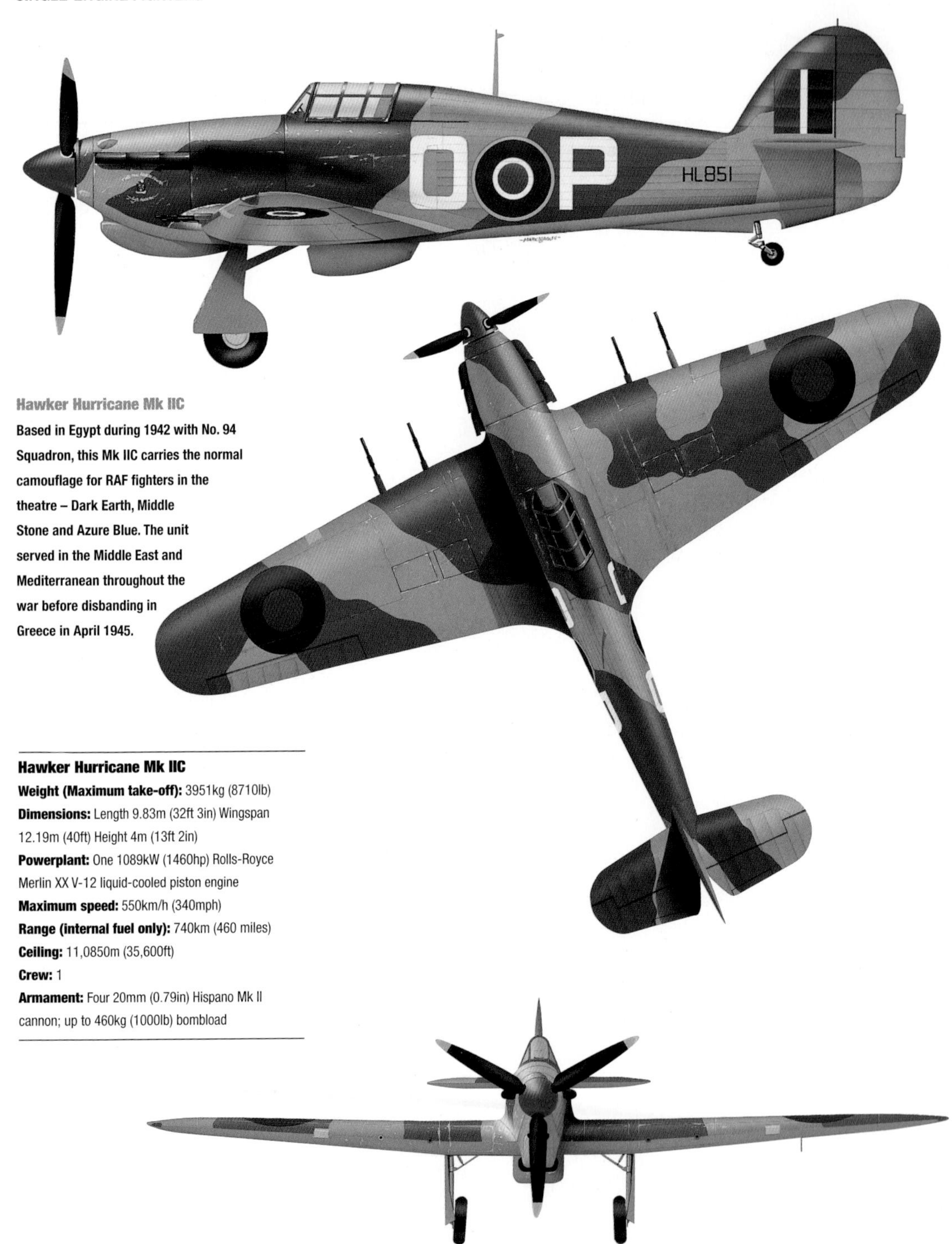

Hawker Hurricane Mk IIC

Based in Egypt during 1942 with No. 94 Squadron, this Mk IIC carries the normal camouflage for RAF fighters in the theatre – Dark Earth, Middle Stone and Azure Blue. The unit served in the Middle East and Mediterranean throughout the war before disbanding in Greece in April 1945.

Hawker Hurricane Mk IIC

Weight (Maximum take-off): 3951kg (8710lb)

Dimensions: Length 9.83m (32ft 3in) Wingspan 12.19m (40ft) Height 4m (13ft 2in)

Powerplant: One 1089kW (1460hp) Rolls-Royce Merlin XX V-12 liquid-cooled piston engine

Maximum speed: 550km/h (340mph)

Range (internal fuel only): 740km (460 miles)

Ceiling: 11,0850m (35,600ft)

Crew: 1

Armament: Four 20mm (0.79in) Hispano Mk II cannon; up to 460kg (1000lb) bombload

---

Supermarine Spitfire

The most famous British aircraft ever built, the Spitfire achieved iconic status in 1940 and has retained that status ever since. Produced in greater numbers than any other British aircraft it remained at the forefront of fighter design from the first day of the conflict to the last.

The Spitfire was the result of the failure of Supermarine's earlier attempt to build a high performance fighter for the Royal Air Force (RAF). The Type 224 was the Supermarine company's first landplane fighter design and combined a fixed undercarriage monoplane airframe with a Rolls-Royce Goshawk engine featuring evaporative cooling. It was designed as a response to Air Ministry specification F7/30, which was ultimately won by the Gloster Gladiator biplane, and the Type 224 had proved disappointing in both top speed and rate of climb. Reginald Mitchell (1895-1937), chief designer at Supermarine, was convinced that Supermarine could build a better fighter. After consultation with the Air Ministry, Supermarine planned an improved aircraft, the Type 300, fitted with one of Rolls-Royce's new P.V.12 engines (soon to be named the Merlin) and featuring a fuselage and straight tapered wing design of much improved aerodynamic form.

New specification

The Air Ministry issued a new specification, F.37/34, explicitly covering the new Supermarine design and issued a contract for a prototype to be built. Between the contract being issued and the emergence of the prototype various refinements were made to the design, by far the most significant being the adoption of a semi-elliptical wing design. This feature would serve to make the aircraft instantly identifiable in service and undoubtedly assisted the popularity of the aircraft within popular culture owing to its aesthetically pleasing shape. However, it was selected for sound aerodynamic reasons, offering the best combination of low drag, strength, and

Supermarine Spitfire Mk I

Weight (maximum take-off): 2651kg (5844lb)

Dimensions: Length 9.12m (29ft 11in), Wingspan 11.23m (36ft 10in, Height 3.86m (9ft 10in)

Powerplant: One 770kW (1030hp) Rolls-Royce Merlin II or III V-12 liquid-cooled piston engine

Maximum speed: 557km/h (346mph)

Range: 1014km (630 miles)

Ceiling: 9296m (30,500ft)

Crew: 1

Armament: Eight 7.7mm (0.303in) Browning machine guns fixed, firing forward in wings

Supermarine Spitfire Mk I

This Spitfire was flown by South African Adolf 'Sailor' Malan, when he was serving with No. 74 Squadron in 1940. Already an 'ace' with five victories before the Battle of Britain even commenced, Malan would ultimately destroy 32 enemy aircraft.

aerodynamic efficiency that could be achieved at that stage of development. In 1936, the Spitfire's wing was likely the most aerodynamically advanced wing yet fitted to any combat aircraft.

Type 300

The Type 300 made its maiden flight on 6 March 1936 and underwent RAF trials in July, demonstrating outstanding performance and resulting in glowing praise from test pilots. The only criticisms being that the flaps were too small and the cockpit canopy was difficult to open above 300mph (483km/h), in the event of an emergency. The Air Ministry responded swiftly to the test pilot's enthusiasm and ordered 310 examples of the new aircraft on 3 June 1936, now officially named 'Spitfire'. Production was severely delayed but the first Spitfire

Supermarine Spitfire Mk I

The head-on view of Malan's Spitfire clearly shows the half-black and half-white underside colours, adopted to allow immediate identification of British aircraft, primarily from the ground. The yellow-green on the upper wing surface consisted of gas-sensitive paint that changed colour in the presence of poison gas.

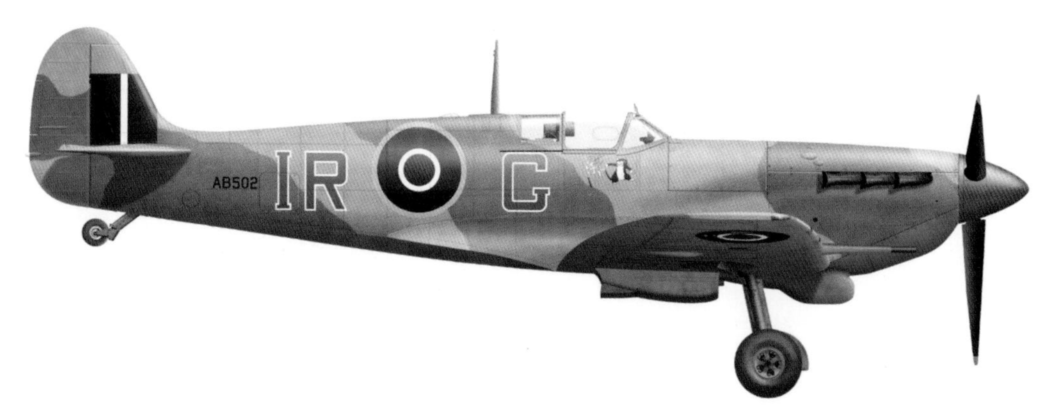

Supermarine Spitfire Mk Vb

AB502 was flown by Wing Commander Ian Gleed in Tunisia and bears his initials 'IRG' in place of squadron codes, a privilege of rank, as well as his personal mascot, Figaro the cat. Gleed downed 13 enemy aircraft before he was himself shot down in April 1943.

Supermarine Spitfire Vb
Weight (maximum take-off): 3071kg (6525lb)
Dimensions: Length 9.12m (29ft 11in), Wingspan 11.23m (36ft 10in), Height 3.02m (9ft 10in)
Powerplant: One 1074kW (1440hp) Rolls-Royce Merlin 45 liquid cooled V-12 piston engine
Maximum speed: 597km/h (371mph) or 564km/h (351mph) with tropical filter
Range: 756km (470 miles)
Ceiling: 10,881m (35,700ft)
Crew: 1
Armament: Two 20mm (0.79in) Hispano cannon and four 7.7mm (0.303in) Browning machine guns in wings; up to 230kg (500lb) bombload

Mk I to be completed was flown on 14 May 1938 and the first Spitfire unit, No. 19 Squadron, received its initial aircraft on 4 August 1938.

Even at this early stage, concerns were being raised about the armament of the Spitfire and a trial installation of two 20mm (0.79in) Hispano cannons was tested, though these weapons proved susceptible to jamming. Despite this issue, a small production run of 30 cannon-armed Spitfire Mk Is was ordered in 1940, seeing limited combat service during the Battle of Britain. By the outbreak of World War II in September 1939, nine squadrons had been equipped with the Spitfire Mk I and two more converted to the type within that month.

The first aerial victory attained by a Spitfire was achieved on 6 September 1939. Unfortunately the aircraft destroyed were two friendly Hurricanes and a Spitfire was shot down in error by British anti-aircraft fire on its return to base.

First kill

A little over a month later however, the Spitfire achieved its first victory over a genuine enemy aircraft when six Spitfires shot down two Ju 88s attacking shipping in the Firth of Forth, Scotland, and sporadic action continued over the next few months of the 'phoney war' period. Spitfires were not involved in the fighting in France (except in the unarmed reconnaissance role), squadrons equipped with the aircraft being deliberately held in the UK for the defence of British targets, though Spitfires were involved with covering the Dunkirk evacuation. The fall of France and subsequent Battle of Britain saw the Spitfire ascend to a level of fame never experienced by a British aircraft before or since.

The relative merits of the Hawker Hurricane and the Spitfire and their contribution to the battle, widely considered to be the first decisive battle fought solely in the air, have been debated from 1940 to the present day. But the fact is that although more aircraft in total were shot down by the Hurricane, the Spitfire achieved more kills relative to its fleet size, 18 squadrons as opposed to 33 of Hurricanes, the two types accounting for 529 and 656 attributed victories respectively.

Battle of Britain

The Spitfires that fought in the Battle of Britain were largely the initial production standard Mk Is, though these had been subject to some improvement. The original flat-topped cockpit canopy had been replaced with a bulged item offering improved headroom as well

Supermarine Spitfire Mk Vc

Spitfire Mk Vc, serial no. A58-254, QY-V, from 452 Squadron RAAF, based at Strauss Airfield, Darwin, Northern Australia, early 1944. At the time, this aircraft was asigned to Squadron Leader LT 'Lou' Spence DFC, who named it 'Rima' for his wife.

Supermarine Spitfire Mk Vc
Weight (maximum take-off): 3346kg (7420lb)
Dimensions: Length 9.12m (29ft 11in), Wingspan 11.23m (36ft 10in), Height 3.02m (9ft 10in)
Powerplant: One 1074kW (1440hp) Rolls-Royce Merlin 45 liquid cooled V-12 piston engine
Maximum speed: 597km/h (371mph) or 564km/h (351mph) with tropical filter
Range: 756km (470 miles)
Ceiling: 11,460m (37,600ft)
Crew: 1
Armament: Four Hispano 20mm (0.79in) cannon, or eight 7.7mm (0.303in) Browning machine guns (both options rarely fitted), or two 20mm (0.79in) Hispano cannon and four 7.7mm (0.303in) Browning machine guns in wings; up to 230kg (500lb) bombload

as better visibility. The fixed pitch, two-blade wooden propeller had been replaced, first by a metal three-blade de Havilland variable pitch unit, offering fine and coarse pitch and then by a constant speed unit. These propellers were heavier but markedly improved climb rate and maximum speed.

An improved Spitfire variant, the Mk II also started to make it to the squadrons before the conclusion of the Battle of Britain. This featured a new Merlin XII engine, the first Merlin intended to use 100 octane fuel, and delivered an increase in power of over 100hp over the Merlin II and III as fitted to the Mk I. Most Mk IIs were of the standard eight machine gun Mk IIA variant but 170 Mk IIB cannon-armed aircraft were also produced, improvements to the ammunition feed having largely solved the earlier stoppage problems.

A few Mk IIs were fitted with a non-jettisonable external fuel tank under the port wing to extend the range. Designated the Mk IIA (LR), these were unpopular due to the deleterious effect of the tank on the aircraft's handling but were quite heavily employed due to their useful range capability.

Mk V

The Mk II was a relatively modest improvement to the basic Spitfire but a more thorough update was schemed with the Mk III which featured a different wing, improved engine, retractable tailwheel and various other detail improvements. However the Mk III would not be produced as the stopgap Mk V was instead built in large numbers (the Mk IV was the prototype Griffon-powered Spitfire, of which more later). This essentially consisted of a Merlin 45 engine fitted to a Mk I airframe and offered roughly the same performance as the Mk III but was much simpler to introduce to production.

The Mk V became the most produced Spitfire variant, with 6,479 built, and was the first of the Spitfires to be exported and see significant service overseas. The 20mm (0.79in) Hispano was now a reliable weapon and nearly all Mk Vs would be fitted with two of these cannons; only 94 Mk VAs with the eight machine-guns were produced. Mk VBs were fitted with two cannon and four machine guns but the later production VC featured the C-type or 'Universal' wing, which was simpler and quicker to build. The

C-type wing was engineered so that either eight machine guns, two cannon and four machine guns, or four cannon could be fitted, though the latter fit was seldom employed. A tropical version of the Spitfire was also introduced with a large dust filter over the carburettor intake, intended for operations in the Middle East and Africa.

Meanwhile, the ongoing issue of short range was eased somewhat by the introduction of a 'slipper' tank that fitted flush to the belly of the aircraft and could be jettisoned in flight. Spitfire Vs with slipper tanks became the first fighter Spitfires deployed beyond the British Isles when in March 1942 three groups of Spitfire VBs, totalling 31 aircraft, fitted with both tropical filters and belly tanks took off from the carriers Eagle and Argus, sailing off the Algerian coast, and flew to Malta to reinforce the fighter defences of the beleaguered island. Malta would also see the first Spitfires to be modified with bomb shackles for the fighter-bomber role. These locally manufactured items prompted Supermarine to design and manufacture definitive bomb racks for the Spitfire for 113kg (250lb) bombs under the wings or a single 227kg (500lb) bomb under the fuselage.

Australian service

Mk Vs were the first Spitfires to serve in quantity with the Royal Australian Air Force (RAAF) in the Pacific with the arrival of 54 Squadron RAF equipped with Spitfire VCs at Darwin, Australia. The squadron became operational during January 1943 and scored the first Spitfire 'kill' against a Japanese aircraft on 6 February 1943. Flying under Australian control, No. 54

Supermarine Spitfire F Mk VIII

No. 457 Squadron RAAF operated the Mk VIII Spitfire from July 1944 to the end of the war. Known as the 'Grey Nurse' squadron after a type of Australian shark, all the unit's Spitfires were adorned with flamboyant sharkmouth markings.

Supermarine Spitfire F Mk VIII

Weight (maximum take-off): 3638kg (8020lb)
Dimensions: Length 9.54m (31ft 4in), Wingspan 11.23m (36ft 10in), Height 3.86m (12ft 8in)
Powerplant: One 1275kW (1710hp) Rolls-Royce Merlin 63 liquid cooled V-12 piston engine
Maximum speed: 657km/h (408mph)
Range: 1062km (660 miles)
Ceiling: 13,106m (43,000ft)
Crew: 1
Armament: Two 20mm (0.79in) Hispano cannon and four 7.7mm (0.303in) or two 12.7mm (0.5in) Browning machine guns or four 20mm (0.79in) Hispano cannon; up to 460kg (1000lb) bombload

Squadron was joined by two RAAF Spitfire VC squadrons to form No 1 Fighter Wing. Later the same year further Spitfire VCs re-equipped three RAF Hurricane squadrons on the Burma (modern-day Myanmar) front with the Indian Air Force (IAF) also receiving Mk Vs during 1944.

The first major use of the Spitfire by a non-Commonwealth power also took place in 1942 when the three 'Eagle' squadrons of the RAF, manned by volunteer US pilots exchanged the British roundels of their Spitfire VBs for American markings when they transferred to United States Army Air Force (USAAF) control, becoming the 334th, 335th and 336th Pursuit Squadrons of the 4th Pursuit Group, and flying their first operational mission on 2 October 1942. Mk Vs were also supplied to the Union of Soviet Socialist Republics (USSR), South Africa, and Yugoslavia, as well as Free French and Italian Co-belligerent units.

High-altitude Spitfire

During 1942, much effort was expended on developing a high-altitude Spitfire to intercept high-flying German Ju 86 bombers and reconnaissance aircraft. On 24 August 1942, a locally modified Mk VC was used to intercept and destroy a Junkers Ju 86P-2 at 12,800m (42,000ft) over the Suez Canal, Egypt, the highest successful interception of the entire war. By this time production of a high-altitude Spitfire variant, the Spitfire Mk VI, later the HF Mk VI, had begun. Featuring a Marshall blower to maintain pressure within the cockpit at 0.91kg (2lb) per square inch higher than the outside atmosphere and a high-altitude Merlin 47 mated to a four bladed propeller, the Mk VI was fitted with extended wingtips, attached to an otherwise standard B-type wing, which increased the span to 13m (40ft 2in). Exactly 100 Mk VIs were built but by the time they entered service, interception of the Ju 86s that were overflying Britain had been proved to be (just) possible by standard Mk IXs. Nonetheless, the Mk VI provided much valuable high-altitude experience to various operational units.

Supermarine Spitfire F Mk VIII

Flown by Flying officer Len Smith with No. 152 Squadron at Sinthe, Burma, in March 1945, MT507 is decorated with the Squadron's leaping panther mascot. RAF predominantly operated the Mk VIII overseas.

Supermarine Spitfire F Mk VIII

Weight (maximum take-off): 3638kg (8020lb)
Dimensions: Length 9.54m (31ft 4in), Wingspan 11.23m (36ft 10in), Height 3.86m (12ft 8in)
Powerplant: One 1275kW (1710hp) Rolls-Royce Merlin 63 liquid cooled V-12 piston engine
Maximum speed: 657km/h (408mph)
Range: 1062km (660 miles)
Ceiling: 13,106m (43,000ft)
Crew: 1
Armament: Two 20mm (0.79in) Hispano cannon and four 7.7mm (0.303in) or two 12.7mm (0.5in) Browning machine guns or four 20mm (0.79in) Hispano cannon; up to 460kg (1000lb) bombload

---

Supermarine Spitfire Mk VIII

Another No. 457 Squadron RAAF aircraft, A58-615 was based at Morotai in the Netherlands East Indies and displays the white leading-edge theatre markings adopted by Allied aircraft flying in the South West Pacific.

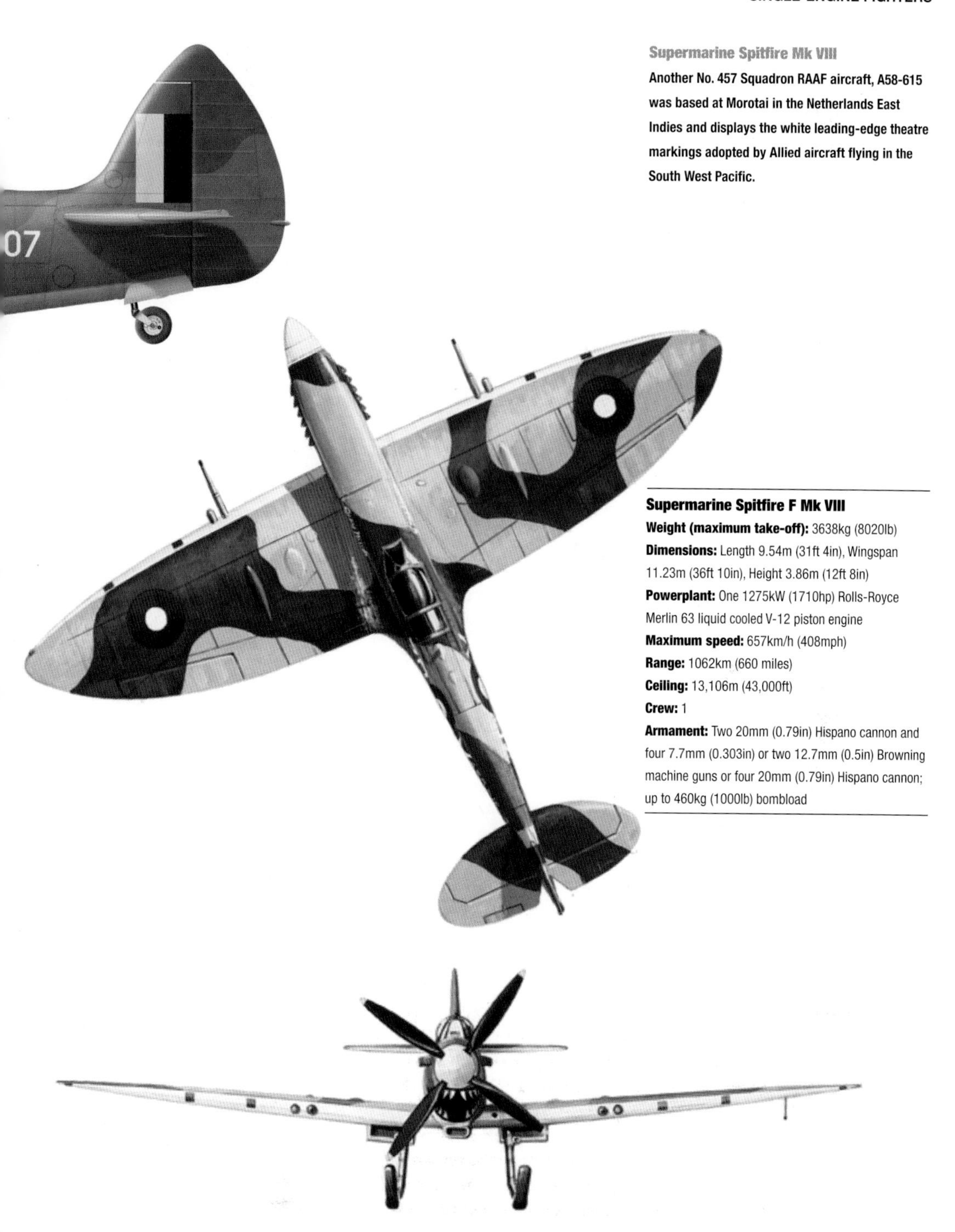

Supermarine Spitfire F Mk VIII

Weight (maximum take-off): 3638kg (8020lb)

Dimensions: Length 9.54m (31ft 4in), Wingspan 11.23m (36ft 10in), Height 3.86m (12ft 8in)

Powerplant: One 1275kW (1710hp) Rolls-Royce Merlin 63 liquid cooled V-12 piston engine

Maximum speed: 657km/h (408mph)

Range: 1062km (660 miles)

Ceiling: 13,106m (43,000ft)

Crew: 1

Armament: Two 20mm (0.79in) Hispano cannon and four 7.7mm (0.303in) or two 12.7mm (0.5in) Browning machine guns or four 20mm (0.79in) Hispano cannon; up to 460kg (1000lb) bombload

Supermarine Spitfire Mk IX

MK392 was used by fighter ace Wing Commander James 'Johnnie' Johnson to destroy the last 12 of his 34 confirmed victories. Wearing full 'invasion stripes', Johnson destroyed a Focke-Wulf Fw 190 in this aircraft on 16 June 1944. As a wing leader, Johnson was able to use his initials "JE-J" in place of squadron code letters.

Supermarine Spitfire Mk IX
Weight (maximum take-off): 4309kg (9500lb)
Dimensions: Length 9.47m (31ft 1in), Wingspan 11.23m (36ft 10in), Height 3.86m (12ft 8in)
Powerplant: One 1151kw (1565hp) Rolls-Royce Merlin 61 liquid cooled V-12 piston engine
Maximum speed: 657km/h (408mph)
Range: 698km (434 miles)
Ceiling: 13,106m (43,000ft)
Crew: 1
Armament: Two 20mm (0.79in) Hispano cannon and four 7.7mm (0.303in) or two 12.7mm (0.5in) Browning machine guns or four 20mm (0.79in) Hispano cannon; up to 460kg (1000lb) bombload

Mk VII

The next significant Spitfire variant was driven by the appearance of a better enemy fighter than the Mk V: the Fw 190. Superior to the Mk V Spitfire in every performance parameter except turn rate and better armed to boot, the Fw 190 prompted the production of a Spitfire variant that was essentially a lash-up: the Mk IX. When the Fw 190 appeared, Supermarine had in fact been working for some time on two new fighters: the Mk VII and Mk VIII.

Developed in parallel, both shared a swathe of improvements but differed in that the Mk VII was intended for the high-altitude role and featured a pressurised cockpit. Neither aircraft was expected to be ready for several months however and the Mk IX was the result of the inspired decision to try fitting a Merlin 61 engine (originally developed for high altitude variants of the Wellington bomber) into a standard Mk V airframe. The new engine resulted in a noticeably longer nose and significantly improved performance: top speed was increased by around 113km/h (70mph) and its fighting altitude was improved by 3050m (10,000ft).

The Mk IX did not enjoy the same advantage over the Fw 190 as the German aircraft did over the Mk V. However, it did deliver parity or a slight superiority over the Focke-Wulf machine. Production was undertaken with such urgency that the first Mk IXs were delivered to No. 64 Squadron at Hornchurch during June 1942 and the Spitfire Mk IX entered combat on 30 July 1942, shooting down three Fw 190s off the French coast on its first operational flight. Initial Mk IXs were converted from Mk V airframes, soon followed by new-build airframes and over 4,000 Mk IXs would be built, serving from mid-1942 to the war's end.

Mk IX

Though early Mk IXs featured the same C-type wing of their Mk VC forebear, the Mk IX was later fitted with the E wing which dispensed with the two outboard 7.7mm (0.303in) machine guns and instead featured one 20mm (0.79in) cannon outboard and one 12.7mm (0.50in) Browning machine-gun immediately inboard on each side. As the pattern of air warfare changed over Western Europe, the Mk IX found itself used less as an air-superiority asset and increasingly as a fighter-bomber with wing bomb racks allowing for the carriage of two 113kg (250lb) bombs under the wings or one 227kg (500lb) weapon under the fuselage. Later production Mk IXs introduced a broad-chord, pointed tip rudder and 'low back' fuselage, which had been trialled on a Mk VIII airframe, allowing for a 360° view teardrop canopy to be fitted.

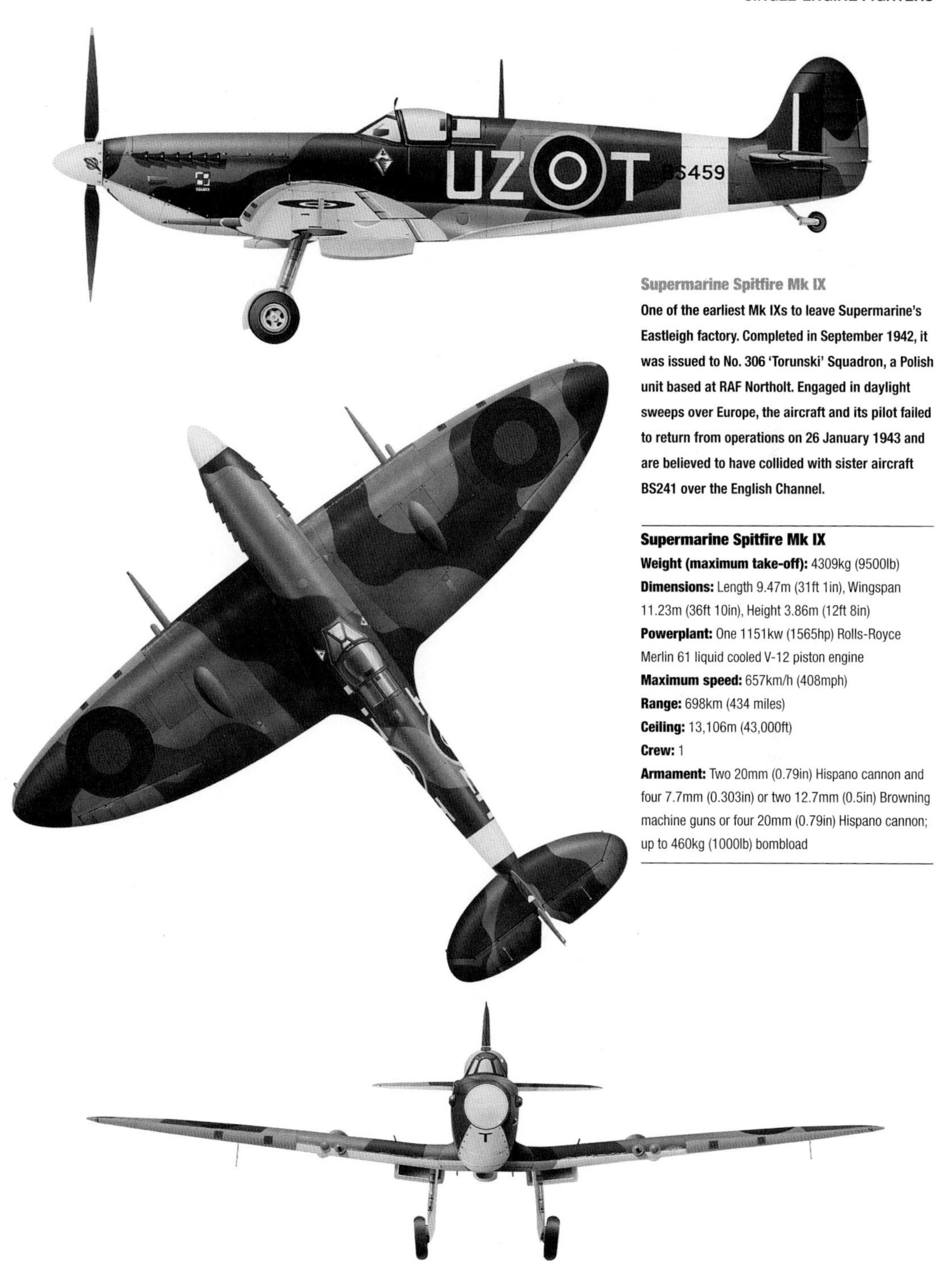

Supermarine Spitfire Mk IX

One of the earliest Mk IXs to leave Supermarine's Eastleigh factory. Completed in September 1942, it was issued to No. 306 'Torunski' Squadron, a Polish unit based at RAF Northolt. Engaged in daylight sweeps over Europe, the aircraft and its pilot failed to return from operations on 26 January 1943 and are believed to have collided with sister aircraft BS241 over the English Channel.

Supermarine Spitfire Mk IX

Weight (maximum take-off): 4309kg (9500lb)
Dimensions: Length 9.47m (31ft 1in), Wingspan 11.23m (36ft 10in), Height 3.86m (12ft 8in)
Powerplant: One 1151kw (1565hp) Rolls-Royce Merlin 61 liquid cooled V-12 piston engine
Maximum speed: 657km/h (408mph)
Range: 698km (434 miles)
Ceiling: 13,106m (43,000ft)
Crew: 1
Armament: Two 20mm (0.79in) Hispano cannon and four 7.7mm (0.303in) or two 12.7mm (0.5in) Browning machine guns or four 20mm (0.79in) Hispano cannon; up to 460kg (1000lb) bombload

---

One of the first units to receive the Mk IX was No. 611 (West Lancashire) Squadron at Biggin Hill. Among the roles added to the Spitfire's repertoire with the Mk IX were Diver patrols to counter the V-1 'flying bomb'.

Despite the success of the Mk IX, the more refined Mks VII and VIII did eventually enter service, though they were never built in the same numbers as the Mk IX. Use of the Mk VII was fairly limited due to the absence of suitable high altitude targets, but the Mk VIII saw widespread service, virtually all examples of which were employed overseas. The first Mk VIIIs were issued to squadrons in the Middle East in mid-1943 and these units would see much action in the invasion of Sicily and the advance up the toe of Italy. As well as RAF units, both US and Free French squadrons flew the Spitfire VIII, and Spitfire Mk IX, in the Italian campaign. Further east, Spitfire Mk VIIIs began to supersede Spitfire Vs in Burma and another major user of the Mk VIII was Australia. No. 1 Fighter Wing, consisting of Nos 452 and 457 Squadrons RAAF and No. 54 Squadron RAF re-equipped with Spitfire Mk VIIIs in 1944. Further squadrons would follow, with the Spitfire Mk VIII deploying for operations in New Guinea. The Spitfire would eventually become the top-scoring Australian fighter in terms of air-to-air victories against the Japanese, accounting for 71 confirmed kills and 17 probables.

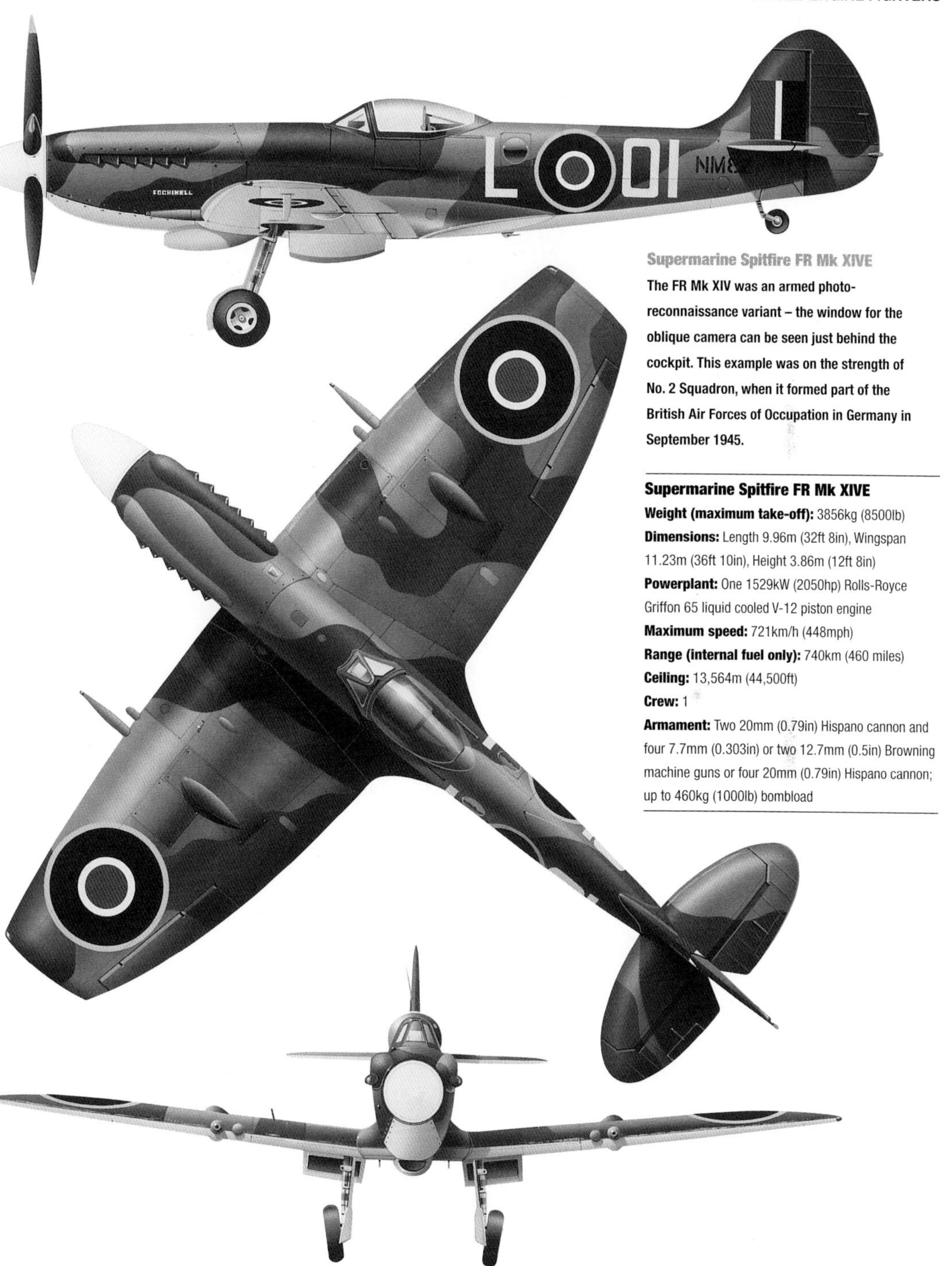

Supermarine Spitfire FR Mk XIVE

The FR Mk XIV was an armed photo-reconnaissance variant – the window for the oblique camera can be seen just behind the cockpit. This example was on the strength of No. 2 Squadron, when it formed part of the British Air Forces of Occupation in Germany in September 1945.

Supermarine Spitfire FR Mk XIVE

Weight (maximum take-off): 3856kg (8500lb)

Dimensions: Length 9.96m (32ft 8in), Wingspan 11.23m (36ft 10in), Height 3.86m (12ft 8in)

Powerplant: One 1529kW (2050hp) Rolls-Royce Griffon 65 liquid cooled V-12 piston engine

Maximum speed: 721km/h (448mph)

Range (internal fuel only): 740km (460 miles)

Ceiling: 13,564m (44,500ft)

Crew: 1

Armament: Two 20mm (0.79in) Hispano cannon and four 7.7mm (0.303in) or two 12.7mm (0.5in) Browning machine guns or four 20mm (0.79in) Hispano cannon; up to 460kg (1000lb) bombload

Supermarine Spitfire Mk XVI

TE311 is painted in the colours of the Polish Commanding Officer of No 131 (Polish) Wing, Group Captain Aleksander Gabszewicz, and features his personal boxing dog motif on the nose.

Supermarine Spitfire F Mk XVI
Weight (maximum take-off): 3946kg (8700lb)
Dimensions: Length 9.47m (31ft 1in), Wingspan 11.23m (36ft 10in) or 9.93m (32ft 7in) wings clipped, Height 3.86m (12ft 8in)
Powerplant: One 1245kW (1670hp) Packard V-1650 Merlin 266 liquid cooled V-12 piston engine
Maximum speed: 657km/h (408mph)
Range: 698km (434 miles)
Ceiling: 13,106m (43,000ft)
Crew: 1
Armament: Two 20mm (0.79in) Hispano cannon and four 7.7mm (0.303in) or two 12.7mm (0.5in) Browning machine guns or four 20mm (0.79in) Hispano cannon; up to 460kg (1000lb) bombload

Rolls-Royce engine

By 1944, the emphasis of Spitfire development had switched to a completely new version with a different engine, the Rolls-Royce Griffon, originally developed for Fleet Air Arm use. In development since mid 1939, the Griffon Spitfire was delayed by the urgency attached to producing Merlin variants, but the Griffon powered Mk IV eventually made its first flight in late 1941. The rapid development of the highly successful Mk IX rendered the Griffon Spitfire less urgently required until the Luftwaffe started using the Fw 190 to deliver 'tip and run' nuisance raids on the British coast.

Whilst the Mk IX was able to deliver a performance as good as or superior to the Fw 190 at medium and high altitude, that advantage fell off at lower altitudes and development of a Griffon powered Spitfire optimised for low level use was suddenly seen as a priority. The result was the Mk XII, an interim variant, which was built using modified Mk Vc and Mk VIII airframes.

The Griffon II engine conferred sparkling performance at low level but at altitude the aircraft was notably inferior to the Mk IX and usage of the Mk XII was therefore limited to low and medium altitude operations. Only 100 were built before production switched to the Mk XIV, once again a conversion from an earlier variant that owed its existence to the definitive Mk 21 running into production delays.

Mk XIV

The Mk XIV was equipped with the Griffon 65 engine delivering 2,035hp and utilising a five bladed Rotol propeller married to a Mk VIII airframe. The first Mk XIVs were fitted with the C-type wing but most Mk XIVs featured the E-type wing with two 20mm (0.79in) Hispano and two 12.7mm (0.5in) Brownings. Later production XIVs were built with the cut-down rear fuselage and many Mk XIVs utilised clipped wings for low-level operations.

The fighter possessed outstanding performance and after comparative tests of contemporary fighters, the Air Fighting Development Unit (AFDU) concluded that the Mk XIV "has the best all-round performance of any present-day fighter". Entering service in January 1944, the Mk XIV served with distinction until the end of the conflict.

Mk 21

Two further Spitfire fighter variants entered service before the end of the war, the Mk XVI, which was identical to the Mk IX except for its use of a

US-built Packard Merlin 266, directly equivalent to a Merlin 66, but requiring a different parts supply chain due to the engine being built to US standards. Most were built with a bubble-canopy and clipped wings for low level operations in Europe.

A total of 1054 of this last Merlin variant were built between late 1944 and the end of production. By contrast, only enough Spitfire Mk 21s were built to equip a single squadron before Victory in Europe (VE) day, No. 91 Squadron flying operations for a month with the type.

The Mk 21 (Roman numerals had by this stage been abandoned for clarity's sake) was the definitive Griffon engine fighter that Supermarine had been developing since 1943 and featured a completely new wing design but serious problems had delayed its service entry until 1945. Only 120 would be built. The postwar Mks 22 and 24 variants were essentially the same as the 21, but featured the bubble canopy and cut-down rear fuselage and a new tail unit in the case of the Mk 24.

Reconnaissance versions

In addition to its service as a fighter, the Spitfire also became one of the most significant Allied reconnaissance aircraft, operated by both the RAF and USAAF. Early efforts saw all armament and radio equipment removed from standard Mk Is, the entire airframe polished to give a highly smooth surface and were finished in a pale blue-green shade, called Camoutint. The Spitfires each carried two F24 cameras with a five inch focal length lens mounted within the wings, one on each side pointing directly downwards, in the space previously occupied by the inboard wing guns and were some 48km/h (30mph) faster than standard fighters. The first reconnaissance missions were flown from bases in France in November 1939 and delivered excellent results.

Further development saw the Spitfire become a very long-ranged aircraft indeed, in stark contrast to famously short-legged fighter variants. Flying from bases in East Anglia, the PR Type F for example, could photograph Berlin, Germany, and return, the first such trip being made on 14 March 1941. Early PR variants were ad hoc conversions made in mere handfuls but 26 PR Mk XIII were built, derived from the Spitfire V to be followed by 471 of the PR Mk XI, derived from the Mk IX airframe, which could cruise at 636km/h (395mph) at 9,800m (32,000ft), rendering them all but immune from interception. Even more successful was the Griffon powered Mk XIX that entered service in May 1944, and which by the end of the war the type had virtually replaced the Mk XI.

A total of 225 were built with production ceasing in early 1946, and they were used in front-line service until April 1954, by which time they were the last operational Spitfires serving with the RAF.

Women's Royal Air Force (WRAF) ground crew work on Spitfire Mk IIAs of No. 411 (Canadian) Squadron at RAF Digby in October 1941. The unit was formed on Spitfires on 16 June 1941 and flew, successively, Mk Vs and IXs until disbanded on 21 March 1946.

Supermarine Spitfire PR Mk I G

Weight (maximum take-off): 2986kg (6584lb)

Dimensions: Length 9.12m (29ft 11in), Wingspan 11.23m (36ft 10in), Height 3.02m (9ft 10in)

Powerplant: One 1074kW (1440hp) Rolls-Royce 45 liquid cooled V-12 piston engine

Maximum speed: 594km/h (369mph)

Range: 1143km (710 miles)

Ceiling: 11,278m (37,000ft)

Crew: 1

Armament: Eight 7.7mm (0.303in) Browning machine guns fixed, firing forward in wings

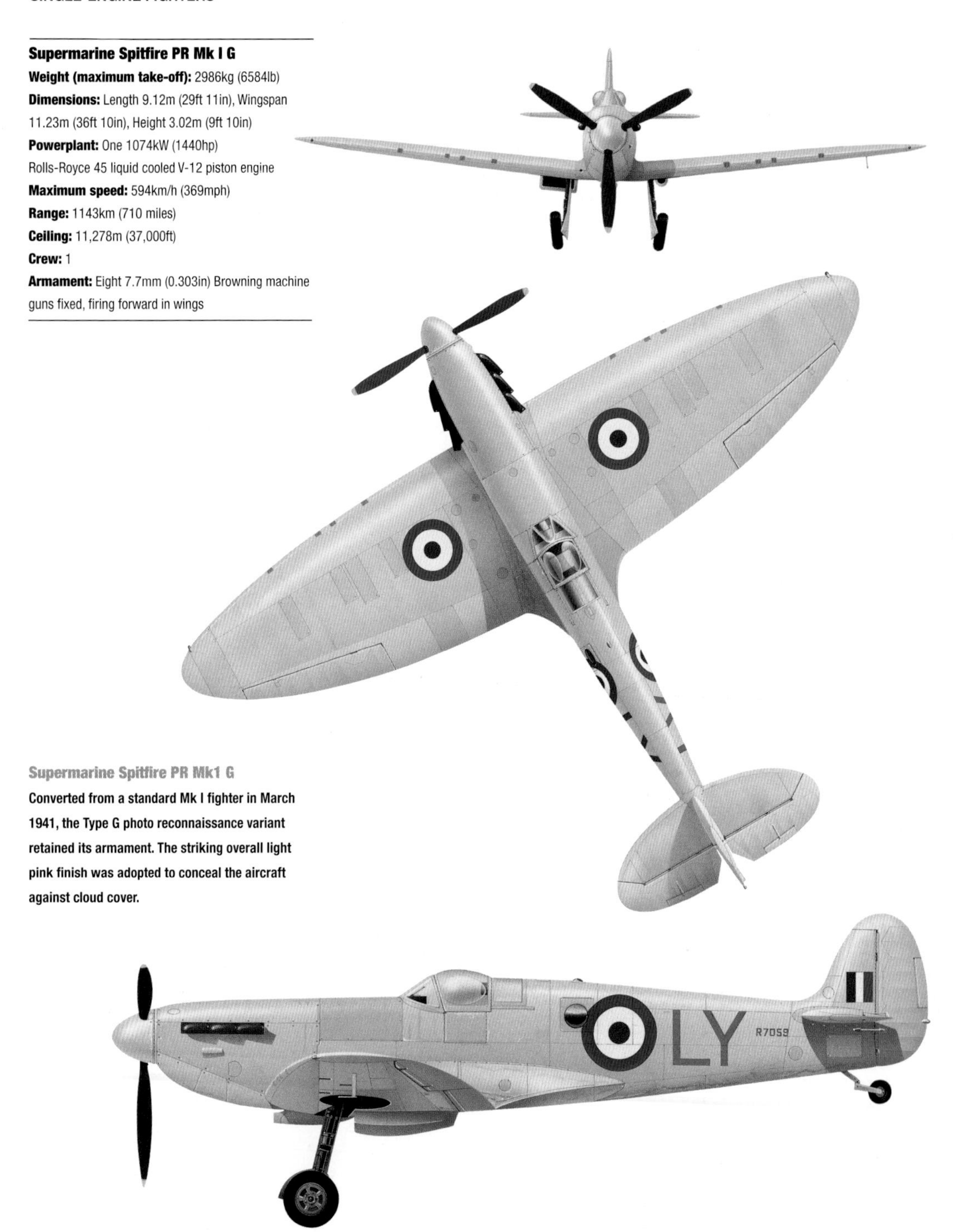

Supermarine Spitfire PR Mk1 G

Converted from a standard Mk I fighter in March 1941, the Type G photo reconnaissance variant retained its armament. The striking overall light pink finish was adopted to conceal the aircraft against cloud cover.

Boulton Paul Defiant

With its entire armament concentrated in a power operated turret, the Defiant was specifically intended to intercept and destroy unescorted bombers.

The two-seat, single-engined fighter had been a feature of the Royal Air Force (RAF) since the highly successful Bristol Fighter of the First World War, and during the early 1930s, the Hawker Demon two-seat fighter biplane entered service. By this time it was becoming clear that the higher speeds at which aircraft were now flying were making it increasingly difficult for a gunner to accurately aim a machine gun from an open cockpit. The Boulton Paul company, who were building Demons under subcontract, were pioneers of the power-operated gun turret in the UK and began discussions with the Air Ministry about the possibility of producing a modern high-performance fighter featuring a powered turret.

New turret

The turreted fighter was primarily intended for use against bomber formations, making beam and cross-over passes from below allowing for accurate, concentrated fire directly into the enemy aircraft's bomb bay and it was envisioned that the aircraft would operate in concert with conventional Hawker Hurricanes. From the outset it was considered inadvisable for the turret fighter to engage in combat with enemy single-seaters but in a future war with Germany, it was expected that France would not fall for some time and unescorted bombing missions would have to be flown against Britain, as no German fighter had the necessary range to fly to Britain and back.

The concept was codified in Specification F.9/35, and attracted considerable attention amongst manufacturers, no fewer than six tendering potential designs. Prototypes of three designs, from Fairey, Hawker, and Boulton Paul were ordered but only the Hawker design (named the Hotspur) and the Boulton Paul, designated P.82 by the company, were destined to be built. Initially the Air Ministry favoured the Hotspur but Hawker-Siddeley's production resources were overburdened with existing projects (not least the Hurricane) whereas Boulton Paul had spare capacity. Once the prototypes had been built the P.82 demonstrated better performance than the Hotspur and proved to possess excellent handling qualities, effectively curtailing any chance that the Hawker aircraft would enter production.

When the P.82 made its first flight on 11 August 1937, an order for 87 production aircraft had already been placed, and the name 'Defiant' had been bestowed on the new fighter. Performance was, as expected, not as good as either the Hurricane or Spitfire and the Defiant, with its second crewman and the hydraulically operated Boulton Paul A Mk IID turret, possessed a power-to-weight ratio some 25 per cent worse than the Hurricane. Nonetheless, during tests at

Boulton Paul Defiant Mk I

Weight (maximum take-off): 3901kg (8600lb)
Dimensions: 10.77m (35ft 4in) Wingspan, 11.99m (39ft 4in) Height, 3.45m (11ft 4in)
Powerplant: One 770kW (1030hp) Rolls-Royce Merlin III V-12 liquid-cooled piston engine
Maximum speed: 489km/h (304mph)
Range: 748km (465 miles)
Ceiling: 9400m (31,000ft)
Crew: 2
Armament: Four 7.7mm (0.303in) Browning machine guns in dorsal turret

Boulton Paul Defiant Mk I

After being withdrawn from daylight operations, the Defiant enjoyed a successful second career as a night fighter. This Mk I was operating with 409 (RCAF) Sqn at RAF Coleby Grange in the late Summer 1941.

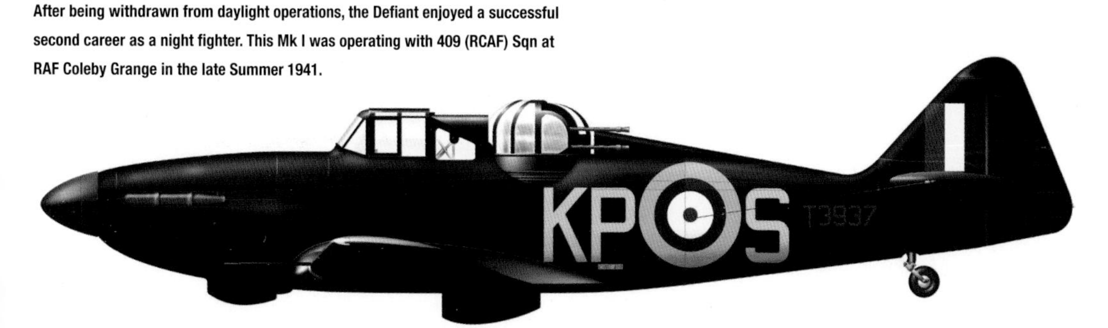

Photographed in 1940, the Defiants of 264 Squadron were led by Squadron Leader Philip Hunter. Hunter and his gunner Pilot Officer FH King had scored nine victories in the Defiant when they took off in pursuit of Ju 88s attacking RAF Manston on 24 August 1940. They were never seen again.

the Aeroplane & Armament Experimental Establishment (A&AEE) in 1939, the production Defiant Mk I managed to clock the respectable speed of 489km/h (304mph) at 5181m (17,000ft).

First combat

The first Defiants began to be taken on strength with No. 264 squadron in December 1939 and operations began to be flown by mid-March 1940. At first, the aircraft did well: in operations covering the Dunkirk evacuation, No. 264 Squadron claimed 37 aircraft shot down without loss but when committed to the Battle of Britain the results were appalling. No. 141 Squadron, the second Defiant unit, suffered nine aircraft losses out of 12 in its first encounter with the Luftwaffe, when it engaged a superior number of Bf 109s.

Meanwhile, the more experienced No. 264 Squadron also suffered, losing all but three of its aircraft in just three combats. Both squadrons were withdrawn from operations during August 1940 and the career of the Defiant as a day fighter came to an end having never operated as originally intended, against unescorted bomber formations.

Night fighter

However, the fighting career of the Defiant was far from over. Nocturnal operations had been intended as a role for the aircraft since its conception and Defiant units started to fly as night fighters from September 1940, claiming their first kills by the middle of the month. Successes were initially a matter of luck but during 1941 airborne radar began to be carried. Initially the rudimentary AI Mk IV set was fitted to a few aircraft but by August 1941 the improved AI Mk VI was being used in quantity. Unusually, the radar set was operated by the pilot, there being no room for its cathode ray tube in the turret. Unlike the ponderous Blenheim, the Defiant had the performance necessary to intercept any German bomber and its turret armament meant the aircraft could attack targets from behind and below to great effect. Production had by this time switched to the Defiant Mk II featuring the Merlin Mk XX for slightly better performance and for a time the Defiant was the most successful RAF night fighter before more powerful aircraft such as the Beaufighter appeared in numbers. By mid-1942 the combat career of the Defiant was effectively over.

Target tug

Further development of the aircraft saw large numbers used in the unglamorous but vital role of high speed target tug but a 12-gun single-seat ‘panic fighter’ version never entered production despite the 586km/h (364mph) top speed demonstrated by a turretless prototype flown during 1940. Production would have been rapid as it required minimal changes to existing tooling but the project did not progress further. Defiants also served as electronic warfare aircraft initially carrying ‘Moonshine’ equipment that re-transmitted German radar signals to simulate large formations of aircraft and later with ‘Mandrel’, a noise jammer which overwhelmed enemy radar signals. Individual Defiants were sent to orbit positions 80km (50 miles) off the enemy coast and with nine aircraft a 320km (200 miles) gap could be made in German radar coverage. Defiants carried out countermeasures work until mid-1943 when the ever-increasing size and power requirements of the increasingly complex electronic equipment required the use of larger aircraft such as the Flying Fortress.

Brewster Buffalo

The Buffalo was the first monoplane fighter ordered by the US Navy though its career with its nation of origin was brief. British and Commonwealth units flew the Brewster against Japanese forces in the brief but fierce fighting in Singapore and Malaya.

Brewster, a coachbuilding company, had not been manufacturing aircraft for very long when they won a contract to supply the US Navy with its first modern monoplane fighter. The US Navy considered that the landing speed of the monoplane was too great for carrier operations. However as the biplane was reaching the realistic limits of its development potential it was decided that a monoplane fighter should be developed and the prototype Brewster XF2A-1 was ordered along with the biplane Grumman XF4F-1 as a back-up. The XF2A-1 that emerged in early 1938 could hardly be called sleek but it possessed advanced features, such as a fully flush riveted stressed skin construction, split flaps and hydraulically powered retractable undercarriage.

First production

First flown on 2 December 1937, the Brewster went into production as the F2A-1, with delivery of the first examples beginning in July 1939. By this time the original prototype had been severely damaged in deck-landing trials and the opportunity was taken to re-engine it as the prototype of the faster and more powerful F2A-2 with the heavier armament of four 12.7mm (0.5in) machine guns, more fuel and other equipment. With the F2A-2 on order the decision was taken to release the balance of the F2A-1 order for export to Finland designated the B-239. Belgium and the United Kingdom ordered a de-navalised F2A-2 under the export designation B-339 during 1940, though the UK would take over the Belgian aircraft after Belgium fell to the Germans, and the Netherlands East Indies government also ordered B-339s shortly after.

Far East action

In British service the aircraft received the official name 'Buffalo', which swiftly became a popular nickname for the aircraft more widely. Royal Air Force (RAF) tests saw the B-339 rejected for use in Europe and nearly all were sent instead to the Far East where they were expected to be superior to any fighter Japan was likely to field in the event of war. Australia also ordered Buffaloes but in the event these were never delivered and the two Royal Australian Air Force (RAAF) Buffalo Squadrons used aircraft drawn from RAF stock, retaining RAF markings and serial numbers. A single Royal New Zealand Air Force (RNZAF) unit also operated the Buffalo, based in Singapore.

When the Japanese onslaught began, the Buffaloes initially fared quite well though it became increasingly clear that the aircrafts were inferior to the latest Japanese fighters. Many of the Buffaloes were destroyed on the ground, and Allied aircraft were outnumbered in the air, resulting in the loss of over 130 Buffaloes in Singapore and Malaya, virtually the entire inventory, between December 1941 and February 1942. Despite their eventual defeat, Buffalo pilots did manage to inflict significant losses on the Japanese during the campaign and four Allied Buffalo pilots became 'aces' during this period.

B-339s of the Netherlands East Indies suffered a similar fate to the Commonwealth Buffaloes, losing 60 of 71 aircraft before surrendering

The majority of Buffaloes were delivered direct from the US to operational squadrons in the Far East but this example, AS430, was retained by the Aeroplane and Armament Experimental Establishment (A&AEE) for testing in the UK.

to the Japanese. Further Brewsters were in the process of being delivered when the Netherlands East Indies was overrun and these 21 aircraft, one B-339 and 20 B-439s with an uprated Cyclone engine, were diverted to Australia and taken on charge by the United States Army Air Force (USAAF). Seventeen of these aircraft were subsequently transferred to the RAAF, receiving Australian markings and serial numbers, and were used as photographic reconnaissance aircraft as well as home-based fighters.

During 1942, these Buffaloes formed the sole fighter defence of Perth in Western Australia, though none were to be used in combat. By mid-January 1944 all the Buffaloes had been transferred to the USAAF's Fifth Air Force (which immediately scrapped them in Brisbane) and the Commonwealth career of the Buffalo was over.

Brewster Buffalo

Like RAF aircraft operating in Europe, the undersides of the Brewster Buffaloes stationed in Singapore were painted half-black for ready recognition. AN210 was on the strength of No. 453 Squadron RAAF in late 1941 and early 1942.

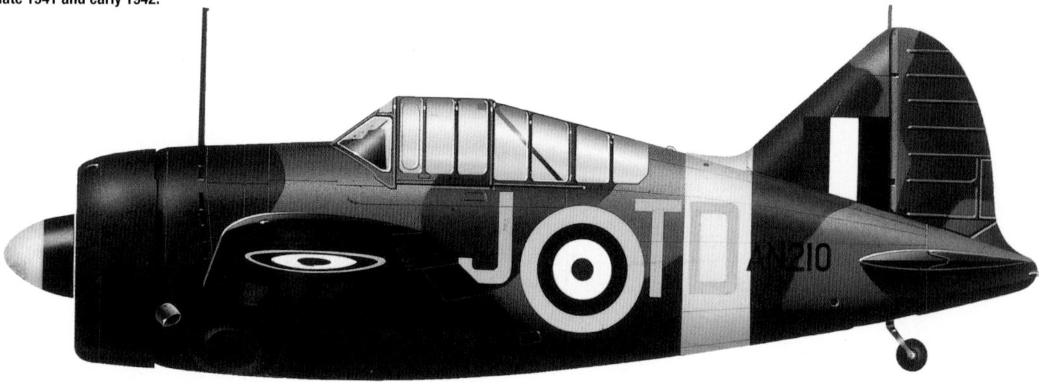

Brewster Buffalo Mk I

Weight (maximum take-off): 3247kg (7159lb)

Dimensions Length: 8.03m (26ft 4in), Wingspan: 10.67m (35ft), Height: 3.66m (12ft)

Powerplant One 890kW (1200hp) Wright R-1820-40 Cyclone 9-cylinder air-cooled radial engine

Speed: 517km/h (321mph)

Range: 1553km (965 miles)

Ceiling: 10,100m (33,200ft)

Crew: 1

Armament: Two 12.7mm (0.5in) M2 Browning machine guns fixed forward firing in wings, two 12.7mm (0.5in) M2 Browning machine guns fixed forward firing in cowling; up to two 90kg (200lb) bombs under wings

Bell Airacobra

Despite delivering exceptional service in the Soviet Union, the career of the Airacobra in the Royal Air Force (RAF) was short and disappointing.

The first single seat fighter design developed by Bell Aircraft, the P-39 Airacobra was of a highly unconventional layout with the engine mounted behind the pilot and driving the propeller by means of a shaft which passed under the cockpit. This unusual arrangement had been adopted to allow for the very heavy nose armament of a 37mm (1.46in) cannon firing through the propeller hub supplemented by two machine guns. The Airacobra had initially flown on 6 April 1938 and 675 examples of a British version were ordered by the British Direct Purchase Commission in 1940, armed with a 20mm (0.79in) cannon in place of the 37mm (1.46in) weapon.

The first examples, briefly named 'Caribou' before the existing Airacobra name was officially adopted, were supplied to 601 Squadron in August 1941 but the aircraft proved inadequate for British needs. Criticisms were levelled at the cockpit layout and the difficulty in bailing out of the aircraft in an emergency as the roof was fixed and the pilot had to get out through one of the automobile-style doors. More serious was the fact that the Airacobra could not meet its specified performance.

Delivery of the Airacobra to the RAF had been contingent on it achieving a speed within 4 per cent of 634km/h (394mph) at 4267m (14,000ft). However, Bell Aircraft had specially prepared an Airacobra with a drag-reducing finish, new engine exhausts with nozzles to increase thrust augmentation, the machine gun ports faired over, and the antenna mast removed. Weight was reduced by 91kg (200lb) and in this form the aircraft achieved 629km/h (391mph). In tests on a standard production Airacobra a maximum of only 578km/h (359mph) could be attained. Combat service with 601 Squadron amounted to a single mission to strafe German invasion barges before the type was removed from service.

All existing Airacobras, except for a single example retained for trials duties, were shipped instead to the Soviet Union. Some British specification Airacobras also made it into operational United States Army Air Force (USAAF) service, designated the P-400, and were used in action in the South Pacific and New Guinea.

Bell Airacobra Mk I

Weight (maximum take-off): 4018kg (8850lb)

Dimensions: Length 9.21m (30ft 2in), Wingspan 10.37m (34ft), Height 3.6m (11ft 10in)

Powerplant: One 858kW (1150hp) Allison V-1710-35 V-12 liquid cooled piston engine

Maximum speed: 579km/h (360mph)

Range: 563km (350 miles)

Ceiling: 9784m (32,100ft)

Crew: 1

Armament: One 20mm Hispano cannon fixed, firing forward through propeller hub, two synchronised 12.7mm (0.5in) Browning machine guns fixed, firing forward in nose and two 7.7mm (0.3in) Browning machine guns fixed, firing forward in wings

RAAF service

This was not quite the end for the Airacobra in Commonwealth service, however, as during 1942 23 P-39s were loaned by the US Fifth Air Force to the Royal Australian Air Force (RAAF) to help bolster fighter forces on the east coast of Australia. No Australian squadron was ever entirely equipped with P-39s, nor did any see combat before the aircraft were replaced, but the aircraft played an invaluable role in supplementing meagre Australian fighter defences during 1942 and 1943.

Bell Airacobra Mk I

Bell Airacobra Mk I, serial no. AH601 of 601 'County of London' Squadron, stationed at RAF Duxford, October 1941. Assigned to the CO, Sqn Ldr EJ Garcie DFC, it carries his personal marking, 'Sklylark XIII' on the cockpit door above a squadron leader's pennant.

Curtiss Mohawk

The first American fighter to shoot down an enemy aircraft in World War II, the Curtiss Hawk 75 proved to be the finest Allied fighter in the Battle for France. In Royal Air Force (RAF) service, the Curtiss fighter served in India and Burma (modern-day Myanmar).

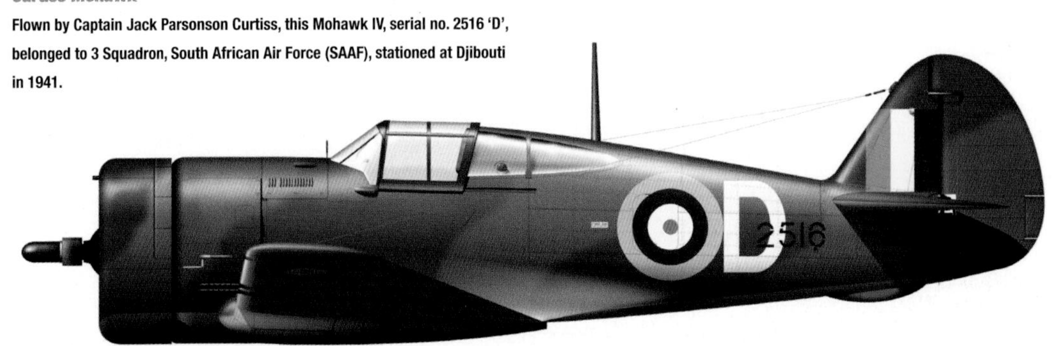

Curtiss Mohawk

Flown by Captain Jack Parsonson Curtiss, this Mohawk IV, serial no. 2516 'D', belonged to 3 Squadron, South African Air Force (SAAF), stationed at Djibouti in 1941.

In competition to select the first 'modern' all-metal low-wing monoplane fighter for the United States Army Air Corps (USAAC), the Curtiss 75 initially lost out to the Seversky P-35 but ultimately proved to be the better aircraft and was produced in greater numbers as the P-36. Two such aircraft managed to achieve the first US victories of the war by shooting down a Nakajima B5N1 each during the Pearl Harbor attack.

Over two years before that however, on 20 September 1939, French Hawk 75s had become the first Allied fighters to shoot down an enemy aircraft on the Western front. In the subsequent Battle for France the French Hawk 75s were responsible for over a third of all German aircraft shot down.

Hawk Model 75A

French aircraft on order when France fell were diverted to the RAF, which named the aircraft the 'Mohawk'. The French had received four subtypes designated the Hawk 75A-1, A-2, A-3 and A-4, and in the expectation that they would receive considerable numbers of these aircraft flown directly from France, the RAF simply designated these Mohawk Mk I, Mk II, Mk III, And Mk IV respectively. In the event, although some aircraft were indeed received in this way, the numbers were small, and the only ex-French Hawk type to enter operational service was the Mk III.

The vast majority of British aircraft were Hawk Model 75A-4s delivered direct from the US to become Mohawk IVs. Considerable interest in the aircraft had been generated in official circles by a report from a British pilot who had flown the Hawk in France and reported that it was "more manoeuvrable at high speed than the Hurricane or Spitfire".

Later, in mock combat with a Spitfire the Mohawk was found to be quite capable of outmanoeuvring the British aircraft and the handling characteristics of the Curtiss aircraft were very highly praised.

Curtiss Mohawk Mk IV

Weight (maximum take-off): 2726kg (6010lb)
Dimensions: Length 8.74m (28ft 8in), Wingspan 11.38m (37ft 4in), Height 2.82m (9ft 3in)
Powerplant: One 149kW (1200hp) Wright R-1820-G205A Cyclone radial nine-cylinder air-cooled radial engine
Maximum speed: 520km/h (323mph)
Range: 1078km (670 miles)
Ceiling: 9967m (32,700ft)
Crew: 1
Armament: Two 7.7mm (0.3in) synchronised Browning machine guns fixed, firing forward in nose and four 7.7mm (0.3in) Browning machine guns fixed, firing forward in wings

East African Campaign

Despite the excellence of the report on the aircraft, the comparatively modest speed performance of the Mohawk resulted in its being judged unsuitable for RAF operations in Europe and many Mohawk IVs were supplied to South Africa. These served in the East African Campaign and later in defence of South Africa itself, mounting anti-shipping and anti-submarine patrols until 1943 and were subsequently used as advanced trainers.

RAF use of the aircraft was limited to India and Burma where the Curtiss fighter was operated for a considerable period. In common with all Cyclone-engined Hawk 75 variants, the Mohawk Mk IV suffered from constant problems with its oil circulation system which tended to be more severe in hotter climates and individual aircraft were regularly grounded as a result. Despite this impediment the Mohawk proved to be quite successful in India, the first unit to convert to the Mohawk IV, No 5 Squadron, exchanged its Hawker Audax biplanes for the new aircraft in India during December 1941 and for a time this unit provided the sole fighter defence of North East India. A second Mohawk unit, No 155 Squadron, converted in April 1942 and utilised the aircraft on bomber escort missions, standing patrols and close support. A Mohawk IV of No. 5 Squadron claimed the type's first air-to-air victory in British service on 20 August 1942 and the aircraft were subsequently committed to the heavy fighting at Imphal, India during early 1943. In May 1943 the Mohawks were used as dive-bombers for the first time using 9kg (20lb) bombs and the aircraft remained in use for ground attack missions until the end of 1944.

Curtiss Tomahawk

An inline engine development of the earlier radial-powered Hawk 75, the Curtiss Tomahawk was used in large numbers by British Commonwealth forces in the Western Desert and Middle East.

The Hawk-75/P-36 had proved to be an excellent handling aircraft but it was somewhat slower than its European contemporaries. Curtiss re-engined the airframe with a turbocharged V-12 Allison engine, promising excellent high altitude performance, to produce the XP-37 in 1937, followed by a small test batch of 13 YP-37s. There were many problems with the turbo superchargers and this development was dropped in favour of a simpler conversion with an Allison V-1710 fitted with a gear driven supercharger. This resulted in a much more reliable system but effectively limited the aircraft to operations below 4,575m (15,000ft), a situation that was acceptable to the US Army Air Corps (USAAC), which at that time regarded coastal defence and ground attack as the primary roles for their fighters.

Flown for the first time on 14 October 1938, the XP-40 as the conversion had been designated, was initially only capable of a highly disappointing 481km/h (299mph).

Curtiss Tomahawk Mk IB

Weight (maximum take-off): 3655kg (8058lb)
Dimensions: Length 9.66m (31ft 9in), Wingspan 11.37m (37ft 4in), Height 3.22m (10ft 7in)
Powerplant: One 813kW (1090hp) Allison V-1710-33 V-12 liquid cooled piston engine
Maximum speed: 555km/h (345mph)
Range: 1287km (800 miles)
Ceiling: 8990m (29,500ft)
Crew: 1
Armament: Two 12.7mm (0.5in) Colt Browning M2 machine guns fixed forward firung in fuselage nose; four 7.62mm (0.3in) Browning M1919 machine guns fixed forward firing in wings

Curtiss Tomahawk Mk IB

More famous for its exploits in the Western Desert, the Tomahawk began its RAF career in the UK in the low-level reconnaissance role. This example was serving with No. 2 Squadron, based at Sawbridgeworth in Essex.

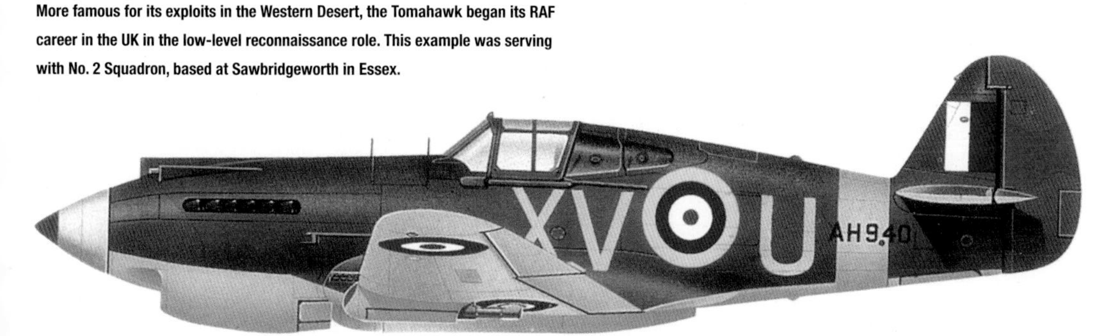

The shark mouth became so synonymous with the Tomahawk and Kittyhawk that virtually all preserved examples are adorned with it. This anonymous 112 Sqn Tomahawk was photographed in North Africa in 1941.

The XP-40s airframe was subjected to a thorough aerodynamic clean-up, during which time the radiator was moved to a chin position, giving the aircraft its distinctive shark-mouthed profile, and speed was improved to 574km/h (357mph).

Production P-40s entered service with the USAAC in September 1940 but as early as October 1939, an order had been placed by the French Purchasing Commission for 230 Hawk 81A-1s (essentially an early production P-40 with French armament and equipment) for use by the Armée de l'Air. Export of these aircraft was delayed by the US government and ultimately none would actually be shipped to France.

British adaption

The entire order was subsequently taken over by the British Purchasing Commission following the fall of France with completed aircraft and those in an advanced state of construction, around 140 aircraft, being shipped to the UK. Fitted with British equipment and armament, four 7.7mm (0.303in) Brownings replaced the 7.5mm (0.29in) FN-Brownings in the wings, but otherwise minimally changed from the French specification, these aircraft were named 'Tomahawk I'. The balance of the French order, consisting of 90 aircraft, followed by the first 20 aircraft built for a direct British order, were completed with further modifications to Royal Air Force (RAF) requirements. They had armour-glass windscreen, self-sealing fuel tanks, armour protection for the pilot and were fitted in the US with four 7.62mm (0.3in) Colt Browning machine guns in the wings. In this revised form it became the Tomahawk IIA but was swiftly followed by the Tomahawk IIB, of which 930 were ordered. The IIB reverted to British 7.7mm (0.303in) wing armament and featured British radio and oxygen equipment rather than the US items fitted to the IIA.

Initial use of the Tomahawk was by seven RAF and two Royal Canadian Air Force (RCAF) squadrons based in the UK for conversion training and for initial operations. The poor altitude performance of the aircraft combined with the lack of self-sealing fuel tanks and armour of the Tomahawk I resulted in the aircraft being considered unsuitable for use as a UK-based interceptor and Tomahawk squadrons were utilised for low-level tactical reconnaissance.

Tropicalised model

The more combat-capable Tomahawk IIA and IIBs gradually supplanted the Tomahawk Is in these units and between March and October 1941, 294 examples of the Curtiss fighter were despatched to the Middle East. Aircraft destined for this theatre were modestly tropicalised with dust filters on the carburettor intake. The first unit to convert to the Tomahawk in the Middle East was 250 Squadron in May 1941, shortly followed by No.3 Squadron of the Royal Australian Air Force (RAAF) and No.2 Squadron of the South African Air Force (SAAF).

Further units converted to the Curtiss in the Western Desert and the aircraft played a significant role as part of the Desert Air Force (DAF) until replaced by the Kittyhawk from early 1942, though some units soldiered on with Tomahawks into 1943. The aircraft was popular due to its pleasant handling, great structural strength, and reliability and at low and medium level was considered roughly equal or slightly superior to both the Messerschmitt Bf 109 and Macchi MC.202. At higher altitudes both enemy fighters were markedly superior to the Tomahawk but most combat in the theatre occurred below or around 14,760ft (4,500m) negating this advantage and the introduction of the Curtiss fighter coincided with a shift in air superiority to the Allies' favour.

'Flying Tigers'

With the lessening of the threat of a German invasion of the British Isles, the RAF released stocks of Tomahawks for other users, the first being 100 Hawk 81A-2s, originally intended to be RAF Tomahawk IIBs that were shipped instead to China and famously used to considerable effect by the American Volunteer Group (AVG), better known as the 'Flying Tigers'. Other Tomahawks were supplied in small numbers to the Egyptian and Turkish Air Forces as well as 195 Tomahawk IIBs that were sent to the Soviet Union in 1941, beginning operations there in October 1941. Curiously, although many P-40s of various subtypes were subsequently supplied directly from the US, the aircraft was always referred to by its British name of Tomahawk, as was the later Kittyhawk, in Soviet service.

Curtiss Kittyhawk Mk IA

No. 112 Squadron was the first to adorn the Tomahawk with the enduring shark's mouth motif, later adopted by the 'Flying Tigers' in China. The shark-like profile of the Curtiss aircraft combined with its large chin intake lent itself to this iconic piece of 'nose art'.

Curtiss Tomahawk Mk IB

Weight (maximum take-off): 3655kg (8058lb)
Dimensions: Length 9.66m (31ft 9in), Wingspan 11.37m (37ft 4in), Height 3.22m (10ft 7in)
Powerplant: One 813kW (1090hp) Allison V-1710-33 V-12 liquid cooled piston engine
Maximum speed: 555km/h (345mph)
Range: 1287km (800 miles)
Ceiling: 8990m (29,500ft)
Crew: 1
Armament: Two 12.7mm (0.5in) Colt Browning M2 machine guns fixed forward firung in fuselage nose; four 7.62mm (0.3in) Browning M1919 machine guns fixed forward firing in wings

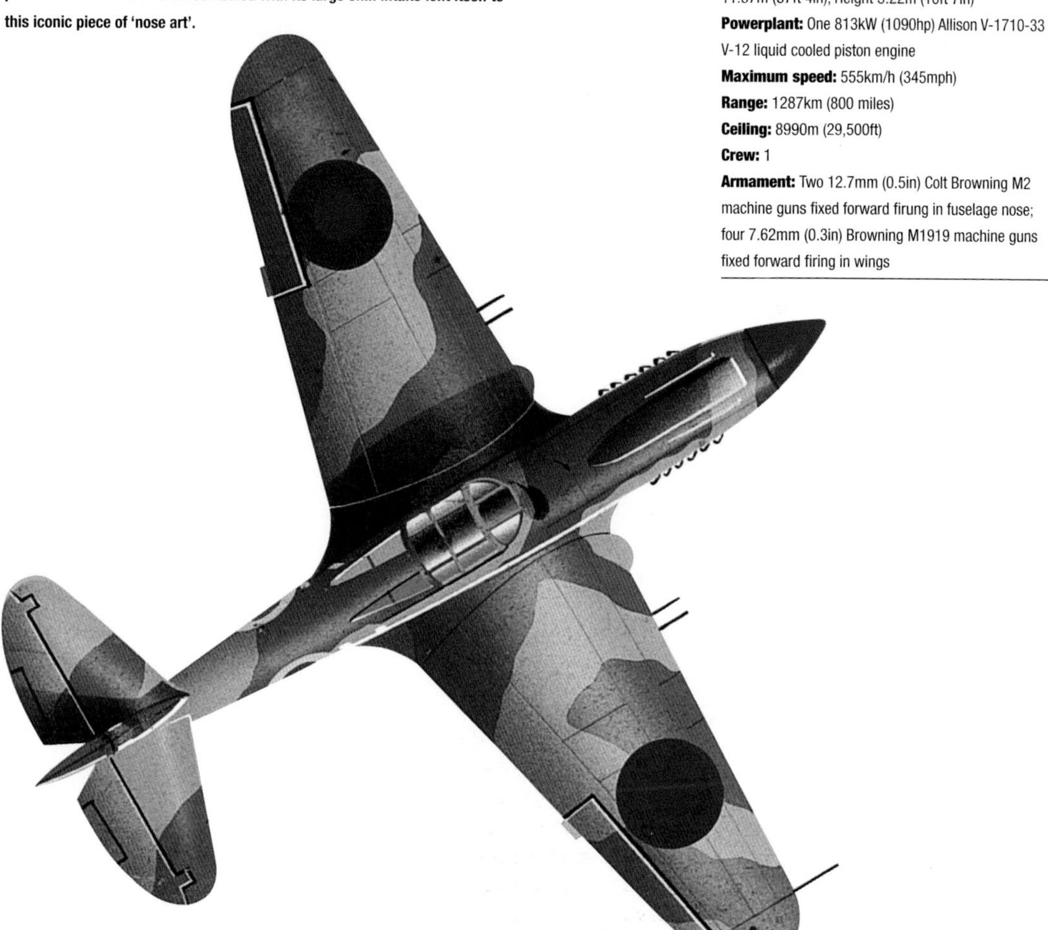

Curtiss Kittyhawk

A relatively modest update to the Tomahawk, the Curtiss Hawk 87 was built in much greater numbers than the earlier aircraft and was to become an important fighter for virtually all the Allied air forces.

The appearance of the Allison V-1710-39 (F3R) variant of the V-1710 engine offered a useful increase in rated power as well as offering a five minute 'war emergency' rating of 1470hp, a feature not available to the V-1710-33 as fitted to the Tomahawk. Curtiss, keen to improve their fighter's performance, duly modified the basic P-40 design to incorporate the new engine. A larger radiator was fitted and the engine's airscrew reduction gear was altered, resulting in a shorter unit and a raised thrust line. As a consequence the aircraft's nose contours had to be significantly revised and there was no longer space for the twin gun nose armament. To make up for the loss of the nose guns the wing armament of the aircraft was increased with four 12.7mm (0.5in) guns fitted in place of the smaller calibre weapons of earlier variants. The entire fuselage was reduced in depth, resulting in a noticeably more slender aircraft and though the US Army Air Corps (USAAC) regarded the Hawk 87 as a new variant of the existing P-40, designating it the P-40D The Royal Air Force (RAF) officially regarded the P-40D as a new type, naming it 'Kittyhawk', after the location of the Wright Brothers' first flight.

Lend-Lease deliveries

The British Purchasing Commission placed the first order for 560 examples of the Hawk 87 in May 1940, with the USAAC following suit shortly after. The new Curtiss fighter flew for the first time a year later on 22 May 1941, the aircraft in question being the first airframe built for the British contract. Two months earlier the Lend-Lease Act had passed

Curtiss Kittyhawk Mk IA

Weight (maximum take-off): 4131kg (9100lb)
Dimensions: Length 9.68m (31ft 9in), Wingspan 11.38m (37ft 4in), Height 3.76m (12ft 4in)
Powerplant: One 858kW (1150hp) Allison V-1710-39 V-12 liquid cooled piston engine
Maximum speed: 582km/h (362mph)
Range (internal fuel only): 845km (525 miles)
Ceiling: 9144m (30,000ft)
Crew: 1
Armament: Six 12.7mm (0.5in) Browning machine guns fixed, firing forward in wings; up to 317kg (700lb) bombload

Curtiss Kittyhawk Mk IA

Another 112 Squadron 'Hawk', Kittyhawks replaced Tomahawks with the unit towards the end of 1941. AK772, which displays some overspray over the fuselage roundel, served with the squadron until it was lost in May 1942.

Curtiss Kittyhawk Mk III

FR243 is pictured as it appeared when serving with No. 250 Squadron in Italy in 1943. By this time the primary role of the Curtiss fighter was ground attack, a role for which the rugged Kittyhawk proved well suited.

allowing future large orders for the Kittyhawk, the first of which being for 1,500 Kittyhawk IAs, equivalent to the United States Army Air Forces's (USAAF) P-40E. These featured a slightly more powerful armament of six 12.7mm (0.5in) machine guns and some were supplied with bomb shackles from the factory.

The first unit to operate the Kittyhawk Mk.I was No. 3 Squadron Royal Australian Air Force (RAAF) which converted from the Tomahawk II during December 1941, becoming operational on the 30th. Shortly afterwards the first RAF Kittyhawk unit, No. 112 Squadron, became operational on the type in January 1942 with conversion of most other squadrons flying Tomahawks proceeding rapidly thereafter. Commanded by the Australian Squadron Leader Clive Caldwell (1911-1994), No. 112 Squadron pioneered the use of the Kittyhawk as a fighter bomber carrying a pair of 114kg (250lb) bombs, thus earning the nickname 'Kittybomber', and saw intensive action in this role, operating in the Western Desert and thence throughout the campaign in Italy. The South African Air Force (SAAF) also operated the Kittyhawk in North Africa, with two Tomahawk units converting to the Kittyhawk I in June 1942. Eventually four South African squadrons would fly the Kittyhawk in action, the last converting from Spitfires as late as November 1944.

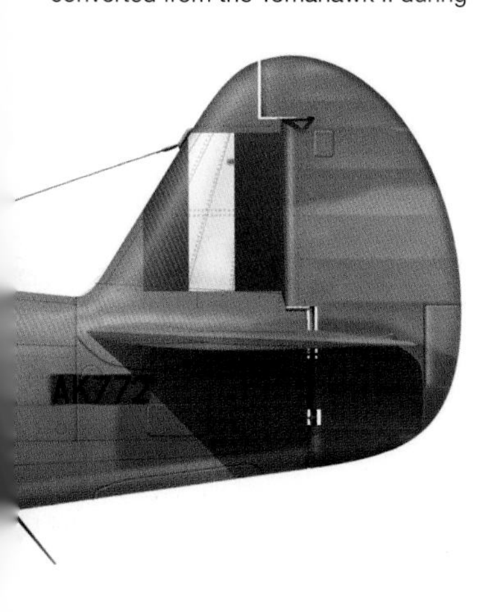

Far East action

The first examples of the updated Curtiss fighter to see Commonwealth service against the Japanese, however, were not British-ordered aircraft at all but American P-40Es. An urgent need to provide fighter defence for Port

Curtiss Kittyhawk Mk III

Weight (maximum take-off): 4131kg (9100lb)
Dimensions: Length 10.16m (33ft 4in), Wingspan 11.38m (37ft 4in), Height 3.76m (12ft 4in)
Powerplant: One 895kW (1200hp) Allison V-1710-81 V-12 liquid cooled piston engine
Maximum speed: 582km/h (362mph)
Range (internal fuel only): 845km (525 miles)
Ceiling: 9449m (31,000ft)
Crew: 1
Armament: Six 12.7mm (0.5in) Browning machine guns fixed, firing forward in wings; up to 317kg (700lb) bombload

Curtiss Kittyhawk Mk IV

Curtiss Kittyhawk IV (P-40N), serial no. NZ3237 'E' from 19 Squadron, Royal New Zealand Air Force (RNZAF), served at Guadalcanal and Torokina in late 1944. It was flown by Allan 'Skip' Watson, who named it "Esma Lee" for a girl he knew in Auckland.

Moresby after the Japanese invasion of New Guinea saw 25 P-40Es transferred from the USAAF to the RAAF, to form the equipment of No. 75 Squadron. This unit arrived in New Guinea on 19 March, claiming its first victory on the 21st, and was subsequently heavily engaged for the next 44 days, claiming 35 confirmed victories for the loss of 22 P-40s. All subsequent RAAF Curtiss fighters were drawn from Lend Lease supplies, the first of which consisting of a batch of 139 Kittyhawk IAs which were supplied to No. 75 Squadron as well as equipping seven further squadrons. Ultimately the Kittyhawk would become the most numerous fighter operated by the RAAF in the Pacific during World War II.

Canada and New Zealand also became major users of the Curtiss fighter, with the Royal Canadian Air Force (RCAF) receiving their first Kittyhawk Is in October 1941 to replace the Goblin and Hurricane. RCAF P-40s supplied from USAAF stocks were used in action to supplement US forces in the defence of Alaska in 1942, scoring the sole victory of a Canadian aircraft operating from North America when a Canadian P-40K shot down a Nakajima A6M2-N 'Rufe' floatplane.

By contrast, the Royal New Zealand Air Force (RNZAF) saw more prolonged and intense action against the Japanese, flying alongside USAAF units in the Solomon Islands. RNZAF Kittyhawks were in the frontline from April 1943 to February 1944 when the last Kittyhawk squadron converted to the Vought F4U Corsair, during which period they destroyed 99 Japanese aircraft.

Upgraded engine

Curtiss meanwhile had sought to improve the P-40's performance, tacitly admitted to be inferior to most of its contemporaries, especially at altitude, by equipping it with a Rolls-Royce Merlin engine. A P-40D was therefore taken from the production line to become the XP-40F when it was fitted with a Rolls-Royce Merlin 28 engine. Performance was sufficiently improved for the type to go into production as the P-40F with a US-built Packard V-1650-1 Merlin.

Only 330 P-40Fs were delivered to Britain and designated Kittyhawk Mk.II, as was the similarly powered P-40L which was a lightened version of the P-40F. The The P-40L dispensed with two of the wing guns, and reduced

Curtiss Kittyhawk Mk IV
Weight (maximum take-off): 4018kg (8850lb)
Dimensions: Length 10.17m (33ft 4in), Wingspan 11.37m (37ft 4in), Height 3.76m (12ft 4in)
Powerplant: One 895kW (1200hp) Allison V-1710-81 V-12 liquid cooled piston engine
Maximum speed: 560km/h (348mph)
Range (max external fuel): 2010km (1250 miles)
Ceiling: 9449m (31,000ft)
Crew: 1
Armament: Four 12.7mm (0.5in) Browning machine guns fixed, firing forward in wings; up to 317kg (700lb) bombload

fuel and ammunition capacity, and so-stripped of equipment was nicknamed 'Gypsy Rose Lee' after the famed contemporary striptease performer.

Merlin-powered Kittyhawks could easily be distinguished from Allison-powered variants by the absence of the carburettor intake atop the nose and were heavily engaged towards the end of the North African campaign with both US and British units. Ultimately, relatively few P-40s received the Merlin as both engines and spares were in short supply due to the demand of other programmes and later Kittyhawks reverted to Allison engines.

P-40M

The P-40M was intended purely for export, though some found their way into US units powered by the Allison V-1710-81, which delivered somewhat improved altitude performance compared to earlier Allison variants. About 466 P-40Ms entered Commonwealth service as the Kittyhawk Mk.III.

Further attempts to wring as much performance out of the P-40 airframe as possible resulted in the lightened P-40N, which was built in greater numbers than any other variant and was instantly identifiable by its much improved and extended cockpit glazing. Of the final P-40 production variant, 586 of them were supplied to British and Commonwealth forces as the Kittyhawk Mk.IV. By the time the Kittyhawk IV was entering service, much superior US fighters were being built and the Curtiss fighter was retained in production primarily for export, in part due to its effectiveness as a fighter-bomber but also because it was cheap.

Production of the P-40 ceased on 30 November 1944, and though largely superseded by the end of the conflict, some examples of the Kittyhawk remained in frontline service until the end of the war, notably in Italy and the South West Pacific.

Considerable numbers of Kittyhawks supplied to the RAF under Lend-Lease were transferred to the RNZAF and RAAF (such as this Australian Mk IV accompanied by three Mk IIIs) for service in the Pacific theatre.

Hawker Typhoon

Originally intended as a successor to the Hurricane, the Typhoon was never able to achieve the same level of success as its redoutable forebear. Nevertheless, it weathered a tortuous development to become one of the Allies' most potent close support assets.

Hawker Typhoon

Wearing full D-Day stripes, this Typhoon is armed with eight 27kg (60lb) RP-3 rockets, the weapon with which the Typhoon is most associated. Typhoons became the scourge of German ground forces in Western Europe.

By 1937, with the Hurricane in production, both the Air Ministry and Hawker were looking at the armament and engine of its replacement. Hawker initially wished to pursue a twelve 7.7mm (0.30in) machine gun arrangement, but the Air Ministry preferred a battery of four 20mm (0.79in) cannon mounted in the wings. At the same time, three engines were in development that had the potential to offer power in the 1471kW (2000hp) class: these were later to become the Bristol Centaurus, Rolls-Royce Vulture and Napier Sabre, the latter two being of a highly unconventional layout. Cognisant of the inherent danger of matching a brand new airframe with a new and unproven engine, the Air Ministry made plain in Specification F.18/37, covering the new fighter, that both the Sabre and Vulture should be considered for the aircraft and in the event, variants of the Typhoon would fly with all three designs. As well as providing for a choice of engine, Sydney Camm's (1893–1966) new fighter, generally resembling a scaled up Hurricane, had a wing design that provided for either the 12 gun armament favoured by Hawker or the four cannon called for in the official specification.

Prototypes

Four prototypes were ordered in early 1938, two to be fitted with the Sabre and two with the Vulture, and named 'Typhoon' and 'Tornado' respectively. Sabre development began to lag behind the Vulture and it was the Rolls-Royce engine that was ready first. As a result, the Tornado was the first of the two fighters to fly, taking to the air for the first time on 6 October 1939. Very quickly it was discovered

Hawker Typhoon Mk IB

Weight (maximum take-off): 6010kg (13,250lb)
Dimensions: Length 9.74m (31ft 11.5in), Wingspan 12.67m (41ft 7in), Height 4.67m (15ft 4in)
Powerplant: One 1630kW (2180hp) Napier Sabre IIA H-24 liquid-cooled piston engine
Maximum speed: 679km/h (422mph)
Range (internal fuel only): 1110km (690 miles)
Ceiling: 9700m (31,800ft)
Crew: 1
Armament: Four 20mm (0.79in) Hispano cannon fixed, forward firing in wings; up to 908kg (2000lb) bombload or eight rockets under wings

Hawker Typhoon Mk IB

This Typhoon IB carries the code letters of No. 181 Squadron. In the early part of 1944 the squadron's Typhoons carried out many attacks on V-1 flying bomb sites before moving to France after D-Day in support of the Allied armies.

that drag increased severely at speeds approaching 643km/h (400mph) and the cause was found to be uneven airflow around the Hurricane style ventral radiator. As a result the radiator was moved to a chin position, a position it already occupied in the as-yet unflown Typhoon prototype, and the two aircraft were externally near identical save for the Tornado featuring two rows of exhaust pipes on each side of the nose as opposed to the Typhoon's single row.

The Typhoon made its maiden flight on 24 February 1940 and although Hawker had received an instruction to proceed with the production of 1,000 examples of the new fighters at the end of 1939, problems with both engines were casting a shadow over planned delivery dates. Nonetheless, at this stage the Vulture was looking like the more promising engine, and of the 1000 aircraft on order, 500 were to be Tornadoes, 250 Typhoons, and the remaining 250 would be decided when it became clear which engine was superior.

Hawker Typhoon Mk IB

Weight (maximum take-off): 6010kg (13,250lb)
Dimensions: Length 9.74m (31ft 11.5in), Wingspan 12.67m (41ft 7in), Height 4.67m (15ft 4in)
Powerplant: One 1630kW (2180hp) Napier Sabre IIA H-24 liquid-cooled piston engine
Maximum speed: 679km/h (422mph)
Range (internal fuel only): 1110km (690 miles)
Ceiling: 9700m (31,800ft)
Crew: 1
Armament: Four 20mm (0.79in) Hispano cannon fixed, forward firing in wings; up to 908kg (2000lb) bombload or eight rockets under wings

Teething troubles

Unfortunately the whole programme was dealt a blow in May 1940 when all aviation development in the UK was paused to concentrate on five existing "super-priority" types, restarting only in the spring of 1941. By this time

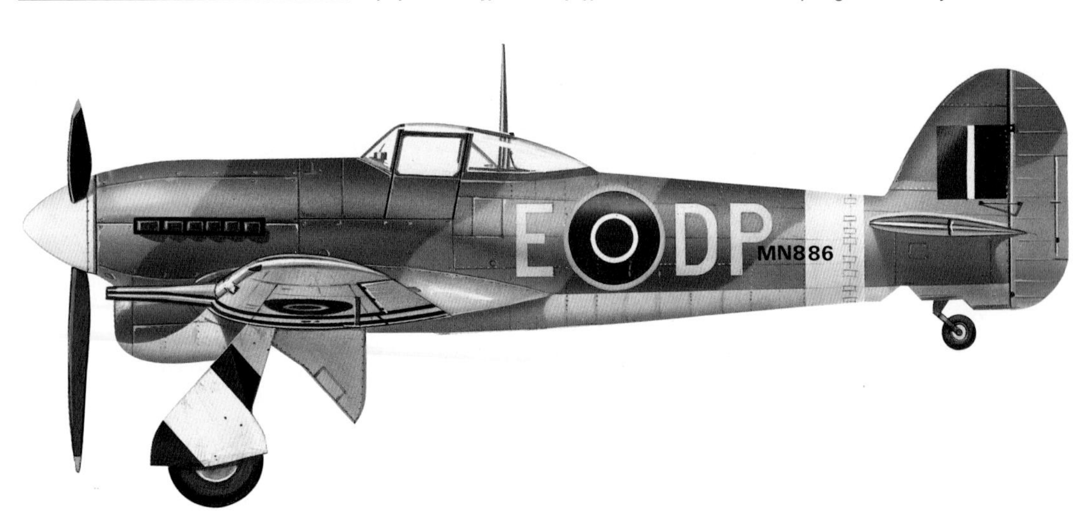

Hawker Typhoon Mk IB

This No. 193 Sqn aircraft is an early production Typhoon Mk IB, as it would have appeared in service during 1942. The 'car door' entry to the cockpit, heavily-framed canopy and three-bladed propeller were typical of early Typhoons.

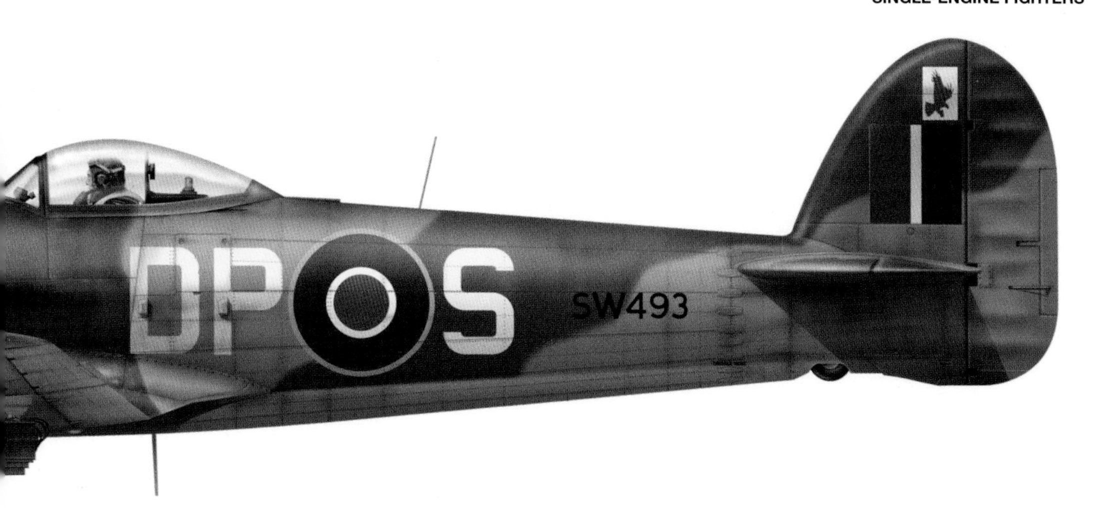

the Vulture no longer seemed so appealing due to its poor reliability when fitted to the Avro Manchester, primarily due to its susceptibility to catastrophic big end failure. With limited resources and constant pressure on Merlin development and production, Rolls-Royce was forced to abandon the Vulture but not before a single production Hawker Tornado had been built.

This aircraft flew for the first time on 29 August 1941 and was used for contra-rotating propeller development trials until 1943, during

Hawker Typhoon Mk IB

No. 193 Squadron was formed in January 1943 and flew Typhoons from February of that year until its disbandment on 31 August 1945. This aircraft, serving with the squadron in early 1945, is a later production example with the four bladed propeller.

Hawker Typhoon Mk IB

Pictured while forming part of the British Air Forces of Occupation in the months immediately following VE Day, this Typhoon of No. 245 Squadron was based at Schleswig, Germany.

Hawker Typhoon Mk IB

Weight (maximum take-off): 6010kg (13,250lb)
Dimensions: Length 9.74m (31ft 11.5in), Wingspan 12.67m (41ft 7in), Height 4.67m (15ft 4in)
Powerplant: One 1630kW (2180hp) Napier Sabre IIA H-24 liquid-cooled piston engine
Maximum speed: 679km/h (422mph)
Range (internal fuel only): 1110km (690 miles)
Ceiling: 9700m (31,800ft)
Crew: 1
Armament: Four 20mm (0.79in) Hispano cannon fixed, forward firing in wings; up to 908kg (2000lb) bombload or eight rockets under wings

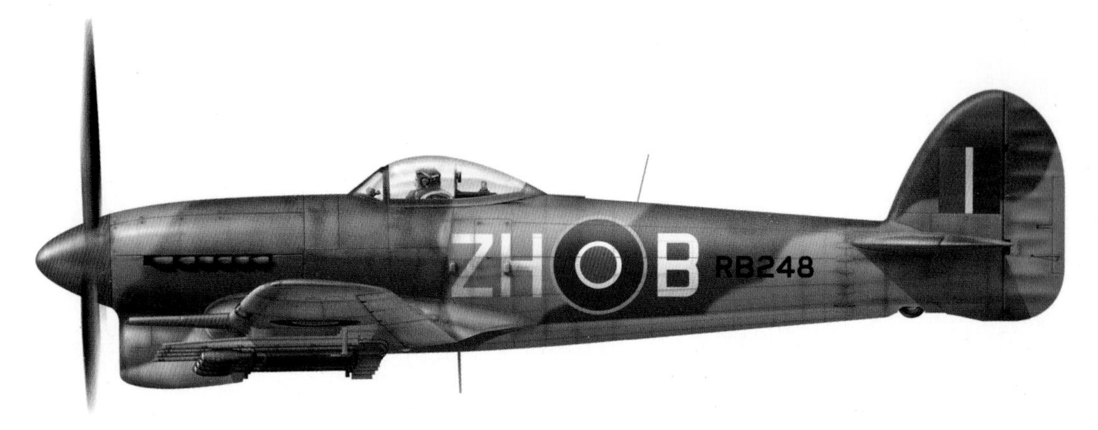

Hawker Typhoon Mk IB

No. 266 Squadron was the first unit to score a combat victory in the Typhoon, when on 9 August 1942 two of the squadron's aircraft shot down a Luftwaffe Junkers Ju 88. RB248 was on strength with the squadron when it was based at Antwerp in the winter of 1944–45.

Hawker Typhoon Mk IB

One of three Royal Canadian Air Force (RCAF) Typhoon units, No. 438 squadron flew the Hawker fighter from January 1944 after previously operating Kittyhawks. By the end of the year, this Typhoon was operating with the squadron from Eindhoven in the Netherlands.

Hawker Typhoon Mk IB
Weight (maximum take-off): 6010kg (13,250lb)
Dimensions: Length 9.74m (31ft 11.5in), Wingspan 12.67m (41ft 7in), Height 4.67m (15ft 4in)
Powerplant: One 1630kW (2180hp) Napier Sabre IIA H-24 liquid-cooled piston engine
Maximum speed: 679km/h (422mph)
Range (internal fuel only): 1110km (690 miles)
Ceiling: 9700m (31,800ft)
Crew: 1
Armament: Four 20mm (0.79in) Hispano cannon fixed, forward firing in wings; up to 908kg (2000lb) bombload or eight rockets under wings

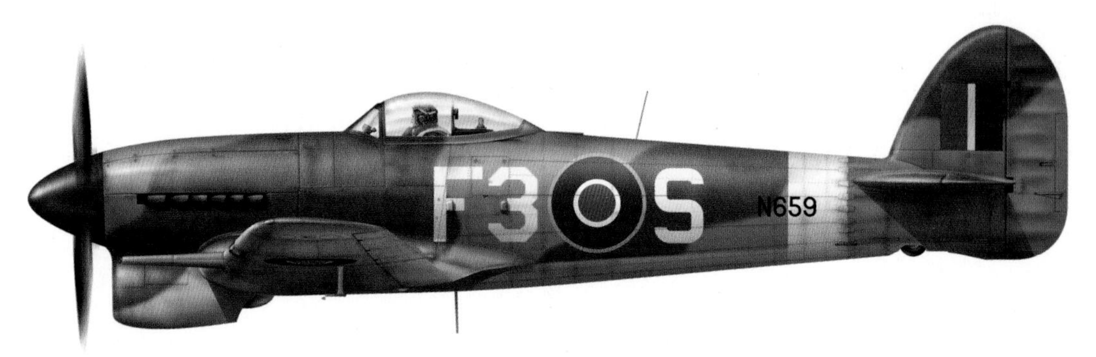

which time its Vulture engine gave no problems at all. On 23 October 1941, a Centaurus-powered version of the Hawker fighter took to the air but this engine too, although it would form an important part of the later Tempest and Fury programmes was enduring developmental problems and this aircraft would remain a one-off.

Typhoon Mk IA

Owing to the pressure of producing ever more Hurricanes, production of the Typhoon was undertaken at the Gloster factory at Hucclecote (Gloster being a subsidiary of the Hawker-Siddeley company), and except for a batch of 15 aircraft built by Hawker, all Typhoons would be constructed there and the first production Typhoon flew at Hucclecote on 27 May 1941.

There were 150 of the early Typhoons built as Typhoon Mk IAs with the 12 machine gun armament, not due to any particular operational need for this variant but because of a shortage of the Chatellerault cannon feed system.

Hawker Typhoon Mk IB

Another RCAF Typhoon, PD389 was flying with No. 440 Squadron in the months following D-Day and had been christened 'Pulverizer IV' by its pilot Flight Lieutenant Harry Hardy.

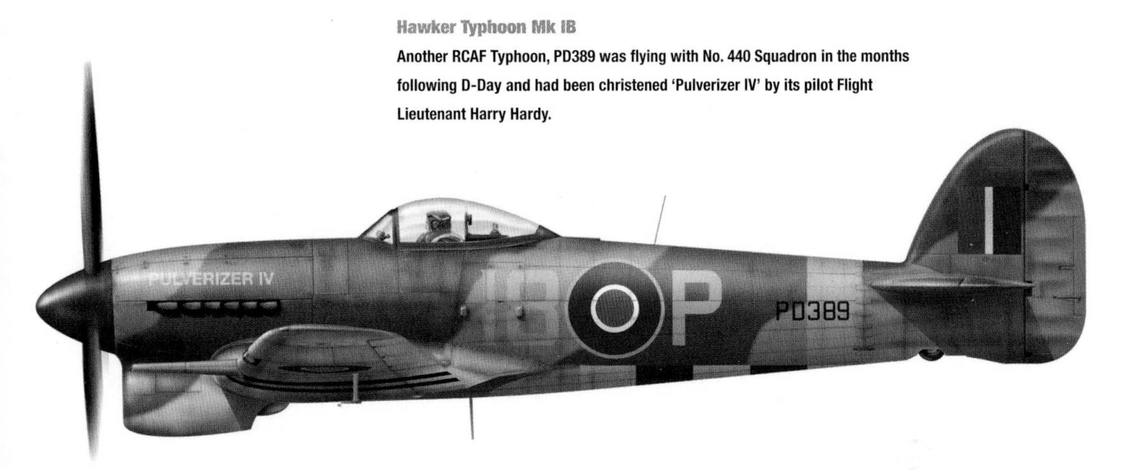

By early September the first Typhoons in service were delivered to No. 56 Squadron and the fact that this was an inadequately developed aircraft became painfully evident: the Typhoon's performance was considerably below expectations due to the overly thick wing, the 'solid' fairing behind the cockpit rendered rearward visibility non-existent, carbon monoxide leaked into the cockpit and the cannons regularly jammed.

Worse still, the Sabre engine was proving desperately unreliable: its time between major overhauls was a mere 25 hours and it frequently failed to achieve even that modest figure. While the 24-cylinder Sabre was an incredibly innovative engine, it was also complex, and its use of sleeve valves, while bold, proved problematic as the sleeves were prone to distort after comparatively short periods.

The engine problems were eventually solved but not until, at the behest of the Ministry of Aircraft Production, the Napier company was taken over by English Electric in 1943 and practical assistance on sleeve valve manufacture had been (grudgingly) provided by Bristol.

Structural weakness

Unfortunately for the Typhoon it also developed a reputation for structural weakness during its early service after several aircraft lost their entire tail units due to failure of the rear fuselage. This problem was easily solved with local strengthening and alteration of the elevator mass balances but discovery of the cause of the failures was far from simple and more pilots lost their lives due to accidents than to enemy action during the first nine months of the Typhoon's operational service.

During 1942, serious consideration was given to cancelling the entire Typhoon programme, and indeed one batch of 270 aircraft was actually cancelled in this period However, as the Royal Air Force's (RAF) first fighter was able to attain 644km/h (400mph) in level flight, the Typhoon suddenly found itself invaluable as the only aircraft capable of intercepting the 'tip and run' bombing attacks on British coastal targets, being made by Fw 190s flying very low to avoid radar detection. The Typhoon squadrons therefore maintained standing patrols over the Channel from dawn to dusk, in all weather, at a mere 200ft (66m).

Hawker Typhoon Mk IB

Weight (maximum take-off): 6010kg (13,250lb)
Dimensions: Length 9.74m (31ft 11.5in), Wingspan 12.67m (41ft 7in), Height 4.67m (15ft 4in)
Powerplant: One 1630kW (2180hp) Napier Sabre IIA H-24 liquid-cooled piston engine
Maximum speed: 679km/h (422mph)
Range (internal fuel only): 1110km (690 miles)
Ceiling: 9700m (31,800ft)
Crew: 1
Armament: Four 20mm (0.79in) Hispano cannon fixed, forward firing in wings; up to 908kg (2000lb) bombload or eight rockets under wings

Hawker Typhoon Mk IB

A Typhoon of No. 175 Squadron unleashes two of its 27kg (60lb) RP-3 rockets. Although the huge Typhoon was envisaged as an interceptor, its lasting fame would derive from its potency as a ground-attack aircraft.

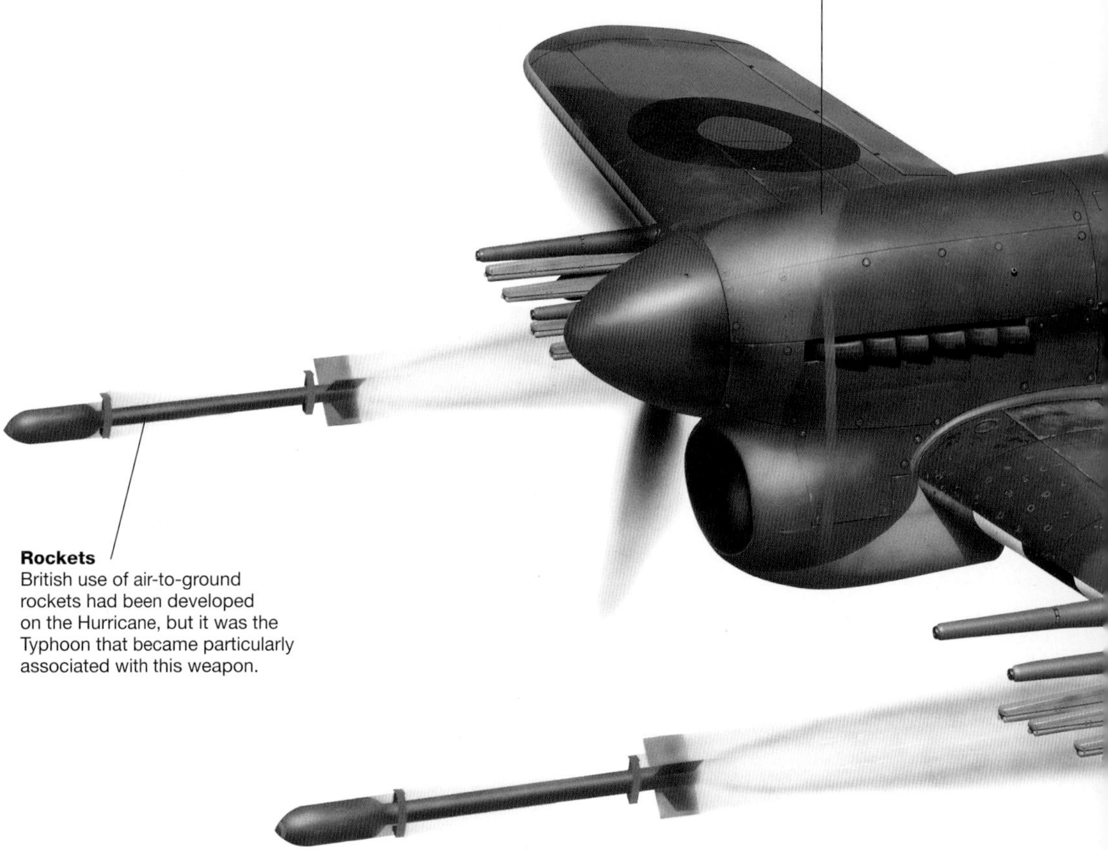

Napier Sabre engine
Crucial to the success of the Typhoon was its awesomely powerful but fiendishly complex Sabre engine. This power unit was at an early stage of development when committed to service and problems were initially serious. By 1944, however, the Sabre was a proven, reliable and remarkably smooth engine.

Rockets
British use of air-to-ground rockets had been developed on the Hurricane, but it was the Typhoon that became particularly associated with this weapon.

Bubble canopy
A blown perspex canopy had been used on the Whirlwind, but the Typhoon was the first Allied aircraft to be built in large numbers with such a feature. The bubble canopy conferred outstanding visibility on the Typhoon, which had initially been criticised for the very poor view from the cockpit.

HH A MN582

Thick wing
The Typhoon ran into aerodynamic problems with its overly thick wing section. Chosen to allow sufficient space for the large cannon and fuel tanks, it limited the top speed of the aircraft and ultimately led to the development of the "thin-wing Typhoon" that became the Tempest.

Hawker Typhoon Mk IB

Weight (maximum take-off): 6010kg (13,250lb)

Dimensions: Length 9.74m (31ft 11.5in), Wingspan 12.67m (41ft 7in), Height 4.67m (15ft 4in)

Powerplant: One 1630kW (2180hp) Napier Sabre IIA H-24 liquid-cooled piston engine

Maximum speed: 679km/h (422mph)

Range (internal fuel only): 1110km (690 miles)

Ceiling: 9700m (31,800ft)

Crew: 1

Armament: Four 20mm (0.79in) Hispano cannon fixed, forward firing in wings; up to 908kg (2000lb) bombload or eight rockets under wings

Hawker Typhoon Mk IB

This Hawker Typhoon Mk IB (serial no. SW393 F3-B) served with 438 (RCAF) Squadron (attached to 2 Tactical Air Force) at B.78 Eindhoven (Holland), Winter 1944/45.

In addition, between November 1942 and April 1943 the Typhoon began its career as a potent ground attack platform, destroying over 100 locomotives during this period, both by day and by night, using its high speed at low altitude to evade interception.

Ground-attack role

The true potential of the Typhoon was realised during 1943, firstly with the addition of bomb racks under each wing, able to carry up to 454kg (1,000lb) each or external fuel tanks, and then with the fitting of rails for four 27kg (60lb) RP-3 rockets under each wing, as pioneered by the Hurricane. By this time, visibility had been much improved, initially by the introduction of a clear fairing behind the pilot's seat whilst retaining the car-style entry doors, followed by a sliding teardrop bubble canopy, which transformed the pilot's view and is credited with inspiring similar installations on the P-51 Mustang and P-47 Thunderbolt. Engine development saw Sabre power increase from 2180hp in Sabre IIA form to 2260hp with the Sabre IIC, and the original three blade propeller was replaced with a four blade unit. With its major problems solved, and operating at the low altitudes that best suited the Sabre with its single-stage supercharger, Typhoon squadrons rampaged across occupied Europe, initially against enemy shipping during 'Channel Stop' operations, then operating in the close support role in support of the Allied armies advancing across France following D-Day.

Eventually 23 squadrons would operate the Typhoon as a fighter-bomber with the Second Tactical Air Force, pioneering the 'cab rank' system wherein standing patrols were available to attack specific targets at short notice at the behest of Army units on the ground. Though Typhoons would be used in this role until the end of the conflict, these operations reached their zenith during August 1944 when rocket-firing Typhoon squadrons wreaked havoc in a series of materially and psychologically devastating attacks on retreating German motorised divisions in the Falaise Pocket, destroying countless vehicles and armour.

Tactical reconnaissance version

With the exception of the Typhoon Mk IAs mentioned earlier, all fighter Typhoons were of the four-cannon Typhoon Mk IB variant. However, the aircraft was also developed and used as a tactical reconnaissance aircraft as the FR Mk IB. There were 60 such aircraft that were modified from stock Mk IBs by replacing the two inboard cannons with forward facing cameras and adding provision for an oblique camera mounting in the port wing and vertical cameras in the fuselage. In total 3,317 Typhoons were built but following the end of hostilities, with the aircraft already being replaced in frontline units by the Tempest, the Typhoon swiftly disappeared from the RAF inventory and the aircraft were scrapped, with only one complete airframe surviving to the present day.

Hawker Typhoon Mk IB

Weight (maximum take-off): 6010kg (13,250lb)
Dimensions: Length 9.74m (31ft 11.5in), Wingspan 12.67m (41ft 7in), Height 4.67m (15ft 4in)
Powerplant: One 1630kW (2180hp) Napier Sabre IIA H-24 liquid-cooled piston engine
Maximum speed: 679km/h (422mph)
Range (internal fuel only): 1110km (690 miles)
Ceiling: 9700m (31,800ft)
Crew: 1
Armament: Four 20mm (0.79in) Hispano cannon fixed, forward firing in wings; up to 908kg (2000lb) bombload or eight rockets under wings

Hawker Tempest

Originally a Typhoon variant, the alterations made to the aircraft were significant enough for it to be considered a completely new type. The result was the outstanding Tempest, arguably the finest British single seat fighter of the war.

Though the Typhoon matured into an effective ground attack aircraft, its development was beset with numerous problems and its performance, though still impressive, was significantly worse than expected. Sydney Camm (1893-1966) and his team had begun work on general studies to improve the Typhoon as early as March 1940 though little practical work was carried out due to the pressing need to develop and produce the Hurricane. One area of development was aimed at producing a much thinner wing, as during 1940 theoretical calculations backed up by test flying carried out with the Typhoon and Tornado prototypes, showed that the aerofoil profile and its 18 per cent thickness to chord ratio at the root limited performance at medium to high altitudes and made the aircraft susceptible to buffeting and aileron reversal in high speed dives.

New wing

A new wing was designed, featuring radiators in the leading edge, and with an overall thickness roughly 12.7cm (5in) less than that of the Typhoon. To allow sufficient space for the Hispano cannons, the chord was increased over much of the span leading to a broadly elliptical planform, not dissimilar to that of the Spitfire, albeit with blunt wingtips to increase the rate of roll.

The thinner wing could no longer contain sufficient fuel so the fuselage was lengthened sufficiently to provide space for fuel tanks directly ahead of the cockpit, adding 53cm (21in) to the aircraft's nose and requiring in turn vertical tail surfaces of greater area. The Ministry of Aircraft Production contracted for two prototypes to be built in November 1941 to be powered by the Sabre IV engine, and the name

Hawker Tempest Mk II
Weight (maximum take-off): 6193kg (13,640lb)
Dimensions: Length 10.49m (34ft 5in), Wingspan 12.5m (41ft), Height 4.42m (14ft 6in)
Powerplant: One (2520hp) Bristol Centaurus V 18-cylinder air-cooled radial piston engine
Maximum speed: 711km/h (442mph)
Range (internal fuel only): 775km (482 miles)
Ceiling: 11,400m (37,500ft)
Crew: 1
Armament: Four 20mm (0.79in) Hispano cannon fixed, forward firing in wings; up to 908kg (2000lb) bombload

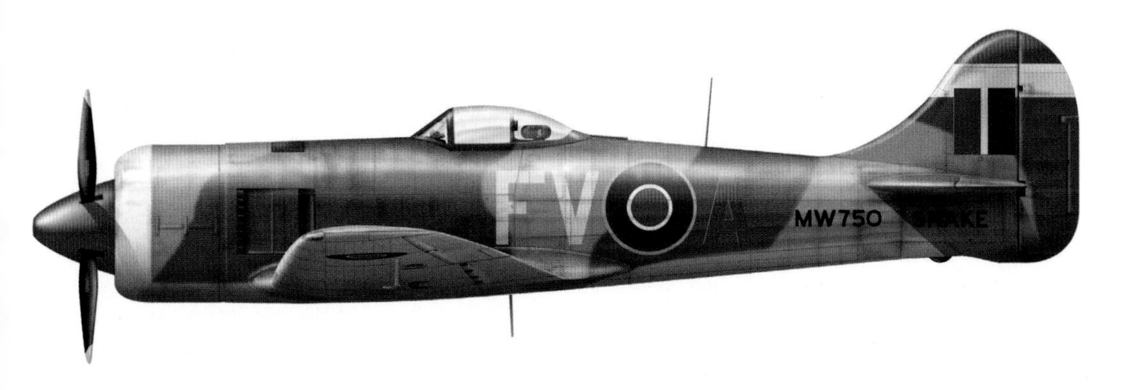

Hawker Tempest Mk II
The codeword 'SNAKE' on the rear fuselage denotes that this is one of the aircraft selected for expedited delivery to the Far East for operations with 'Tiger Force' against Japan in 1945. In the event, the war ended before any Tempest IIs began operational service.

Hawker Tempest Mk V

A New Zealand manned unit, No. 486 Squadron exchanged the Typhoon for the Tempest in May 1944 and operated the type until the end of the conflict. As well as attacking V-1 launch sites immediately following D-Day, the squadron destroyed over 200 of the missiles in flight.

Hawker Tempest Mk V
Weight (maximum take-off): 6340kg (13,977lb)
Dimensions: Length, 10.26m (33ft 8in), Wingspan: 12.5m (41ft), Height 4.52m (14ft 10in)
Powerplant: One 1800kW (2420hp) Napier Sabre IIB H-24 liquid-cooled piston engine
Maximum speed: 700km/h (435mph)
Range (internal fuel only): 680km (420 miles)
Ceiling: 11,100m (36,500ft)
Crew: 1
Armament: Four 20mm (0.79in) Hispano cannon fixed, forward firing in wings; up to 908kg (2000lb) bombload

'Tempest' Mk I was bestowed on the new fighter at the start of 1942. The Mk II was to be powered by the Bristol Centaurus and the planned Mks III and IV were to be fitted with different versions of the Rolls-Royce Griffon.

First flight

The first prototype made its maiden flight on 2 September 1942 fitted with a standard Typhoon installation of a Sabre II and chin radiator as the Sabre IV and its leading edge radiators were suffering delays. The second prototype followed it into the air on 24 February 1943 and was to Mk I standard with Sabre IV and wing radiators fitted. Both prototype Tempests featured the early Typhoon cockpit arrangement with 'car-door' entry and, initially at least,

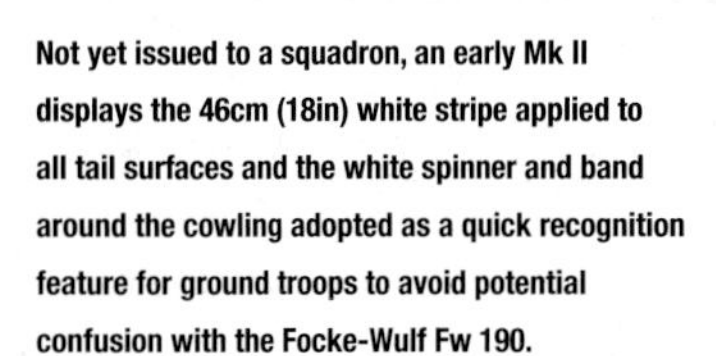

Not yet issued to a squadron, an early Mk II displays the 46cm (18in) white stripe applied to all tail surfaces and the white spinner and band around the cowling adopted as a quick recognition feature for ground troops to avoid potential confusion with the Focke-Wulf Fw 190.

were fitted with a standard Typhoon tail unit. Flight testing revealed that the new wing markedly improved handling and performance was greatly improved, especially that of the second prototype, which benefited from the low drag of the buried radiators and recorded the impressive speed of 750km/h (466mph) in June 1943.

Unfortunately, development of the Sabre IV was still problematic and with a pressing need for an improved interceptor to replace the Typhoon, the decision was taken to place a Sabre IIA-powered variant into production as the Tempest Mk V. An order for 400 Mk Is was altered to cover Mk Vs instead, and the first production Tempest V flew on 21 June 1943. Production aircraft all featured the sliding teardrop canopy developed for the Typhoon and the elegantly curved fin and rudder of increased area that was developed during flight testing of the Tempest prototypes.

D-Day role

Production built up slowly during the latter half of 1943 but by the time the aircraft was cleared for service in April 1944 around 250 had been completed. The first two Tempest squadrons, Nos 3 and 486, received their aircraft later that month with No. 56 Squadron joining them in July to form 150 Wing. All three squadrons were former Typhoon units and initial operations saw them continue with ground-attack strikes in the lead up to D-Day. On 8 June,

Hawker Tempest Mk V
Weight (maximum take-off): 6340kg (13,977lb)
Dimensions: Length, 10.26m (33ft 8in), Wingspan: 12.5m (41ft), Height 4.52m (14ft 10in)
Powerplant: One 1800kW (2420hp) Napier Sabre IIB H-24 liquid-cooled piston engine
Maximum speed: 700km/h (435mph)
Range (internal fuel only): 680km (420 miles)
Ceiling: 11,100m (36,500ft)
Crew: 1
Armament: Four 20mm (0.79in) Hispano cannon fixed, forward firing in wings; up to 908kg (2000lb) bombload

Hawker Tempest Mk V

Based at Hawkinge in Kent, this Tempest of No. 501 Squadron was engaged in Operation Diver, the UK defence against V-1 flying bombs. Squadron Leader Joe Berry assumed command of 501 in August 1944 and became the top scorer against V-1s, with 59 destroyed.

Hawker Tempest Mk VI

Weight (maximum take-off): 6655kg (14,672lb)
Dimensions: Length 10.26m (33ft 8in), Wingspan 12.5m (41ft), Height 4.52m (14ft 10in)
Powerplant: One 1939kW (2,600hp) Napier Sabre VA H-24 liquid-cooled piston engine
Maximum speed: 772km/h (480mph)
Range (internal fuel only): 680km (420 miles)
Ceiling: 11,582m (38,000ft)
Crew: 1
Armament: Four 20mm (0.79in) Hispano cannon fixed, forward firing in wings; up to 908kg (2000lb) bombload

Hawker Tempest Mk VI

The last Tempest variant to enter service, the majority of the Mk VI's service took place overseas. This example in desert camouflage was serving with No. 249 Squadron at Habbaniyah, Iraq, in 1948.

Tempests encountered enemy aircraft for the first time, claiming four Bf 109s destroyed and two damaged without loss whilst flying an air superiority patrol over the Normandy beachhead. However, eight days later they were reassigned to a new role as part of 'Operation Diver', the British defence against the V-1 guided missile.

The Tempest would prove to be the most effective of the fighter aircraft assigned to intercept the flying bombs, due mainly to its excellent speed at low altitude, and further Tempest squadrons were rapidly formed to deal with this threat. Between June and August 1944, when the main V-1 campaign ended, 1,771 of the missiles had been downed by aircraft of which 638 were accounted for by Tempests, more than any other aircraft type. Sporadic V-1 attacks would continue until March 1945 and No. 501 Squadron was retained in the UK on interception duties until the spring of 1945, whilst the other Tempest units provided close support in Europe as part of the Second Tactical Air Force, replacing or supplementing Typhoons, until the end of the war. German aircraft were encountered in ever decreasing numbers by this stage of the conflict but the Tempest proved formidable in air-to-air combat, including against jets, attaining 239 confirmed victories for 31 losses, a kill-to-loss ratio of approximately 8:1. A total of 800 Mk Vs were built.

Tempest II

Whilst the Mk V was the only Tempest variant to see combat during World War II, the Bristol Centaurus-powered Mk II was in full production and about to enter service by VE day, 500 of this variant having been ordered as early as September 1942, to be built by Gloster. The first prototype Tempest II flew on 28 June 1943 but Gloster were preoccupied with work on the Meteor and the contract passed to Bristol, the manufacturers of the Centaurus, but only 50 were actually built there and the majority of Mk IIs were built by Hawker themselves, a total of 452 ultimately being produced.

The Tempest II was faster than the Mk V as well as possessing a longer range and better ceiling and was planned to operate as a long-range escort fighter for the Avro Lincoln in operations against Japan but the war

ended before this could happen. The Tempest II equipped eight squadrons postwar and some saw operational service in Malaya during Operation Firedog, during which the last combat sortie by a Royal Air Force (RAF) Tempest was flown on 6 June 1951. Tempest IIs also served with the air forces of India and Pakistan, remaining in service with both nations until 1953.

Another postwar variant, the Tempest Mk VI, featuring the more powerful Sabre V engine became the last piston engine fighter type to enter service with the RAF, 142 of which were built. The Mk VI was only distinguishable from the Tempest Mk V by the installation of an oil cooler in the starboard wing, freeing up the entire chin intake for the radiator. Tempest VIs saw some action in the Middle East during the turbulent postwar years before its replacement by the Vampire in 1950.

No. 501 Squadron received the Tempest Mk V in August 1944. During this month it absorbed the Fighter Interception Unit (FIU), a technological evaluation unit, and became the only Tempest unit specialising in night operations against the V-1 flying-bombs using 'Monica' radar to determine target range.

North American Mustang

Despite its status as the most famous American fighter of World War II, the Mustang owes its existence to British requirements and only succeeded as an escort fighter due to being fitted with a British-designed engine.

In 1939, officials from the British Purchasing Commission, an organisation founded to obtain war materials from US companies, met with representatives of the North American Aviation Inc to discuss the prospect of the company building Curtiss P-40s under licence. General Manager James 'Dutch' Kindelberger (1895–1962) proposed instead that North American design a better fighter, powered by the same V-1710 engine, for British needs.

Innovative features

In fact, a design for just such an aircraft had already been prepared by North American, featuring such innovative features as a laminar flow aerofoil section and engine and oil cooling radiators mounted in a ventral duct for maximum efficiency. Impressed by the plans, the British assented to the project in April 1940, stipulating a delivery date of January 1941. As it turned out, a mere 102 days would elapse between the commencement of work and the roll-out of the prototype, though a further 20 days would then pass before the engine was delivered and fitted. Designated NA-73X by North American, the aircraft was flown for the first time on 26 October 1940 but was badly damaged in a crash landing less than a month later.

Although the aircraft was subsequently repaired, flight testing had to be completed using some of the first of the 320 production aircraft on order for the British and by the end of 1940 the suitably American sounding name 'Mustang' had been officially adopted by the Royal Air Force (RAF).

Mustang Mk I

The first Mustang Mk I was tested in Britain during the summer of 1941 and was described by the Aeroplane and Armament Experimental Establishment (A & AEE) as the best fighter aircraft so far received from the USA. Speed, handling and manoeuvrability were all considered outstanding, though the V-1710 suffered from rapidly diminishing performance at altitudes above 13,000ft (3,965m) due to the engine's lack of a two-stage supercharger. Most aerial combat over Western Europe took place above that altitude so it was decided that the aircraft would best be used as a tactical reconnaissance platform with RAF Army Cooperation Command. Fitted with a single F-24 camera mounted at an oblique angle directly behind the cockpit, the Mustang retained its armament of four 12.7mm (0.50in) and four 7.62mm (0.30in) Browning machine guns and the first Mustang reconnaissance missions were flown during May 1942.

Mustang squadrons supported the Dieppe landings three months later, during the course of which the first air-to-air victory was achieved when a Focke Wulf Fw 190 was shot down on 19 August 1942. As a foretaste of what was to come, the aircraft's long-range capability was demonstrated to great effect when the Mustang became the first UK-based single engined

aircraft to fly over Germany, flying a mission to reconnoitre the Dortmund-Ems canal, Germany. A further batch of 150 aircraft was ordered by the RAF with four 20mm (0.79in) cannon replacing the machine guns and designated the Mustang IA. The Mustang Mk II was identical to the US P-51A and saw a return to the original armament, featured a slightly more powerful engine, and could carry drop tanks, but only 50 were built before production switched to the Merlin-powered Mustang III. So effective were the Allison-powered variants at low level that the RAF retained the aircraft in service until the conclusion of hostilities.

New Merlin engine

In April 1942, Ronnie Harker, a test pilot for Rolls-Royce flew a Mustang I for 30 minutes and came to the conclusion that the aircraft would be better still if fitted with a Rolls-Royce Merlin, which could deliver high performance at altitudes unattainable by the Allison V-1710. Engineers at Rolls-Royce calculated a top speed of 695km/h (435mph) could be achieved at 7772m (25,500ft), generating considerable enthusiasm for a Merlin-Mustang and Rolls-Royce were contracted to convert

North American Mustang Mk I

AM101, the 364th Mustang I built for the UK, commenced operations with No. 26 Sqn from RAF Gatwick in January 1942. The aircraft was involved in Rhubarbs and Poplars (photographic reconnaissance along the French coast).

North American Mustang Mk I

Weight (maximum take-off): 4808kg (10,600lb)
Dimensions: Length 9.83m (32ft 3in), Wingspan 11.28m (37ft), Height 3.71m (12ft 2in)
Powerplant: One 895kW (1200hp) Allison V-1710-81 V-12 liquid cooled piston engine
Maximum speed: 628km/h (390mph)
Range (with external fuel): 2011km (1250 miles)
Ceiling: 9555m (31,350ft)
Crew: 1
Armament: Two synchronised 12.7mm (0.5in) Browning M2 machine guns fixed forward firing under nose, two 12.7mm (0.5in) Browning M2 machine guns and four 7.7mm (0.303in) Browning machine guns fixed forward firing in wings

three Mustang Is to Merlin power. The company also promoted the aircraft to the United States Army Air Force (USAAF), which duly contracted with North American to re-engine two P-51s with Merlins. Whilst it is unlikely the USAAF would have accepted an aircraft powered by a British built engine, a Merlin production line had already been established at the Packard car company in Detroit to provide a local engine source for Canadian production of the Lancaster bomber.

The Rolls-Royce built aircraft was the first to appear, designated the Mustang X, and performance was only 2km/h (1.5mph) less than forecast. Six weeks after the first flight of the Mustang X, the first XP-51B was completed by North American. This aircraft featured the supercharger intercooler and radiator in a deepened ventral scoop, a much more aerodynamically efficient solution than that of the Rolls-Royce machine and was considerably faster, stock P-51Bs demonstrating a speed of 729km/h (453mph) at 8778m (28,800ft). As a result the Mustang X was not required and did not enter production.

Mustang Mk III

The P-51B and P-51C models were identical aircraft, the suffix denoting only their factory of origin and no distinction was made between them in British service which designated the new aircraft the Mustang Mk III, of which 944 were delivered to the RAF, entering service with 65 Squadron at the end of 1943. A further 12 squadrons would convert to the Mustang, and though some Mustang IIIs were utilised for tactical reconnaissance, like the Allison powered variants before them.

Most Mustangs were employed in escort duties, covering the increasing number of daylight raids being undertaken by RAF Bomber Command during 1944 and 1945, as well as escorting strike missions by Coastal Command. Some units were attached to Second Tactical Air Force and moved to France following D-Day but the three remaining in the UK were employed as part of Operation Diver, the defence against V-1 flying bombs, and accounted for 232 shot down.

The Mustang III was not normally fast enough to intercept the low-flying, high speed missiles and the aircraft's engines had to be specially tuned to permit them to catch the V-1s.

Although it had proved highly effective from the moment it was introduced, the Mustang Mk III suffered from limited visibility due to the heavily framed cockpit canopy. As a result, a bulged clear-view perspex canopy was developed by the British Malcolm company and fitted to hundreds of Mustangs in the UK.

New canopy

A better solution was introduced with the P-51D which introduced a large teardrop-shaped clear canopy (reportedly inspired by that fitted to the Typhoon) and cut-down rear fuselage allowing for 360-degree visibility. Towards the end of the war the P-51D and K, differing only in the type of propeller fitted, began to arrive

North American Mustang Mk III

Weight (maximum take-off): 5352kg (11,800lb)
Dimensions: Length 9.83m (32ft 3in), Wingspan 11.28m (37ft), Height 4.16m (13ft 8in)
Powerplant: One 1208kW (1620hp) Packard V-1650-3 Merlin V-12 liquid cooled piston engine
Maximum speed: 708km/h (440mph)
Range (with external fuel): 2655km (1650 miles)
Ceiling: 12,800m (42,000ft)
Crew: 1
Armament: Four 12.7mm (0.5in) Browning M2 machine guns machine guns fixed forward firing in wings, two; up to 908kg (2000lb) bombload; modification in field to permit carriage of three rocket launch tubes under each wing

North American Mustang Mk III

No. 306 'Torun' Polish Fighter Squadron flew the Mustang from March 1944 until the end of the conflict. During this period it was based at RAF Brenzett in Kent, engaged in V-1 interception duties, destroying 59 flying bombs.

North American Mustang

No. 112 Squadron exchanged the Kittyhawk for Mustang IIIs in 1944, but continued to adorn their aircraft with the unit's famous shark mouth motif, as displayed by this Mustang Mk IV operating with the squadron in 1945.

in RAF units and were designated the Mustang Mk IV and IVA respectively, supplementing the Mustang IIIs already in service. On the other side of the world, Australia selected the P-51D to produce under licence as the Commonwealth Aircraft Corporation (CAC) Mustang. The first 100 were assembled in Australia from kits of parts sent from the US and were designated the CA-17, these were followed by 120 CA-18s which were manufactured locally. The first CA-17 flew in April 1945 though none had been delivered to units by VJ Day.

North American Mustang Mk III

Weight (maximum take-off): 5352kg (11,800lb)
Dimensions: Length 9.83m (32ft 3in), Wingspan 11.28m (37ft), Height 4.16m (13ft 8in)
Powerplant: One 1208kW (1620hp) Packard V-1650-3 Merlin V-12 liquid cooled piston engine
Maximum speed: 708km/h (440mph)
Range (with external fuel): 2655km (1650 miles)
Ceiling: 12,800m (42,000ft)
Crew: 1
Armament: Four 12.7mm (0.5in) Browning M2 machine guns machine guns fixed forward firing in wings, two; up to 908kg (2000lb) bombload; modification in field to permit carriage of three rocket launch tubes under each wing

North American Mustang Mk IV

Weight (maximum take-off): 5493kg (12,100lb)
Dimensions: Length 9.83m (32ft 3in), Wingspan 11.28m (37ft), Height 4.16m (13ft 8in)
Powerplant: One 1263kW (1695hp) piston engine
Maximum speed: 703km/h (437mph)
Range (with external fuel): 2655km (1650 miles)
Ceiling: 12,800m (42,000ft)
Crew: 1
Armament: Six 12.7mm (0.5in) Browning M2 machine guns fixed forward firing in wings; up to 908kg (2000lb) bombload; later production aircraft fitted with provision for three rocket launch tubes under each wing

North American Mustang Mk III

A Mustang III (serial no. HB866), from 133 (Polish) Wing at RAF Coolham, West Sussex, in October 1944. This is the personal aircraft of (Acting) Group Captain Tadeusz Nowierski, in which he shot down a V1 flying bomb on 5th August 1944. It carries his initials (TN) and group captain's pennant.

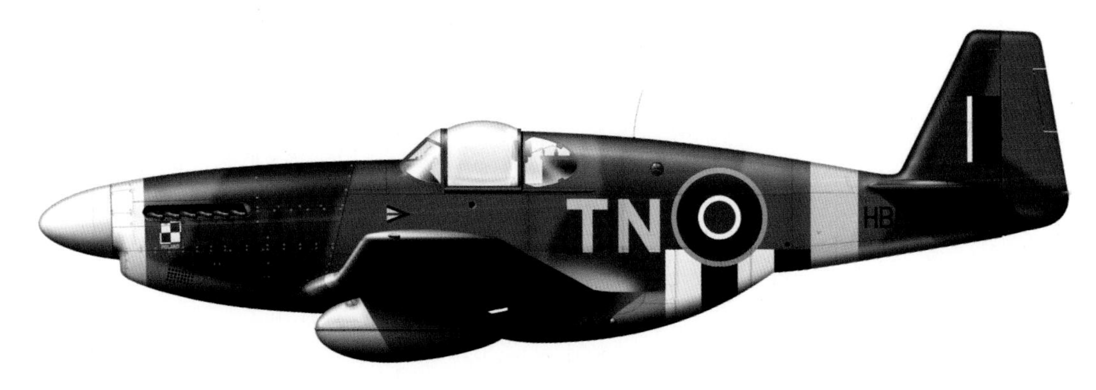

Republic Thunderbolt

The most produced US fighter of the war, the huge and powerful Thunderbolt saw widespread service with the United States Army Air Force (USAAF) but was employed solely in Burma (modern-day Myanmar)and India by the Royal Air Force (RAF).

Republic Thunderbolt Mk I

Based at RAF Fayid in Egypt, this Thunderbolt Mk I was utilised by No. 73 Operational Training Unit. This unit trained pilots transferring to South East Asia Command to fly the Thunderbolt under frontline conditions.

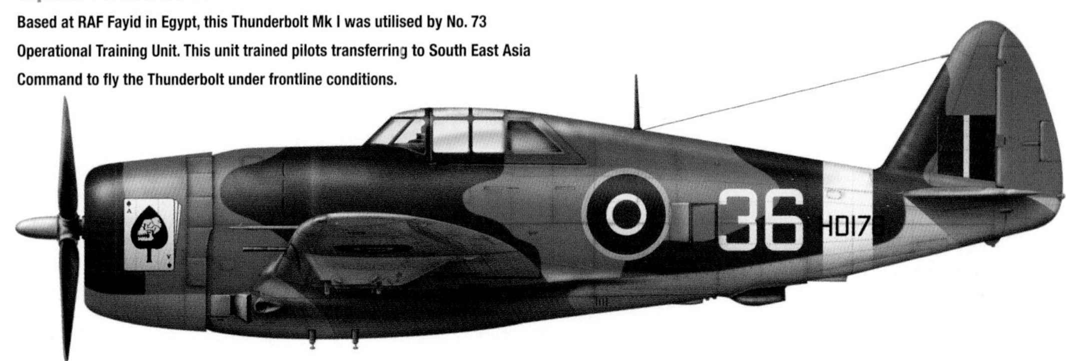

The prototype of the Thunderbolt, the XP-47B flew for the first time on 6 May 1941 and benefitted from reports of fighter combat in Europe. As a result, the P-47 utilised a General Electric turbo-supercharger in the rear fuselage to help the engine maintain an adequate power output at height. The installed armament of eight 12.7mm (0.5in) machine guns, all in the wings, was considerably heavier than the norm for contemporary United States Army Air Corps (USAAC) fighters and the aircraft was protected with self-sealing fuel tanks and armour.

Early production P-47B aircraft were retained in the US for training, with the more capable P-47C becoming the initial operational Thunderbolt variant when the first were received by the Fourth Fighter Group of the Eighth Air Force during January 1943. These were replaced by the slightly improved P-47D, later examples of which were built with a clear vision bubble canopy, though there was no separate designation reflecting this change, and early P-47Ds without the bubble canopy were retrospectively referred to as 'Razorback' models, referring to the sharp-edged fairing behind the cockpit. With the Eighth and Ninth Air Forces in Western Europe the Thunderbolt demonstrated its worth as a high altitude escort fighter and, once it was sidelined by the Mustang due to the latter aircraft's superior range, as a remarkably successful fighter bomber. In total 15,863 P-47s were built and the aircraft was supplied to five other nations through lend-lease channels.

The UK was the second non-US operator of the P-47, Free French forces having been supplied with Razorback P-47Ds as early as August 1943. British use of the Thunderbolt began the following year though the RAF had little use for the aircraft in the European theatre as its needs were well-covered by domestically produced aircraft. In India however, there existed an urgent need for modern aircraft for use as fighter-bombers in the escalating campaign against the Japanese in Burma, and the Republic fighter was shipped to the Far East.

Republic Thunderbolt Mk I

Weight (maximum take-off): 7938kg (17,500lb)

Dimensions: Length: 10.99m (36ft 1in), Wingspan: 12.43m (40ft 9in), Height: 4.44m (14ft 7in)

Powerplant: One 1500kW (2000hp) Pratt & Whitney R-2800-59 18-cylinder air-cooled radial piston engine

Speed: 686km/h (426mph)

Range (with external fuel): 1660km (1030 miles)

Ceiling: 13,000m (42,000ft)

Crew: 1

Armament: Eight 12.7mm (0.5in) M2 Browning machine guns; up to 1,100kg (2,500lb) of bombs or six zero-length rockets under wings with drop tanks or 10 rockets without drop tanks

Thunderbolt Mk I

All Thunderbolts taken on strength by Britain were P-47Ds, comprising 240 Razorback P-47s, referred to as the Thunderbolt Mk I in British service, and 590 bubble cockpit aircraft which became the Thunderbolt II. Conversion of Hurricane units in India began in May 1944 and by the late summer of that year four squadrons had re-equipped with Thunderbolt Is. Thunderbolt IIs began to arrive at around the same time and all four Thunderbolt units began operations with a mixture of both types. The first operational mission was an armed reconnaissance of the Chudwin River, Burma on 14 September 1944 with bombing and strafing attacks beginning two days later in attacks south of Imphal, India. Japanese aerial activity had dwindled by this stage of the war so opportunities for air combat were scarce but the first air-to-air victory by an RAF Thunderbolt occurred on 4 November 1944 when a Ki 44 was shot down.

Burma service

Further squadrons became operational on the Thunderbolt and eventually the type would equip 12 RAF units operating over the Arakan and Central Burmese fronts, seeing heavy fighting in early 1945 in support of Allied ground forces advancing into Burma. Losses were generally light and the Thunderbolt endeared itself to pilots due to its remarkable ability to absorb battle damage and keep flying.

Following the capture of Rangoon, Burma in May, some Thunderbolt squadrons were withdrawn to India for the planned invasion of Malaya (modern-day Malaysia), but four units remained in Burma until the end of hostilities, and in the days that followed these dropped leaflets on isolated Japanese troops, informing them of the end of the war.

RAF Thunderbolts also flew missions in support of Dutch efforts to retain Batavia (modern-day Jakarta) against Indonesian freedom fighters following the Japanese surrender, but the type disappeared from British service fairly rapidly thereafter; the last unit, No. 60 Squadron, converted to Spitfire Mk 24s in Singapore during October 1946.

Republic Thunderbolt Mk I

This Thunderbolt Mk I of No. 135 Squadron displays the characteristic blue roundels adopted by South East Asia Command (SEAC) to avoid any confusion with the Japanese 'Hinomaru' marking.

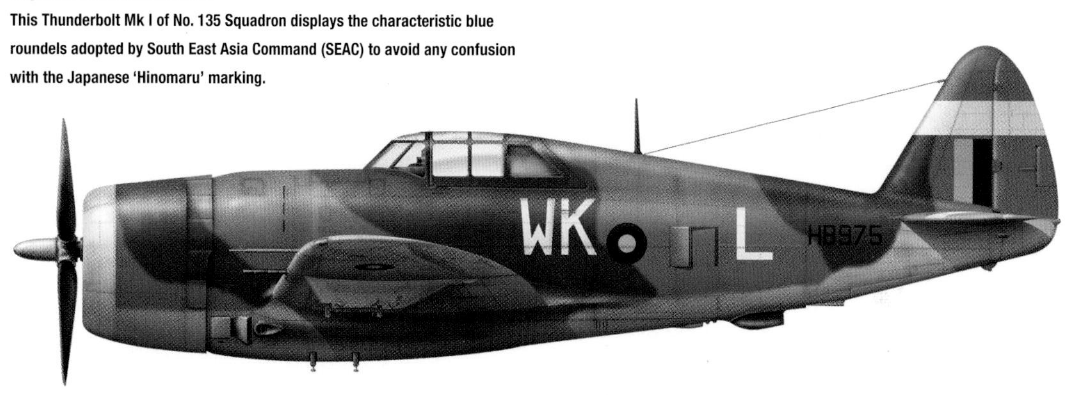

Republic Thunderbolt Mk II

This Thunderbolt Mk II of No. 134 Squadron based at Kyaukpyu, Burma, in May 1945, displays the blue identification stripes and front cowling and a small, repeated serial on the base of the fin, peculiar to the type in SEAC operations.

Commonwealth Boomerang

The only Australian designed and built fighter to enter production and see combat service, the Boomerang was tough, manoeuvrable, and versatile.

Following the attack on Pearl Harbor, Australia found itself thrust into the frontline of the Pacific war and desperately short of modern fighters. To answer this deficiency, Lawrence Wackett (1896–1982), the influential manager and chief designer of Commonwealth Aircraft Corporation (CAC) enlisted Fred David (1898–1992), an Austrian engineer with recent experience at Heinkel as well as Aichi and Mitsubishi to help design a stop-gap fighter. Powered by the 895kW (1200hp) Pratt & Whitney R-1830 Twin Wasp engine, which was then being licence-produced in Sydney for local manufacture of the Bristol Beaufighter, the design incorporated as many parts as possible from the existing Wirraway. The Defence Department authorised CAC to proceed in late December and work went ahead swiftly, greater impetus being added following the Australian War Cabinet's decision to order 105 examples of the new aircraft 'off the drawing board' on 2 February 1942, conferring the name 'Boomerang' on the aircraft shortly after. The first 105 CA-12 Boomerangs (sometimes referred to as the Mk I), would be built followed by 95 of the slightly improved CA-13 (or Mk II).

First combat

The prototype Boomerang flew for the first time on 29 May 1942 and during flight testing the aircraft proved to be easy to handle and manoeuvrable, as well as being well-armed, with two 20mm (0.79in) cannon and four 7.7mm (0.303in) machine guns all mounted in the wings. In mock combat against a lightened Brewster Buffalo, intended to approximate the flight characteristics of the Mitsubishi A6M Zero, the Boomerang proved the faster aircraft, though the Buffalo could outmanoeuvre it, but compared to other contemporary fighters the Boomerang was undeniably slow.

Initial Boomerang deliveries began in October 1942 to operational training units with the first fighter squadron, No. 83, receiving aircraft from April 1943, to replace the unit's Airacobras. Sporadic encounters with Japanese bombers occurred over the next few months but no successful interceptions were made as the Boomerang simply wasn't fast enough to catch the enemy aircraft. With Curtiss Kittyhawks available in greater numbers from September 1943, the Boomerang was transferred to the close support role, serving with Nos 4 and 5 (Army Co-operation) Squadrons in the Solomon Islands from November 1944, where the disappointing interceptor became an extremely effective light attack aircraft.

Commonwealth CA-12 Boomerang
Weight (maximum take-off): 3742kg (8249lb)
Dimensions: Length 7.77m (25ft 6in), Wingspan 10.97m (36ft), Height 2.92m (9ft 7in)
Powerplant: One 890kW (1200hp) Pratt & Whitney R-1830 Twin Wasp 14-cylinder air-cooled radial piston engine
Maximum speed: 491km/h (305mph)
Range: 1500km (930 miles)
Ceiling: 8800m (29,000ft)
Crew: 1
Armament: Two 20mm (0.79in) Hispano or CAC cannon and four 7.7mm (0.303in) Browning machine guns fixed, firing forward in wings

Commonwealth CA-12 Boomerang

'Phooey' was serving with No. 4 Squadron RAAF at Labuan in North Borneo during 1945 in support of the Australian Army's Borneo campaign.

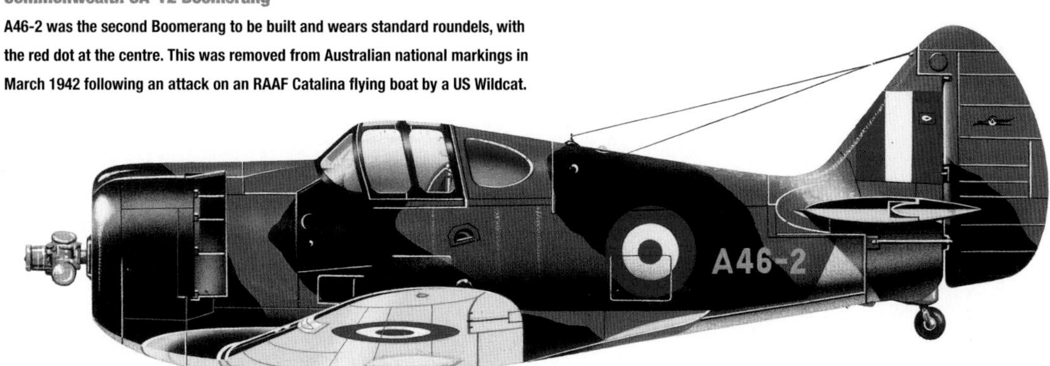

Commonwealth CA-12 Boomerang

A46-2 was the second Boomerang to be built and wears standard roundels, with the red dot at the centre. This was removed from Australian national markings in March 1942 following an attack on an RAAF Catalina flying boat by a US Wildcat.

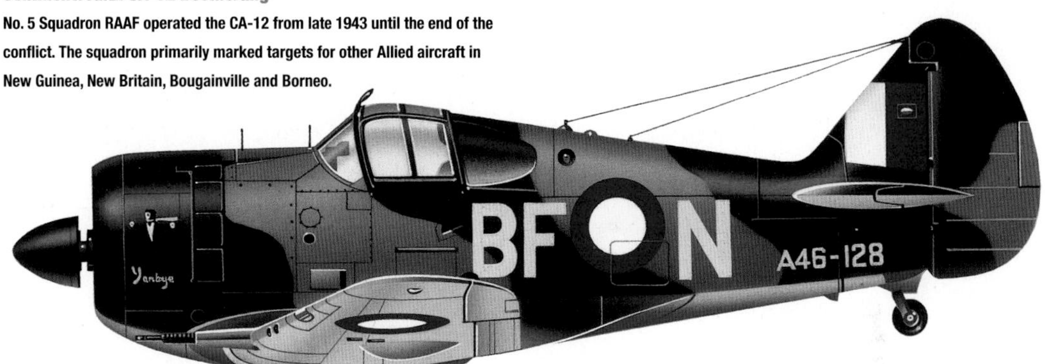

Commonwealth CA-12 Boomerang

No. 5 Squadron RAAF operated the CA-12 from late 1943 until the end of the conflict. The squadron primarily marked targets for other Allied aircraft in New Guinea, New Britain, Bougainville and Borneo.

Agile, easy to fly, possessing heavy armament, featuring extensive armour plating, and able to withstand significant battle damage, the Boomerang proved to be ideally suited to the ground war in the South West Pacific where widely dispersed, small actions were typical, fought at close quarters and with vague front lines. Boomerangs were also used for artillery spotting, aerial supply drops, tactical reconnaissance, and anti-malarial spraying, as well as marking targets with a 9kg (20lb) smoke bomb for other, larger aircraft to attack, No. 5 Squadron formed a particularly effective partnership marking targets for Royal New Zealand Air Force (RNZAF) Corsairs during the Bougainville Campaign, and the Boomerang would continue in the close support role until the end of hostilities. Late production CA-19 variants were also equipped with vertical cameras and were in considerable demand for reconnaissance missions.

CA-14

Cognisant of the Boomerang's pedestrian speed performance, particularly at altitude, CAC developed the CA-14, later developed into the square-tailed CA-14A which also utilised fan cooling for its R-1830 engine. The CA-14 featured a General Electric B-2 turbo supercharger from a B-24 Liberator, and a Harrison intercooler taken from a B-17 Flying Fortress. Performance was greatly improved, the CA-14 proving 122km/h (76mph) faster than the CA-12 and demonstrating a climb rate more than triple that which could be achieved by the earlier aircraft. Despite an order for 50 turbocharged Boomerangs to be powered by the enlarged R-2000 Twin Wasp being placed, better performing fighters from the US and Britain were already arriving in Australia, and this, coupled with the decision to locally manufacture P-51D Mustangs saw the 50 aircraft on order completed as the CA-19 tactical reconnaissance variant instead, with similar performance to the standard CA-12.

UB-E

TWIN-ENGINE FIGHTERS

Although the radical Westland Whirlwind was developed as a particularly heavily armed daylight air superiority fighter, the use of larger twin-engined fighters in the RAF was primarily driven by the specific requirements of night fighting. In the form of the Beaufighter and the superlative Mosquito, the RAF possessed two of the world's finest nocturnal combat aircraft, both of which would excel in a variety of challenging combat roles. The following aircraft are featured in this chapter:

- Bristol Blenheim
- Westland Whirlwind
- Douglas Havoc
- Bristol Beaufighter
- de Havilland Mosquito

Apart from night-fighting, the role with which the Beaufighter became most associated was that of maritime strike. Here, an early production Beaufighter TF Mk X of No. 455 Sqn, RAAF, based at Langham in Norfolk, releases all eight of its rockets for the benefit of the press.

Bristol Blenheim

Although lacking the necessary performance to act as a truly effective fighter, the Blenheim made history by achieving the first air-to-air interception in history assisted by airborne radar.

Bristol Blenheim Mk IF

Serving with No. 25 Squadron, based at Northolt in the summer 1939, this Blenheim wears the squadron badge on its fin depicting a hawk rising from a gauntlet in a spearhead cartouche, this shape signifying a fighter squadron. This aircraft was lost on 17th December 1939 after an engine failure on take off and subsequent belly landing.

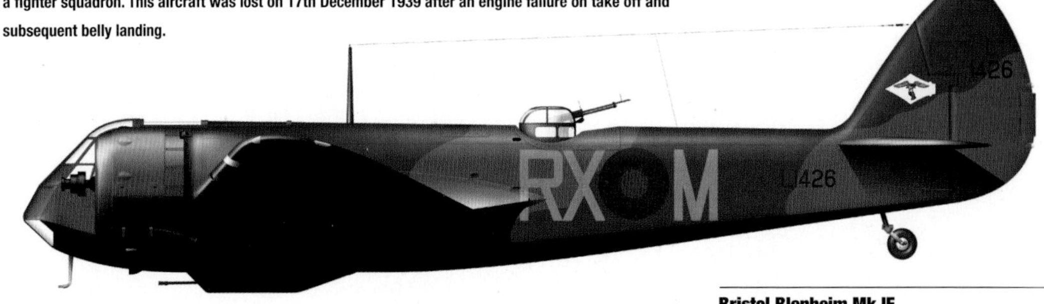

Bristol Blenheim Mk IF
Weight (maximum take-off): 5942kg (13,100lb)
Dimensions: Length 12.11m (39ft 9in), Wingspan 17.14m (56ft 4in), Height 3m (9ft 10in)
Powerplant: Two 626kW (840hp) Bristol Mercury VIII nine-cylinder air-cooled engines
Maximum speed: 426km/h (265mph)
Range: 1481km (920 miles)
Ceiling: 7772m (25,500ft)
Crew: 2–3
Armament: four 7.7mm (0.303in) machine guns in ventral pack and one 7.7mm (0.303in) Vickers K gun flexibly mounted in dorsal turret

In 1937, the Blenheim bomber entered service with the Royal Air Force (RAF) and its then exceptional performance prompted the decision to develop a heavy fighter version, the Blenheim Mk IF. All fighter Blenheims were converted from standard bombers by the simple addition of a self-contained gun pack under the fuselage containing four 7.7mm (0.303in) Browning machine guns. A total of 1,375 of these gun packs were made by the Southern Railway company and the aircraft were converted at RAF Maintenance units between 1938 and 1940. The Blenheim IF entered service with No. 600 Squadron in September 1938, replacing the Hawker Demon biplane but by the outbreak of war a year later, the Blenheim's performance was no longer particularly impressive though the Blenheim IFs were utilised quite intensively. In the UK, 10 squadrons were equipped with Blenheim fighters and often operated in concert with bomber variants to attack ground targets.

By the time of the Battle of Britain, however, the Blenheim was being withdrawn from daylight fighter operations just as a new important role appeared, that of radar equipped night fighter. The Blenheim IF was both immediately available and large enough to carry the initial AI Mk III radar equipment and the crewman required to operate it, and during mid-1940 three radar equipped Blenheims conducted successful field trials.

On the night of 23 July, a Blenheim IF made radar contact with a Dornier Do 17 and then closed to make a successful attack, the world's first airborne radar-guided interception. Subsequently, six squadrons would fly radar equipped Blenheim IFs in the nocturnal interception role, although the appearance of the vastly more effective Beaufighter at the end of 1940 meant that the Blenheim's night fighting career would remain brief. The Blenheim IF was also flown by day in Singapore, though these were swiftly destroyed by Japanese fighters in early 1942, and with rather greater success against the Italians in Greece and Crete.

Further fighter conversions were applied to the “long-nose” Blenheim Mk IV using the same gun pack design. The Blenheim IVF supplemented Mk IFs in several squadrons in the UK but only No. 600 Squadron was ever wholly equipped with the type, with a second unit, No. 203 Squadron, operating it with some success in the Middle East and Mediterranean until mid-1941. Coastal Command also used the Blenheim IVF in conjunction with its bomber Blenheims employing both on attacks on invasion barges in Channel ports during 1940 and 1941.

Bristol Blenheim Mk IVF
Weight (maximum take-off): 6583kg (14,500lb)
Dimensions: Length 12.98m (42ft 7in), Wingspan 17.17m (56ft 4in), Height 3m (9ft 10in)
Powerplant: Two 690kW (920hp) Bristol Mercury XV 9-cylinder air-cooled radial piston engines
Maximum speed: 428km/h (266mph)
Range: 1867km (1160 miles)
Ceiling: 6706m (22,000ft)
Crew: 2–3
Armament: Four 7.7mm (0.303in) machine guns in ventral pack and one 7.7mm (0.303in) Vickers K gun flexibly mounted in dorsal turret

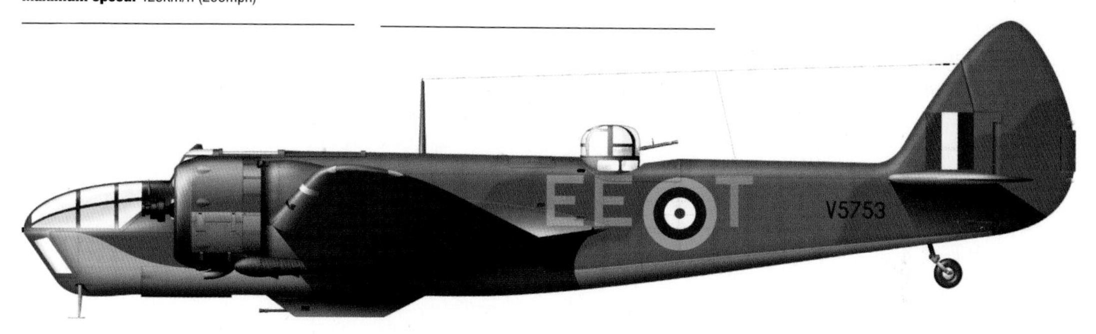

Bristol Blenheim Mk IVF

This Blenheim Mk IVF of 404 (RCAF) Squadron claimed the first air-to-air victory for the unit on 18th December 1941 while being flown by Wing Commander PH Woodruff, with Pilot Officer JRA Matthews as air gunner and Flight Sergeant IR Sims as navigator. They successfully intercepted a Junkers Ju 88 80km (50 miles) east of their base at Sumburgh in the Shetland Isles.

Westland Whirlwind

A highly advanced design, the Whirlwind was the first cannon-armed fighter to enter the Royal Air Force's (RAF) service yet despite combat success, the cancellation of its engine meant that the aircraft was built only in trivial numbers.

The Whirlwind was a response to Air Ministry Specification F.5/34 calling for a single-seat day and night fighter armed with four cannon with a top speed of at least 531km/h (330mph) at 4,600m (15,000ft). Designer Edward 'Teddy' Petter (1908–68) came up with a very small twin-engine fighter bristling with radical features such as the first clear-view perspex bubble canopy seen on a British aircraft, a monocoque fuselage, T-tail, and the new fighter was the first aircraft to possess ducted radiators fitted in the wing leading edge. It was powered by two Rolls-Royce Peregrine engines, an aggressively supercharged Kestrel derivative that was considered highly promising in the late 1930s. The Whirlwind flew for the first time on 11 October 1938 and demonstrated excellent handling qualities and performance. When fitted with its intended armament of a quartet of Hispano 20mm (0.79in) cannon in the nose, it was, for a time, the most heavily armed fighter in the world. Orders were placed for 200 aircraft from Westland with a further 800 to be built at the new Castle Bromwich Shadow Factory. Unfortunately, the Peregrine was subject to delays and though the first production Whirlwinds were delivered to the initial unit, No. 263 Squadron in July 1940 the unit was declared operational with the Whirlwind only in December. Initial operations consisted of convoy patrols and anti E-boat missions, and the Whirlwind scored its first confirmed victory on 8 February 1941, shooting down an Arado Ar 196 floatplane.

Peregrine engine

Unfortunately, with Rolls-Royce concentrating on Merlin development, the company had little time to develop or mass produce the Peregrine, and given that the Whirlwind was the only production aircraft to use it, the decision was taken to cease Peregrine production. This effectively ended production of the

Whirlwind as the design was too closely tailored to the Peregrine engine to be readily altered for any other powerplant. Furthermore, Hurricanes and Spitfires fitted with 20mm (0.79in) Hispanos were in service by the end of 1941, thus answering the need for a cannon-armed fighter, and the Whirlwind essentially became superfluous.

The 114 examples that were constructed were used by only two squadrons but in service the Whirlwind proved highly effective. Underwing bomb racks were added during 1942, allowing the carriage of either two 227kg (500lb) or two 113kg (250lb) bombs. In this guise, unofficially named "Whirlibombers", the aircraft engaged in ground attack duties against targets in occupied Europe until the aircraft was replaced in November 1943 by the Typhoon.

A frontline aircraft type serving for three years during this period of the war without significant modification was virtually unheard of, speaking to for the Whirlwind's excellence as a combat aircraft. If the aircraft had been powered by a different engine it would seem likely that it would have become a significant asset to the RAF rather than languishing in relative obscurity.

Westland Whirlwind Mk I

Weight (maximum take-off): 5191kg (11,445lb)

Dimensions: Length 9.83m (32ft 3in), Wingspan 13.72m (32ft 3in), Height 3.35m (11ft)

Powerplant: Two 660kW (885hp) Rolls-Royce Peregrine V-12 liquid-cooled piston engines

Maximum speed: 580km/h (360mph)

Range: 1300km (800 miles)

Ceiling: 9200m (30,300ft)

Crew: 1

Armament: Four 20mm (0.79in) Hispano cannon fixed firing forward in nose; up to 460kg (1000lb) bombload under wings

Westland Whirlwind Mk I

One of the first four Whirlwinds built, P6969 served with No. 263 Squadron and scored the type's first confirmed victory in February 1941. Unfortunately this aircraft was lost on the same mission for unknown reasons, possibly shot down by the Arado floatplane it was attacking.

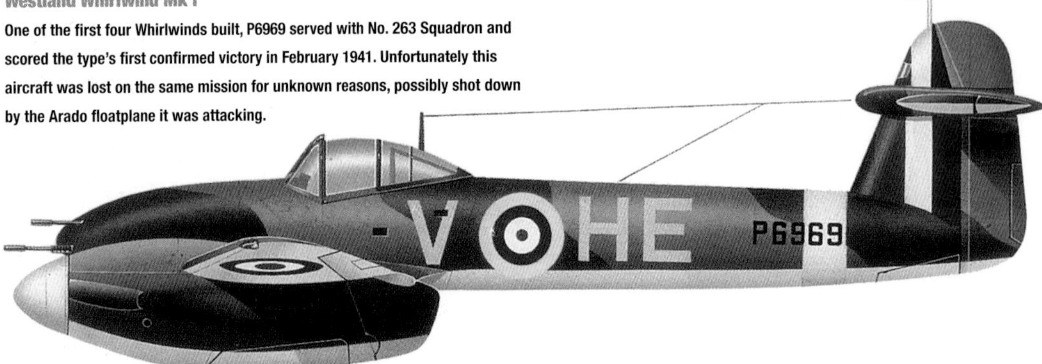

Westland Whirlwind Mk I

P6974 HE 'M' from 263 Squadron, based at RAF Warmwell (Dorset), detached to RAF Manston (Kent) between 7th and 10th September 1942 for Operation Starkey. Operation Starkey was a large scale deception raid, designed to convince the Germans of an amphibious assault being mounted on Boulogne.

Douglas Havoc

A variant of the prolific Douglas DB-7 family, the Havoc night fighter derived from a tactical bomber aircraft and although soon superseded, it formed an important part of the UK's defences when domestically produced night fighters were scarce.

Douglas Havoc Mk II

AH470 from 1459 (Fighter) Flight based at RAF Hibaldstow, Lincolnshire, in Spring 1942. Around 30 Havocs were converted into Turbinlite aircraft, equipped with a 2.7 million candera searchlight in the nose and AI Mk IV radar.

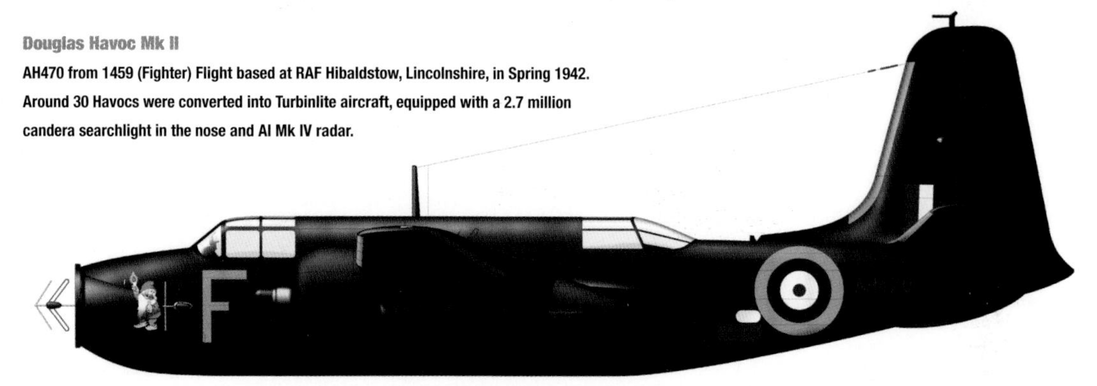

The Douglas Model 7B had initially flown on 26 October 1938 and was designed as a response to a US Army Air Corps (USAAC) specification calling for a fast attack aircraft. The design had attracted the attention of the French Purchasing Commission and French observers were present during testing, one of whom died when the prototype crashed in January 1939.

Despite this setback the French were impressed with the aircraft and ordered 100 production DB-7 aircraft on 15 February 1939, followed by 170 more in October 1939. The French order was followed by orders for the US, designated the A-20, and Britain, which named the aircraft 'Boston'.

Havok Mk I night fighters

Those French DB-7s that had been delivered before the fall of France were used briefly against the advancing Germans before being evacuated to North Africa. The remaining undelivered aircraft built on the French order were then transferred to the Royal Air Force (RAF). Unfortunately, the aircraft possessed far too short a range to be used effectively as a bomber operating from UK bases against targets in Europe, so the decision was taken to modify these aircraft into night-fighters, becoming the Havoc Mk I. The DB-7 offered good performance, excellent handling, the ability to carry bulky radar equipment and tricycle undercarriage making for easier night operations when landing and taxiing. Of the 150 ex-French aircraft, around 100 were modified to Havoc standard with flame-damping exhausts and a 'solid' nose containing eight 7.7mm (0.30in) machine guns and an AI Mk IV or V radar set. Some aircraft however retained the glazed nose and were fitted with four machine guns in the lower nose to be used on night intruder missions from early 1941 onwards.

Havoc Mk IV

Initially designated the Havoc Mk IV, these aircraft later became known as the Havoc I (Intruder). The slightly improved DB-7A was also inherited from a French contract, becoming the Havoc Mk II when fitted with radar and a 12-gun nose developed by the Martin-Baker Aircraft Company. Many Havocs were modified to carry the 2.7 million candlepower Helmore/GEC searchlight, known as the 'Turbinlite', in the nose to illuminate enemy aircraft for an accompanying single seat fighter to attack but this scheme achieved scant success. Later, Boston bombers built on British contract and converted to the night intruder role with a ventral pack containing four 20mm (0.79in) cannon were given the designation Havoc II C-B and Havoc II C-D, the two designations reflecting whether the cannon were drum- or belt-fed.

Douglas Havoc Mk II

Weight (maximum take-off): 9654kg (21,264lb)
Dimensions: Length 14.5m (47ft 7in), Wingspan 18.69m (61ft 4in), Height 5.36m (17ft 7in)
Powerplant: Two 1177kW (1600hp) Wright R-2600-A5B Cyclone 14-cylinder air-cooled radial piston engines
Maximum speed: 529km/h (329mph)
Range: 1706km (1060 miles)
Ceiling: 8611m (28,250ft)
Crew: 2–3
Armament: None when equipped with Helmore Turbinlite; otherwise 12 7.7mm (0.303in) Browning machine guns fixed firing forward in nose

Bristol Beaufighter

Derived from the Beaufort torpedo bomber, the Beaufighter was developed in great haste to fill a critical gap in the Royal Air Force's (RAF) fighter defences, yet became one of the most successful aircraft of the conflict.

Bristol Beaufighter Mk IF

Beaufighter R2059 made the first sortie of the type in RAF service on 5 September 1940 by Flight Lieutenant Glyn Ashfield and Flight Sergeant Reginald Leyland of the Fighter Interception Unit, before the type entered regular squadron service in the same month.

Bristol Beaufighter Mk IF

Weight (maximum take-off): 9435kg (21,000lb)
Dimensions: Length 12.6m (41ft 4in), Wingspan 17.63m (57ft 10in), Height 4.82m (15ft 10in)
Powerplant: Two 1163kW (1560hp) Bristol Hercules XI 14-cylinder air-cooled radial piston engines
Maximum speed: 520km/h (323mph)
Range: 1883km (1170 miles)
Ceiling: 8077m (26,500ft)
Crew: 2
Armament: Four 20mm (0.79in) Hispano cannon fixed firing forward in nose and six 7.7mm (0.303in) Browning machine guns fixed firing forward in wings

---

The Bristol company had submitted unsuccessful proposals to Air Ministry Specifications F.37/35 and F.18/37, both calling for a cannon-armed fighter, which ultimately resulted in production of the Westland Whirlwind and Hawker Typhoon respectively. However, during late 1938 those aircraft were either suffering from severe delays or had yet to even fly, and the Bristol design team led by Leslie Frise (1895–1979) made the remarkably inspired suggestion that a two seat fighter derivative of their Beaufort torpedo bomber, first flown on 15 October 1938 and itself derived from the Blenheim, might offer a suitable cannon-armed aircraft to fulfil the requirements of both specifications. Bristol proposed two variants, the Type 158 "sports model" with a slimmer fuselage than the Beaufort and the Type 156 which featured a fuselage the same width as the Beaufort and thus could utilise more of the existing jigs and tooling and be ready more quickly. The proposal was submitted to the Air Ministry in October 1938 and the response was both rapid and enthusiastic, four prototypes of the Type 156 were ordered in February 1939, and a contract for 300 production aircraft was placed in July, the name 'Beaufighter' (a portmanteau of 'Beaufort' and 'Fighter') having been officially adopted in the previous month.

Hercules engine

The Beaufighter retained much of the Beaufort's structure: the wings and tail were essentially the same, as was most of the rear fuselage. However, the Beaufighter utilised Bristol's own Hercules engine in place of the lower-powered Taurus of the Beaufort. These engines necessitated the use of greater diameter propellers, in turn requiring that the fuselage stopped short of the propeller disc, resulting in the aircraft's distinctive snub-nosed profile. From the outset the Beaufighter was armed with four 20mm (0.79in) Hispano cannon in the lower front fuselage, which apart from the first 50 production aircraft, was supplemented by six 7.7mm (0.303in) machine guns, four in the starboard wing, two to port, this armament making the Beaufighter the most heavily armed fighter used by the RAF during the war. The cannon were initially fed by 60-round drum magazines which were to be changed by the observer in lieu of a servo feed mechanism that Bristol intended to develop. Production delays to the Hercules Mk VI intended for the aircraft saw it substituted with the Hercules III resulting in reduced performance estimates, though shortages of even this engine variant resulted in the prototype being fitted with the earlier Hercules I-SM when it first flew on 17 July 1939.

The Beaufighter was never a particularly fast fighter but when the first prototype fitted with the definitive Hercules III engines could only manage 497km/h (309mph), and with delivery of the Hercules VI not expected for another two years, serious questions were asked about the wisdom of producing the aircraft in this form. Although production did go ahead, the Rolls-Royce Griffon was seen as a potential alternative for the Beaufighter; but the Fairey Firefly had priority for that engine and as a stopgap a Merlin powered Mk II variant was designed, utilising the Merlin XX combined engine and nacelle 'power egg' that had already been designed for the Avro Lancaster. The first Mk II was completed rapidly, and the first example flew in July 1940 before the Beaufighter I had even entered service. In total 450 Mk IIs were built , all delivered in overall matt black finish as night fighters. At around the same time the Mk III and Mk IV designations were reserved for the slim-fuselage Type 158 Beaufighter to be powered by the Hercules and Griffon respectively but in the event neither of these types was built.

Bristol Beaufighter Mk IF

R2069, one of the first production Beaufighters, was taken on strength by No. 25 Squadron, based at North Weald in Kent in September 1940 and wears the standard daylight fighter scheme applied to operational Beaufighters.

Night-fighter role

Night fighting was initially the most important role for the Beaufighter and the first squadrons to use the type were selected from those currently flying Blenheim IFs, five units taking delivery of the Beaufighter during September 1940 with No. 29 Squadron flying the type's first operational sortie on 17 September. This coincided both with the introduction of airborne radar and the German night blitz reaching its greatest intensity. On 25 October 1940, Sgts Hopkinson and Benn of No. 219 Squadron managed to shoot down a German bomber without the aid of radar, but teething troubles combined with the very limited numbers of the new AI Mk IV radar resulted in the aircraft having to wait until 19 November before an airborne radar-guided victory was achieved. The first such were scored by Flt Lt John Cunningham (1917–2002) and Sgt J Phillipson of No. 604 Squadron, who were credited with the destruction of a German Junkers Ju 88.

With the efficacy of the night fighters enhanced by the commission of six ground-controlled interception (GCI) radar stations, the Beaufighter squadrons gradually proved ever more effective until on 10 May 1941, 14 enemy bombers were shot down during the last major Luftwaffe attack on London, the largest number brought down on any single night of the offensive. By this time a further four Beaufighter I units had formed, as well as 10 squadrons operating Merlin-powered Beaufighter Mk IIs, including Polish, Canadian and Australian manned units.

Bristol Beaufighter Mk IF

Weight (maximum take-off): 9435kg (21,000lb)

Dimensions: Length 12.6m (41ft 4in), Wingspan 17.63m (57ft 10in), Height 4.82m (15ft 10in)

Powerplant: Two 1163kW (1560hp) Bristol Hercules XI 14-cylinder air-cooled radial piston engines

Maximum speed: 520km/h (323mph)

Range: 1883km (1170 miles)

Ceiling: 8077m (26,500ft)

Crew: 2

Armament: Four 20mm (0.79in) Hispano cannon fixed firing forward in nose and six 7.7mm (0.303in) Browning machine guns fixed firing forward in wings

Bristol Beaufighter Mk 21

Australian Mk 21 Beaufighters were similar to the TF Mk X but lacked radar and the provision to carry a torpedo. A8-146 'Beau-Guns-Ville' (a play on Beaufighter and Bougainville) was on the strength of No. 22 Squadron RAAF and flew that unit's last wartime sortie, over Ambon, then part of the Netherlands East Indies.

Autopilot
Australian Beaufighters are easily identified by the bulged fairing just ahead of the cockpit. This contained a Sperry autopilot adopted as a pilot aid, as the RAAF expected its Beaufighters to spend a greater amount of time flying over open water than their European counterparts.

"BEAU-GUNSVILLE"

Firepower
On its introduction, the Beaufighter possessed the greatest weight of fire of any aircraft in the world. Australian-built Beaufighters featured fewer wing machine guns than British aircraft, but these were the harder hitting 12.7mm (0.5in) Brownings, rather than the rifle calibre 7.7mm (0.303in) fitted to British 'Beaus.

Instability
The Beaufighter garnered a reputation for difficult handling, which only increased as the aircraft gradually gained weight, and was never entirely eradicated. The addition of significant dihedral on the horizontal tail surfaces helped somewhat and the TF Mk X added a large dorsal fin, though the latter feature was not adopted for Australian production.

Hercules engine
Key to the Beaufighter's performance was its Bristol Hercules engines. More generally used by bombers, the Hercules was an outstanding radial engine produced throughout the World War II but never achieved the same sort of fame as the Spitfire-powering Rolls-Royce Merlin.

Bristol Beaufighter Mk 21

Weight (maximum take-off): 11,521kg (25,400lb)

Dimensions: Length 12.60m (41ft 4in), Wingspan 17.63m (57ft 10in), Height 4.83m (15ft 10in)

Powerplant: Two 1200kW (1600hp) Bristol Hercules XVIII 14-cylinder air-cooled radial piston engines

Maximum speed: 515km/h (320mph)

Range: 2820km (1750 miles)

Ceiling: 5800m (19,000ft)

Crew: 2

Armament: Four 20mm (0.79in) Hispano cannon fixed firing forward in nose and four 12.7mm (0.5in) Browning machine guns fixed firing forward in wings; up to 220kg (500lb) bombload or eight RP-3 rockets

Mk V variant

During the summer of 1941 two examples of a second Merlin powered variant, the Mk V, were given field trials with Nos 29 and 406 Squadrons. The Mk V dispensed with the rear observer's cockpit and featured a Boulton Paul BPA.1 power operated turret installed just behind the pilot's cockpit instead. The fact that emergency escape from the turret was nigh on impossible predictably saw the Mk V find little favour with crews and production did not proceed. Later Mk I and IIs were fitted with a tailplane featuring 12 degrees of dihedral as a solution to the aircraft's low-speed longitudinal instability and this tailplane would be fitted to all subsequent production aircraft except for the very first Mk VIs.

German nocturnal activity over the UK tailed off towards the end of 1941 and the Beaufighter began to be used in roles other than defensive night fighting; consequently, Beaufighter units in the UK increasingly flew intruder missions over occupied Europe attacking targets of opportunity. One spectacular morale-boosting mission in June 1942 saw a single Beaufighter of No. 263 Squadron despatched to Paris to fly the length of the Champs Elysee at low altitude, disrupting the daily German parade, before dropping the French *tricouleur* over the Arc de Triomphe and then strafing the German navy headquarters.

Mk IC

The Mk IC was developed specifically for the needs of Coastal Command, (resulting in the retrospective designation of Mk IF for the night fighter Beaufighters) featuring greater fuel capacity, a direction-finding (D/F) loop, and navigators table and instruments provided for the second crewman. The first Mk IC unit, No. 252 Squadron commenced operations with the type from Malta in May 1941, swiftly joined by No. 272 Squadron. The latter unit provided support for the 'Crusader' offensive in the Western Desert, Egypt, destroying 44 enemy aircraft on the ground and in the air in just four days of operations. Local modifications saw Beaufighters in the Western Desert, Egypt, fitted with under fuselage bomb shackles allowing them to carry a single 227kg (500lb) or two 113kg (250lb) bombs and the considerable success of these two units in attacking land-based and shipping targets in the Mediterranean resulted in a greater demand for production of the Beaufighter as a strike fighter.

Bristol Beaufighter TF Mk X

Weight (maximum take-off): 11,521kg (25,400lb)

Dimensions: Length 12.60m (41ft 4in), Wingspan 17.63m (57ft 10in), Height 4.83m (15ft 10in)

Powerplant: two 1200kW (1600hp) Bristol Hercules XVII or XVIII 14-cylinder air-cooled radial piston engines

Maximum speed: 515km/h (320mph)

Range: 2820km (1750 miles)

Ceiling: 5800m (19,000ft)

Crew: 2

Armament: Four 20mm (0.79in) Hispano cannon fixed firing forward in nose, six 7.7mm (0.303in) Browning machine guns fixed firing forward in wings, and one 7.7mm (0.303in) Browning machine gun flexibly mounted in rear cockpit; up to 220kg (500lb) bombload or one 45cm (18in) torpedo or eight RP-3 rockets

Bristol Beaufighter TF Mk X

Based at Langham, Norfolk, UK, between April and October 1944, the Beaufighters of No. 455 Squadron RAAF were utilised on highly successful but hazardous anti-shipping operations.

Early 1942 finally saw a reliable supply of the Hercules VI engine materialize and the Beaufighter Mk VI, the aircraft that had been envisaged back in 1938, finally began rolling off the production lines in VIF and VIC forms for night-fighting and Coastal Command use respectively, supplementing and then replacing earlier models in operational units. Mk VIF night fighters were initially fitted with the AI Mk IV radar, but this was gradually replaced by the greatly improved AI Mk VII and the mass produced AI Mk VIII, as these radar sets began to appear in early 1942 and most Beaufighter VIFs would be fitted with the later radar.

The newer radars worked on a wavelength of 10cm (3.94in), rather than the 1.5m (4ft 11in) of AI Mk IV resulting in a single small aerial being used both for transmitting and receiving rather than the widely separated aerials of the earlier version. Fitted with a reflector dish behind the aerial to focus the beam and allow it to scan a 90° cone ahead of the aircraft, both aerial and dish could be fitted within a distinctive compact 'thimble' fairing on the nose of the aircraft. The first victory for a Beaufighter fitted with the new centimetric radar occurred on the night of 5 April 1942 when a Do 217 was destroyed. The Beaufighter also appeared in a new theatre during 1942, when Mk VIFs were supplied to three RAF squadrons in India, though these were not used as night fighters and subsequently engaged in interdiction of Japanese lines of communication in Burma (modern-day Myanmar) to great effect. The Mk VIF was also utilised by four squadrons of the United States Army Air Force (USAAF), operating initially in North Africa – two re-equipped with the P-61 Black Widow. The remaining two units retained the Beaufighter until the end of hostilities.

'Interim Torpedo Fighter'

Closer to home, Coastal Command's use of the Beaufighter spread from the Mediterranean to operations over the Bay of Biscay and North Sea and by 1942 it was apparent that the aircraft was superior in every regard to the RAF's standard torpedo bomber and progenitor of the Beaufighter, the Bristol Beaufort. As a result Bristol proposed a Beaufighter that could carry a torpedo externally, under the fuselage. Following the construction of a suitably modified Mk VIC as a torpedo-carrying prototype, Bristol built 50 examples of the Mk VI (ITF) which entered service towards the end of 1942, 'ITF' standing for 'Interim Torpedo Fighter'.

These were soon followed by the definitive TF Mk X (Mks VII, VIII, and IX were reserved for unbuilt Australian variants) which, in addition to its torpedo carrying gear, was fitted with the Hercules XVII engine, optimised for maximum performance at low altitude. Early production TF Mk Xs were fitted with standard ASV radar as carried by other Coastal Command aircraft but it was soon discovered that the night fighting AI Mk VIII could be utilised effectively against surface targets and this radar in its thimble nose radome became standard. The TF Mk X also introduced armament for the observer for the first time with a 7.7mm (0.303in) Vickers K machine gun flexibly mounted in the rear cockpit canopy. This gun and its mounting were fitted retrospectively in many earlier Mk VIs. Other armament changes saw Beaufighters adapted to carry a 227kg (250lb) bomb under each wing, or from late 1942 onwards, four 41kg (90lb) rockets under each wing instead. With torpedo and additional other equipment fitted the TF Mk X was some 50 per cent heavier than the original prototype when loaded and handling was compromised as a result. To cure this a long dorsal fin was fitted, originally developed for the Mk II but never adopted for production, as well as enlarged elevators.

These modifications did much to cure the issues but the Beaufighter was nonetheless noted for its capricious handling qualities throughout its service life. The final production variant to appear in the UK was the Mk XIC, intended for the strike role and identical to the TF Mk X in all respects except that it lacked torpedo carrying provision. Coastal Command usage of the Beaufighter was intense and highly successful with squadrons combining to form Beaufighter Strike Wings. Attacking initially with rockets to silence anti-aircraft fire, a second wave would strike with torpedoes before all aircraft strafed with cannon. The Strike Wings began by attacking shipping targets in the North Sea before moving southwards to support the D-Day operations.

Australian service

On the other side of the world, the Royal Australian Air Force (RAAF) was

Flying over the Botanic Gardens in Melbourne, A8-95 was one of the 364 Beaufighters to be delivered from the Department of Aircraft Production factory a mere 7km (4 miles) away in Fishermans Bend. The transparent fairing above the fuselage contains a direction-finding loop aerial.

becoming an enthusiastic Beaufighter operator and Australia would put the type into production before the war's end. Two RAAF Beaufighter units, equipped with Mk ICs were operational by August 1942 and these moved to New Guinea in September 1942 where they mostly flew missions against Japanese land forces. Further squadrons converted to the type and anti-shipping sorties began to be flown in the Timor Sea.

RAAF Beaufighter operations reached their zenith in the Battle of the Bismarck Sea in March 1943 when, operating in concert with attack aircraft of the US Fifth Air Force (5AF), all eight transport ships of a Japanese convoy critical to continuing efforts on the New Guinea campaign were sunk, as well as four escorting destroyers.

At around the same time the Australian government decided to place the Beaufighter into production at the Department of Aircraft Production factory, a process made easier by the fact that the factory was already producing the Beaufort. The first Mk 21, derived from the TF Mk X, though devoid of torpedo gear, radar, or dorsal fin, was flown on 26 May 1944 and 364 examples were built. Five squadrons would operate Mk 21s before VJ day, though two of these units were equipped with the aircraft very late in the war and saw little action.

The Beaufighter was withdrawn from British and Australian service fairly rapidly following the end of the war, both nations retaining a few examples for target towing. In the UK, TF Mk Xs modified as target tugs were redesignated the TT Mk 10, and one of these flew the last Beaufighter sortie on 12 May 1960.

Despite its somewhat makeshift origins the Beaufighter had proved immensely successful, 5,928 were built in total and the type was the third most successful British aircraft in terms of the total number of enemy aircraft shot down during the war.

de Havilland Mosquito

Of wooden construction, the remarkable Mosquito was schemed as a bomber but its performance was such that it was adapted into an exceptional fighter, becoming the finest night-fighter fielded by any nation during the war.

The radical concept of using a relatively small aircraft carrying no defensive armament that relied on speed and altitude to evade interception was proposed by de Havilland in the late 1930s. The idea was met with much scepticism in official circles, scepticism that was bolstered by the company's intention to build this high-speed aircraft out of wood, a material considered obsolete for modern high performance combat aircraft. Yet de Havilland's proposal did not fall entirely on deaf ears and thanks largely to Sir Wilfred Freeman (1888–1953), the Air Member for Development at the Air Ministry, championing the unconventional aircraft in government circles, a prototype was ordered in March 1940 to Specification B.1/40 calling for a high speed bomber, with a secondary role as a reconnaissance aircraft, which had been written around de Havilland's proposal, designated D.H.98 by the company. Even before this point had been reached, however, although defensive weaponry had been consistently eschewed, the prospect of fitting offensive guns to transform the design into a heavy fighter had been taken into account. De Havilland designers deliberately provided enough room under the cockpit floor for a quartet of 20mm (0.79in) Hispano cannon and a prototype D.H.98 in fighter configuration was ordered in July 1940 with an official specification, F18/40, drawn up to cover de Havilland's design.

D.H.98

The first flight by the D.H.98, soon to be named 'Mosquito', was made on 25 November 1940 and the first fighter prototype followed it into the air on 15 May 1941. Externally, the fighter did not differ greatly from the standard Mosquito, but featured a strengthened main wing spar and four 7.7mm (0.303in) machine guns in the extreme

de Havilland Mosquito FB Mk VI

Wearing full 'invasion stripes', this FB Mk VI was serving with No. 235 Squadron, which converted to the Mosquito in June 1944. Forming part of the 'Portreath Wing', 235 Squadron's Mosquitoes flew long-range missions to counter Luftwaffe sorties over the Bay of Biscay.

de Havilland Mosquito FB Mk VI

Weight (maximum take-off): 10,124kg (22,300lb)
Dimensions: Length 12.34m (40ft 6in), Wingspan 16.51m (54ft 2in), Height 4.66m (15ft 4in)
Powerplant: Two 1206kW (1640hp) Rolls-Royce Merlin 25 V-12 liquid-cooled piston engines
Maximum speed: 608km/h (378mph)
Range: 2990km (1860 miles)
Ceiling: 10,520m (34,500ft)
Crew: 2
Armament: Four 20mm (0.79in) Hispano cannon fixed, firing forward in lower forward fuselage and four 7.7mm (0.303in) Browning machine guns fixed, firing forward in nose; up to 440kg (1000lb) bombload in bomb bay and up to 440kg (1000lb) bombload or eight RP-3 27kg (60lb) rockets under wings

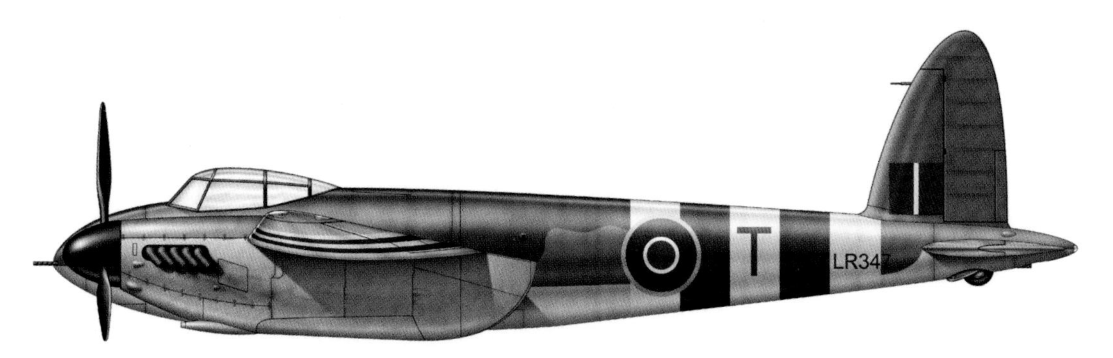

de Havilland Mosquito NF Mk II

Pictured in late 1942, this Mosquito of No.23 Squadron features "Smooth Night" undersurfaces and standard daylight camouflage on the upper surfaces. As night fighter Mosquitoes were increasingly used also by day, black finishes were gradually dropped.

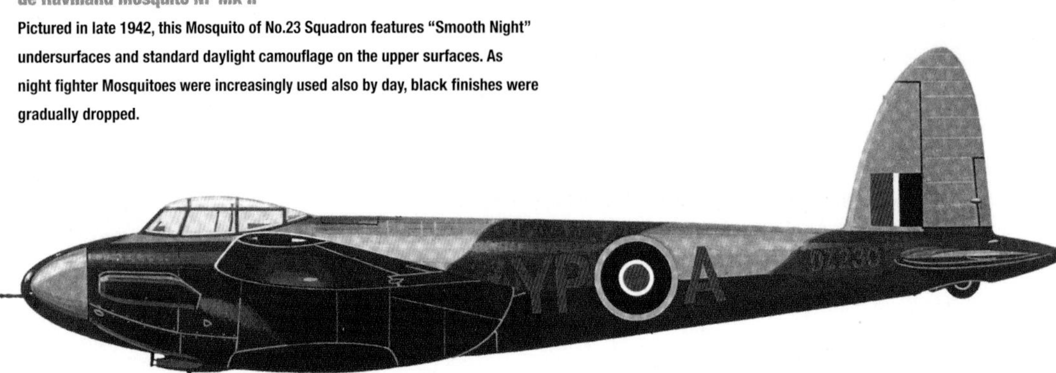

nose as well as the aforementioned 20mm (0.79in) cannon in the lower fuselage. The cannon precluded the use of the ventral crew hatch of the bomber Mosquito so a side door was fitted instead and the vee-shaped windscreen was replaced by a single flat pane for better visibility, especially at night.

Rapid production

Production was rapid, largely due to the type's wooden construction, and the first Mosquito F Mk IIs, as the fighter was initially designated, began to be received by No. 157 Squadron in December 1941, followed by Nos 141 and 264 Squadrons in April 1942. Even before the fighter Mosquito had entered service, a modified version fitted with a two gun Bristol power-operated turret manned by a third crew member had been built and flown but production of this version did not proceed, official enthusiasm for the 'turret fighter' concept having finally waned.

Fitted with AI MK IV or V radar and finished in all-over matt lamp-black paint, the Mosquito fighters were also given exhaust shrouds to reduce glare, all of which knocked 26mph (42km/h) off the F Mk II's top speed. Despite this, the Mosquito possessed a performance comfortably in excess of all other night fighters and after teething troubles with both the aircraft and the AI Mk V radar were overcome the Mosquito achieved its first confirmed air-to-air 'kills' during June 1942. By this time the centimetric wavelength AI Mk VII was beginning to be used on operations by Beaufighters and an improved AI Mk VIII was fitted to a Mosquito II in July 1942. As a result the next batch of 97 new-production Mk IIs were instead completed with AI Mk VIII radar and designated the Mosquito NF Mk XII, entering service with No. 85 Squadron in February 1943.

In the same month the first trial installation of the American SCR 720 radar, designated AI Mk X in the UK, went ahead and a batch of 99 aircraft with this equipment mounted in a large 'bullnose' radome was ordered, becoming the NF Mk XVII. Both centimetric radar equipped night fighter Mosquitoes required the entire nose be given over to the radar installation and so these and later night fighting Mosquito variants dispensed with the nose machine guns, though on operations the enhanced capability of the new radar more than compensated for the loss of firepower.

de Havilland Mosquito NF Mk II

Weight (maximum take-off): 9080kg (20,000lb)
Dimensions: Length 12.34m (40ft 6in), Wingspan 16.51m (54ft 2in), Height 4.66m (15ft 4in)
Powerplant: Two 1089kW (1480hp) Rolls-Royce Merlin 21 V-12 liquid-cooled piston engines
Maximum speed: 595km/h (370mph)
Range (internal fuel only): 1432km (890 miles)
Ceiling: 10,520m (34,500ft)
Crew: 2
Armament: Four 20mm (0.79in) Hispano cannon fixed, firing forward in lower forward fuselage and four 7.7mm (0.303in) Browning machine guns fixed, firing forward in nose

The first two victories by the Mosquito NF Mk XII were achieved on the night of 14 April 1943 and the type was subsequently committed to combating the Fw 190 'tip-and-run' raids then making attacks on London and the South of England, achieving considerable success against these high-speed, low-altitude raiders. By June 1943 there were 11 squadrons of night fighter Mosquitoes in the UK, nine engaged in defensive operations and the other two primarily undertaking intruder missions. Mosquitoes would provide the main nocturnal defence of the UK for the rest of the war.

A separate area of activity that was to become a major role for the Mosquito began in July 1942 when Mosquitoes of No. 23 Squadron commenced making low-level attacks on enemy airfields, communications, and other targets in occupied Europe. Two further units were formed for this activity in early 1943 and subsequently several night fighting squadrons adapted their Mk IIs to perform daylight 'Ranger' sorties over Europe. Mosquitoes began to operate overseas for the first time when night intruder missions began to be flown from Malta during December 1942 against targets in Sicily. The first use of the Mosquito by Coastal Command took place in 1943, with aircraft patrolling the Bay of Biscay to protect other Coastal Command aircraft from shore-based Luftwaffe fighters.

FB Mk VI fighter-bomber

A Mosquito variant tailored for fighter-bomber missions had been under development since July 1941, and the appearance of the FB Mk VI in February 1943 allowed the Mosquito to realise its full potential in the strike role. The FB Mk VI retained the full machine gun and cannon armament of the Mk II but could also carry two 227kg (500lb) bombs modified with telescopic fins in

Starting its engines at Hatfield, where the prototype Mosquito made its first flight, this NF Mk II was photographed in November 1941 while the aircraft was still under development. The arrowhead transmitting aerial of the AI Mk IV radar is visible between the centre guns in the nose of the aircraft.

de Havilland Mosquito NF Mk II

No. 157 Squadron was formed specifically to become the first Mosquito night fighter unit, taking the brand-new Mosquito NF Mk II into operational service during April 1942, though the first victory over German aircraft did not occur until late August.

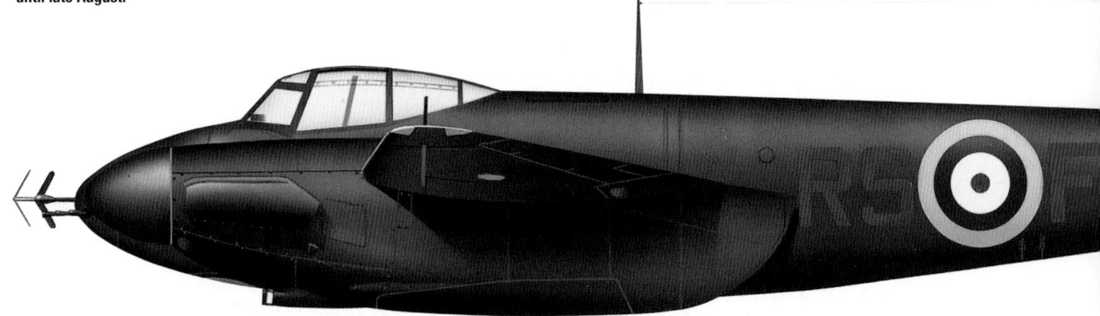

de Havilland Mosquito NF Mk II
Weight (maximum take-off): 9080kg (20,000lb)
Dimensions: Length 12.34m (40ft 6in), Wingspan 16.51m (54ft 2in), Height 4.66m (15ft 4in)
Powerplant: Two 1089kW (1480hp) Rolls-Royce Merlin 21 V-12 liquid-cooled piston engines
Maximum speed: 595km/h (370mph)
Range (internal fuel only): 1432km (890 miles)
Ceiling: 10,520m (34,500ft)
Crew: 2
Armament: Four 20mm (0.79in) Hispano cannon fixed, firing forward in lower forward fuselage and four 7.7mm (0.303in) Browning machine guns fixed, firing forward in nose

a bay behind the cannons. The aircraft also benefited from uprated Merlin engines and the wing was modified to a standard known as the "basic" wing allow the carriage of a 113kg (250lb) bomb on an underwing rack each side, or alternatively a flush fitting 227 litre (50 gallon) external tank. It was subsequently found that a pair of 227kg (500lb) bombs could be carried instead without difficulty or eight 27kg (60lb) RP-3 rockets. The "basic" wing was also combined with an NF Mk XII fuselage to produce the NF Mk XIII, of which 270 were built, the type evolving into the NF Mk XIX when fitted with Merlin 25 engines and "universal" radome which could house either AI Mk VIII or SCR 720 radar.

A total of 280 of the latter variant were built before production switched to the last wartime night fighter mark to see service, the NF Mk 30, 530 of which were built, first flown in April 1944 and fitted with two-stage Merlin 72s conferring outstanding performance at all altitudes.

The first action the NF Mk XIXs were assigned to was combatting the V-1 flying bomb, the Mosquito being one of the few aircraft with the necessary performance at low level to be able to catch these guided missiles, which Mosquitoes intercepted primarily at night. Second only in success to the Hawker Tempest, Mosquitoes accounted for 623 V-1s destroyed.

Later, night fighter Mosquitoes took on an offensive role, flying missions within the bomber stream and intercepting enemy night fighters by homing in on German radio and radar emissions utilising an array of electronic equipment, such as 'Perfectos' which detected Luftwaffe IFF signals, as well as 'Monica' and 'Serrate' which were tuned to locate airborne radar sets. Such was the success of these efforts that by the end of 1944, German night fighter losses during raids were greater than those of British bombers.

An earlier urgent effort to develop a high altitude Mosquito to counter the perceived threat of high-flying Junkers Ju 86P bombers over the UK had seen a development airframe, of no specific subtype, which had been engaged in the testing of a pressure cabin modified within the space of seven days to become the prototype NF Mk XV fitted with long span wings, a Mk II nose

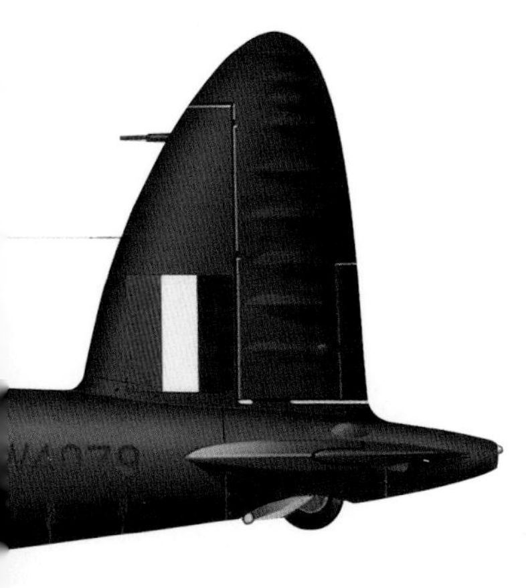

and much unnecessary equipment discarded. In this form it was found capable of reaching 13,716m (45,000ft).

Four further NF Mk XVs were converted from Mk IIs and served with No. 85 Squadron but enemy high altitude activity had ceased by the time these were available in 1943 and no interceptions were carried out.

Low-level sweeps

Meanwhile, the FB Mk VI was rapidly becoming one of the Royal Air Force's (RAF) most potent assets and was used for some of the war's most spectacular raids. Entering service simultaneously in the UK and Malta with three units, all operating Mk IIs on intruder duties, FB Mk VIs were subsequently issued to six squadrons, forming part of the newly created Second Tactical Air Force (2TAF).

The first FB Mk VI operations were flown on 3 October 1943 and the aircraft played an ever-increasing role in attacks on tactical targets until the war's end, all six 2TAF Mosquito squadrons operating the FB Mk VI exclusively until Victory in Europe (VE) Day. A particularly impressive mission saw FB Mk VIs attack Amiens prison at low level, knocking down the walls to allow 258 prisoners to escape, 79 of whom were resistance members. Proving this level of accuracy was no fluke – FB Mk VIs also destroyed a building housing German records of resistance activity in the Hague, leaving the buildings on either side undamaged, and followed this up with similar attacks on offices housing Gestapo archives in Denmark at both Aarhus and Copenhagen.

Coastal Command

In 1944, the FB Mk VI entered service with Coastal Command, with three squadrons so equipped forming the Banff Strike Wing which mounted a major offensive on shipping and coastal targets in the Bay of Biscay, North Sea and in the Channel until the end of the war. An FB Mk VI derivative was also developed specifically for attacking shipping, the FB Mk XVIII which featured a 57mm (2.24in) Molins gun in the fuselage replacing the four cannon, though the four machine guns were retained, primarily to sight the large weapon. Although some successes were achieved with the Mk XVIII, conventional rocket-armed FB Mk VIs claimed the type's first U-boat 'kills' when three submarines were discovered on the surface on 9 April 1945 and all were sunk by the collective action of 37 Mosquitoes. Mosquitoes would account for 10 U-boats sunk by the end of the war.

Far East service

Doubts over the ability of the Mosquito's wooden structure to stand up to a tropical environment resulted in a small sample of Mk IIs and FB Mk VIs undergoing operational trials in India, which proved successful. Subsequently five units flew the FB Mk VI against Japanese targets in Burma, before Victory over Japan (VJ) Day with a further three units, including two equipped with NF Mk XIXs, forming too late to see action. However, a few Royal Australian Air Force (RAAF) Mosquito squadrons did take part in fighting just before the war's end, equipped with the FB Mk 40, an Australian-built derivative, equivalent to the FB Mk VI, which utilised Australian coachwood in its construction in place of the birch used in British-built aircraft.

British-made Merlin engines were too scarce to be spared for shipping to Australia so de Havilland Australia utilised the US-built Packard Merlin 31, and later the Merlin 69 when it became available. The first FB Mk 40 flew at Bankstown near Sydney 23 July 1943 but production proceeded slowly, with Australian Mosquitoes being supplied to Nos 1, 87, and 94 Squadrons by VJ day. Canada too built Mosquitoes, most of which were bomber variants for service in Europe but de Havilland Canada also produced 337 examples of the Packard Merlin 225 powered FB Mk 26, equivalent to the FB Mk VI, 140 of which were despatched to the UK, though none had entered service by the conclusion of hostilities. FB Mk 26s were also flown at home by No. 133 Squadron Royal Canadian Air Force (RCAF), their sole action against an enemy 'aircraft' being an attempted interception of an unmanned Japanese Fu-go incendiary balloon.

Postwar developments

Two further Mosquito fighters were developed after the war, the NF Mk 36, with slightly more powerful Merlin 113 engines but otherwise similar to the NF Mk 30, this being the last variant to see widespread RAF service. The NF Mk 38 was the last of all but stability problems meant it was never used by the RAF although 60 were sold to Yugoslavia.

NAVAL FIGHTERS

The performance of British carrier fighters at the start of the war was hamstrung somewhat by the requirement that a second crewman be carried, primarily to perform navigation over the open ocean. All of the Royal Navy's wartime single-seat fighters were either conversions of RAF types, such as the Sea Hurricane and Seafire, or the more capable American designs, such as the Martlet and Corsair. The following aircraft are featured in this chapter:

- Blackburn Skua
- Blackburn Roc
- Fairey Fulmar
- Hawker Sea Hurricane
- Grumman Martlet/Wildcat
- Vought Corsair
- Grumman Hellcat
- Supermarine Seafire
- Fairey Firefly
- Hawker Sea Fury

An 807 Squadron Fulmar begins its take-off run as a second Fulmar and the Skuas of 800 Squadron warm up on HMS *Ark Royal* in the Atlantic in 1941.

Blackburn Skua

Intended to fulfil the roles of both fighter and dive bomber, the Skua was responsible for the first British air-to-air victory of the war, as well as becoming the first aircraft in history to sink an enemy capital ship during wartime.

In 1934 Specification O.27/34 was issued calling for a dive bomber that could also function as a fighter. It was believed that, at sea, a solo pilot could not navigate with sufficient accuracy and thus a two-seater aircraft was considered essential, a design philosophy that would later compromise the performance of both the Fairey Fulmar and Firefly. Blackburn Aircraft's response to O.27/34 was judged sufficiently impressive for 150 production machines to be ordered in March 1936 along with two prototypes, the first of which flew on 9 February 1937. Stability issues resulted in the aircraft's nose being lengthened by 73cm (29in) and the aircraft also proved difficult to recover from a spin. As an interim measure an anti-spin parachute was fitted in the extreme tail but this 'interim' feature was subsequently installed on all production Skuas as the aircraft's spin recovery characteristics remained problematic.

The dihedral of the wing was found to be too shallow in testing but rather than redesign the entire wing, which would have delayed production, Blackburn instead fitted the Skua with upturned wingtips which had much the same effect with no major disruption to production plans. The aircraft went into production as the Skua Mk II, the prototype becoming the solitary Mk I, and in late 1938, No. 800 Squadron became the first unit to receive the Skua, subsequently taking the aircraft to sea for the first time aboard HMS *Ark Royal* in the spring of 1939.

During its early service life, the Skua was found to be a good deck landing aircraft, possessing pleasant handling characteristics and whilst its performance was somewhat pedestrian, it was generally considered unlikely that it would have to deal with shore-based

Blackburn Skua Mk II

Never a particularly effective fighter, the Skua was, however, an excellent dive bomber. L2987 was serving aboard HMS *Ark Royal* in June 1940 when it was lost after running out of fuel escorting Hurricanes to Malta.

Blackburn Skua Mk II

Weight (maximum take-off): 3732kg (8228lb)

Dimensions: Length 10.85m (35ft 7in), Wingspan 14.07m (46ft 2in), Height3.81m (12ft 6in)

Powerplant: One 660kW (890hp) Bristol Perseus XII 9-cylinder air-cooled radial piston engine

Maximum speed: 362km/h (225mph)

Range: 1220km (760 miles)

Ceiling: 6200m (20,200ft)

Crew: 2

Armament: Four 7.7mm (0.303in) Browning machine guns fixed firing forward in wings, one 7.7mm (0.303in) Vickers K or Lewis machine gun flexibly mounted in rear cockpit; up to 227kg (500lb) bomb-load under fuselage

Skuas were extremely busy during the early war years. L2928, seen here serving with No. 759 Squadron, the Fleet Fighter School, had earlier seen action with 801 Squadron during the Norwegian campaign and flown from RAF Detling in Kent to cover the Dunkirk evacuation.

single-seat fighters. During the prewar period dive bombing techniques were developed, using its patented Zap flaps as dive brakes, and the Skua proved to be an excellent dive bomber.

Norway campaign

By the outbreak of war three squadrons were flying Skuas and on 26 September 1939, three Skuas intercepted and shot down a Dornier Do 18 flying boat, the first confirmed British air-to-air victory of the war. At first, the Skua's performance as a fighter was quite successful, with the aircraft downing 28 German aircraft in air combat off Norway, and the first Royal Navy (RN) 'ace' of the war was a Skua pilot, Lt William Lucy, who scored all five of his confirmed victories in the aircraft. Just over six months later, a force of 16 Skuas, led by Lucy, successfully attacked the cruiser *Königsberg* in Bergen harbour. At least five 227kg (500lb) bombs directly hit the ship, and two near misses tore further holes in the hull, causing the vessel to capsize and sink, becoming the first ship to be lost to dive bombing and the first capital ship to be sunk by aircraft during wartime. Further dive bombing attacks were made during the Norwegian campaign, including a daring but costly raid on the battleship *Scharnhorst* in Trondheim.

The Skua saw more action as a fighter covering the Dunkirk evacuation and during operations in the Mediterranean but it was becoming increasingly clear that the Skua, whilst effective enough against German bombers and flying boats, could not successfully cope with modern enemy fighters, mainly due to its comparatively low speed, and the aircraft was gradually withdrawn from frontline use.

The last Skua dive bombing mission was flown on 19 February 1941 by No. 801 Squadron and in May this unit was re-equipped with recently introduced Sea Hurricanes.

After its frontline career ended, the Skua served on in considerable numbers as a target tug with both the Navy and the RAF. It proved well suited to the target tug role, possessing good handling, a reliable engine, and an incredibly strong airframe, and served until March 1945 in this unglamorous but essential task.

Blackburn Roc

A development of the Skua fitted with a four gun powered turret, the Blackburn Roc was even slower than the earlier aircraft and proved to be a dismal fighter aircraft.

The Air Ministry issued specification O.30/35 for a naval turret fighter at the end of 1935, intended to complement conventionally armed fighter aircraft. A turret equipped variant of the Skua was proposed by Blackburn Aircraft and 136 examples of the 'Roc', as it was named, were ordered off the drawing board in July 1937. The Skua was slow and not particularly impressive in the air-to-air combat role and it seems the Air Ministry began to have second thoughts about producing an untested turret fighter development of that aircraft as 127 examples of the conventional Fairey Fulmar were ordered in 1938 as an insurance should the Roc prove a failure.

New contract

Blackburn Aircraft had no spare capacity available to construct the Roc so production was contracted to Boulton Paul Aircraft, who made the turret and who by this time had already flown the turret equipped Defiant which was around 130km/h (80mph) faster than the lacklustre Roc. The first Roc flew on Christmas Eve 1938 and proved to possess pleasant handling characteristics. Unfortunately it could barely exceed 200mph (320km/h) and its endurance was compromised due to the turret replacing the fuselage fuel tanks as fitted to the Skua. Issued to Nos 800, 801 and 803 Naval Air Squadrons during 1939, Rocs supplemented the Skua in all three units and on operations Rocs had to return to their base or carrier over an hour earlier than Skuas due to their reduced fuel capacity.

Norwegian campaign

Nonetheless, both Nos 800 and 801 Squadrons flew Rocs in combat during the Norwegian campaign from HMS *Ark Royal*. Unable to intercept any German aircraft over Norway due to their slow speed, Rocs were later used along with Skuas to cover the Dunkirk evacuation during May 1940. It was during the course of one of these missions that the Roc scored its one confirmed 'kill', a Junkers Ju 88, a surprising victim as the Ju 88 was one of the fastest aircraft in the world and well able to escape from a Roc.

Later the same year Rocs performed useful work attacking moored E-boats and gun emplacements at Cap Gris-Nez in concert with Skuas, but the low performance of the Roc saw it transferred to non-operational roles by mid-1940.

Blackburn Roc

Few Rocs saw frontline operational service, but L3075 flew patrols and ground attack sorties over the Dunkirk evacuation beaches with No. 806 Squadron.

Blackburn Roc

Weight (maximum take-off): 3606kg (7950lb)
Dimensions Length: 10.85m (35ft 7in), Wingspan: 14.03m (46ft), Height: 3.68m (12ft 1in)
Powerplant: One 675kW (905hp) Bristol Perseus XII 9-cylinder air-cooled radial engine
Speed 359km/h (223mph)
Range 700km (434 miles)
Ceiling 5486m (18,000ft)
Crew 2
Armament: Four 7.7mm (0.303in) Browning machine guns in Boulton Paul Type A power operated dorsal turret; up to eight 14kg (30lb) bombs on underwing carriers

---

Fairey Fulmar

The first 'modern' eight-gun monoplane fighter of the Royal Navy (RN) and derived from a cancelled light bomber design, the Fulmar ultimately shot down more enemy aircraft than any other Fleet Air Arm (FAA) fighter.

Even before the outbreak of war the Admiralty had realised that the Blackburn Skua lacked the necessary speed to intercept several contemporary German bombers, let alone fighters, and the stop-gap biplane Gloster Sea Gladiator, was only marginally better. In 1938 the Air Ministry issued Specification O.8/38 calling for a two-seat fighter/observation aircraft conforming to the then prevailing view that a second crew member was necessary for navigation at sea as well as allowing the aircraft to be used for other roles such as reconnaissance, a useful quality on a carrier where space is limited. The Fairey company, which had a long history of providing aircraft to the Navy, proposed a fighter version of their pre-existing light bomber design which had been designed to Specification P.4/34 but hadn't entered production yet. As an adaptation of an extant design, valuable time could be saved in development and the fact that the aircraft was stressed to undertake dive bombing meant that the structure was of sufficient strength to withstand the rigours of carrier operations. The aircraft also possessed a good range capability, and a stable, wide-track undercarriage ideal for deck handling.

The first Fulmar flew on 4 January 1940 and demonstrated a maximum speed of only 370km/h (230mph) which was disappointing, even allowing for the penalty imposed by the two-seat layout. An engine change to the Rolls-Royce Merlin VIII saw this improved to 426km/h (265mph), which although hardly spectacular was judged sufficient for an aircraft that was generally not expected to meet enemy single-seaters.

Clearance for service use was extremely rapid, deck landing trials began during May of 1940, and although production built up relatively slowly at first, No. 886 Squadron aboard HMS *Illustrious* had received three Fulmars by June, replacing Blackburn Rocs. By the end of the year, seven squadrons were operating the type. By then the Fulmar had made its combat debut – four Italian Savoia Marchetti SM.79 torpedo bombers and a Cant Z.501 flying boat were all shot down on 2 September by Fulmars flying off *Illustrious* while the ship was en route to join the Mediterranean Fleet.

Mk II variant

During January 1941 the Mk II variant replaced the Mk I on the production line which featured a more powerful Merlin 30 engine delivering an additional 265hp, sufficient to raise the maximum speed slightly and allow extra stores and equipment to be carried. A heavier armament of four 12.7mm (0.5in) Browning machine guns in place of the eight 7.7mm (0.303in) guns was fitted to most Mk II Fulmars, although some aircraft featured an unusual asymmetric arrangement of four 7.7mm (0.303) guns in one wing and two 12.7mm

Fairey Fulmar Mk II

Weight (maximum take-off): 4627kg (10,200lb)
Dimensions: Length 12.24m (40ft 2in), Wingspan 14.14m (46ft 4.5in), Height 3.25m (10ft 8in)
Powerplant: One 970kW 1300hp Rolls-Royce Merlin 30 V-12 liquid-cooled piston engine
Maximum speed: 440km/h (272mph)
Range: 1255km (780 miles)
Ceiling: 8300m (27,200ft)
Crew: 2
Armament: Eight 7.7mm (0.303in) Browning machine guns fixed firing forward in wings; up to 227kg (500lb) bombload

Fairey Fulmar Mk II

Serving with No. 808 Squadron in the spring of 1941, N1860 displays the distinctive slender profile of the type. Most of 808's Fulmars were lost when HMS *Ark Royal* was torpedoed and sunk by the German U-boat *U-81* on 13 November 1941.

A Fulmar of an unknown unit cruises over the battlecruiser HMS *Renown*. The Fulmar's two-seat layout hampered its performance as a pure fighter but did lend it the versatility to operate effectively in many other roles such as convoy escort.

(0.5in) weapons in the other. Fulmars saw a lot of use over the following three years, including at the Battle of Cape Matapan (March 1941), where they provided cover to Swordfish and Albacore torpedo bombers. They also operated from escort carriers defending convoys making the bitterly cold trip across the Arctic Sea to the USSR, as well as in the more temperate conditions of the Mediterranean, and formed part of the fighter force during Operation Torch (November 1942), the Allied landings in North Africa. The Fulmar also saw considerable service from shore bases, flying as fighter bombers from the UK during 1942, as well as serving in the Western Desert, Egypt, and against the Japanese in Malaya. True to the multi-role nature of the original specification, the Fulmar was regularly employed as both a convoy escort and high-speed reconnaissance machine, roles for which its excellent range rendered it highly suitable, with external fuel tanks fitted, the Fulmar's endurance was of the order of five and a half hours.

Second-line role

During 1942, however, as carrier fighters of superior performance such as the Martlet started to become available in numbers, the Fulmar was gradually transferred into second-line roles, serving until the end of the war as an advanced trainer and as a high-speed courier aircraft. The final frontline role of the aircraft was as a night-fighter: 100 NF Mk.IIs were converted using Mk.II airframes by fitting AI Mk.IV radar. However, the three radar aerials fitted to each wing reduced the already unimpressive maximum speed of the Fulmar by 20mph (32km/h) and no night kills are known to have been achieved by the aircraft. Despite its slow speed, however, the Fulmar was the RN's most successful fighter of the war, scoring 112 victories. With 17 'kills', Commander Stanley Orr (1916–2003) was both the top-scoring British naval pilot of the war, and the most successful Fulmar ace, having scored 12 of his victories with the aircraft.

Hawker Sea Hurricane

Despite never being completely adapted for carrier operations, the Hawker Sea Hurricane enjoyed a surprisingly successful career, providing the Fleet Air Arm (FAA) with a better fighter than the Fulmar at its moment of greatest need.

During 1940, Focke Wulf Fw 200 Condors were becoming a serious problem for Atlantic convoys as they transmitted details of a convoy's position to U-boats and directly attacking shipping. With inadequate numbers of Royal Navy (RN) carriers to protect the convoys, the Hawker Hurricane made its debut at sea launched from a crude, rocket-powered catapult on a cargo ship specifically to combat the Fw 200. Standard Royal Air Force (RAF) Hurricane Mk Is were fitted with catapult spools and minimal naval equipment, designated the Sea Hurricane Mk Ia, and the Merchant Ship Fighter Unit (MSFU) was hastily formed with volunteer pilots from both the RAF and Navy to fly these aircraft from Catapult Aircraft Merchant (CAM) ships. When a Condor was sighted, the Sea Hurricane was fired off the catapult to either shoot down or chase away the enemy aircraft. There was no way to recover the aircraft once it had completed its mission, the pilot could either bail out, fly to land if close enough, or ditch near the convoy and hope to be picked up. Although only nine German aircraft are known to have been shot down by CAM ship Hurricanes, many more were driven off and the system effectively brought the use of Focke Wulf Fw 200 Condors over the North Sea to an end – a remarkably successful, if extemporised, maritime debut for the Hawker Hurricane.

The Sea Hurricane subsequently appeared in a more thoroughly navalised form as the Sea Hurricane Mk IB, of which 340 were converted, with an arrestor hook and strengthened structure for carrier landings. Entering service in July 1941, the Sea Hurricane Mk IB was in action almost immediately, scoring its first victory on the last day of that month when a Dornier Do 18 was shot down by aircraft from HMS *Furious*. The Sea Hurricane was very active over the next two years but the most notable action in which it was involved was probably Operation Pedestal of August 1942, when a convoy of 14 fast merchant ships fought their way through near constant attacks to Malta with desperately needed supplies. No fewer than four fleet carriers were provided for escort and most of the fighter force consisted of Sea Hurricanes that were heavily engaged for the duration of the voyage. During this action Lieutenant Richard Cork (1917–44) became the only RN

Hawker Sea Hurricane Mk IB
Weight (maximum take-off): 3511kg (7740lb)
Dimensions: Length 9.83m (32ft 4in), Wingspan 12.2m (40ft), Height 4m (13ft 1in)
Powerplant: One 954kW (1280hp) Rolls-Royce Merlin XX V-12 liquid-cooled piston engine
Maximum speed: 505km/h (314mph)
Range: 1207km (750 miles)
Ceiling: 10,516m (34,500ft)
Crew: 1
Armament: Eight 7.7mm (0.303in) Browning machine guns fixed firing forward in wings

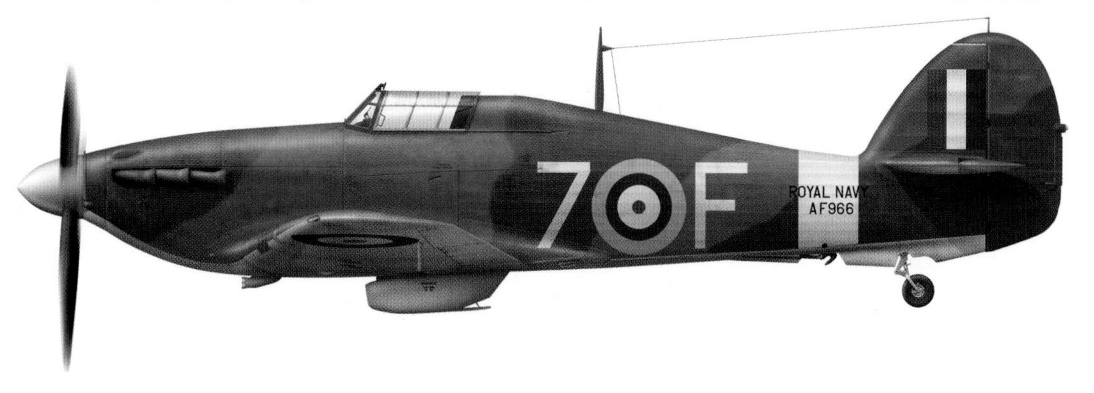

Hawker Sea Hurricane Mk IB
One of only four Sea Hurricanes that survive today, Z7015 is shown here in the colours of No. 880 Squadron with whom it served in 1941. This airframe was built in Canada as a standard Hurricane and modified for naval use in the UK.

Hawker Sea Hurricane Mk IIC

No. 835 Squadron adopted an all-over white scheme appropriate for concealing their aircraft against the prevailing overcast of the North Atlantic.

Hawker Sea Hurricane Mk XII

JS327 was operating with No. 800 Squadron during the Operation Torch landings of November 1942. All aircraft during Torch received US markings to make it easier for US forces to recognise the friendly aircraft and also as an attempt to ameliorate the suspected anti-British sentiments of the Vichy French.

pilot to achieve 'ace in a day' status by shooting down five enemy aircraft.

Sea Hurricane Mk IIC

The following variant, the Sea Hurricane Mk IIC was cannon-armed. Converted from the standard land-based Mk IIC, 81 airframes were diverted for naval use in May 1942 and featured the 1460hp Merlin XX engine, which raised the maximum speed to 550km/h (342mph). As with other variants, the Mk IIC never received folding wings. The possibility of designing such a wing was considered but the urgency attached to getting Hurricanes onto carriers as quickly as possible combined with concerns over the weight penalty of the folding wing and the plans were abandoned. This proved to be the Sea Hurricane's Achilles heel as only two carriers, HMS *Eagle* and *Ark Royal* had deck lifts big enough to accommodate the Hurricanes and both had been lost by August 1942. The newer Illustrious class fleet carriers had to store Sea Hurricanes, exposed to the elements, on deck, limiting the amount that could be carried to approximately six aircraft. Despite this, serviceability rates were comparatively good attesting to the durable nature of the Hurricane. The Sea Hurricane IIC saw action during Operation Torch, the Allied invasion of North Africa when around 40 operated off the escort carriers HMS *Biter*, *Avenger* and *Dasher*. The final Sea Hurricane deliveries were made in August 1943 by which time adequate stocks of the superior F4F Martlet were available for RN use and the last unit to fly the Sea Hurricane, No. 835 Squadron aboard the escort carrier *Nairana*, converted to the Wildcat VI in September 1944.

Hawker Sea Hurricane Mk IIC

Weight (maximum take-off): 3511kg (7740lb)
Dimensions: Length 9.83m (32ft 4in), Wingspan 12.2m (40ft), Height 4m (13ft 1in)
Powerplant: One 954kW (1280hp) Rolls-Royce Merlin XX V-12 liquid-cooled piston engine
Maximum speed: 505km/h (314mph)
Range: 1207km (750 miles)
Ceiling: 10,516m (34,500ft)
Crew: 1
Armament: Four 20mm Hispano cannon fixed firing forward in wings

Grumman Martlet/Wildcat

The most important Allied carrier fighter of the first half of the war, the Grumman F4F delivered adequate performance, docile handling and an incredibly robust airframe. The Royal Navy (RN) was the first air arm to use the pugnacious Grumman fighter in combat.

Despite losing to the Brewster F2A in the competition to build the US Navy's first monoplane fighter, the F4F would become one of the most significant combat aircraft in history. Curiously, the aircraft began life as a biplane, the XF4F-1, but was modified to a monoplane design as the XF4F-2, before construction even began as a reaction to the predicted performance of the Brewster F2A. Although Grumman started building the XF4F-2 some time later than the Brewster aircraft, the prototype XF4F-2 was completed first and made its first flight on 2 September 1937. Despite the US Navy selecting the Brewster aircraft to enter production in April 1938 Grumman remained convinced that the basic F4F design possessed potential and proposed fitting a more powerful version of the Pratt & Whitney Twin Wasp incorporating a two-speed, two stage supercharger. This proposition was met with enthusiasm by the Navy and work on the updated aircraft proceeded rapidly. The updated XF4F-3 flew for the first time on 12 February 1939 and swiftly demonstrated a performance superior to both the earlier XF4F-2 and the Brewster F2A. An initial batch of F4F-3s was ordered in August 1939 and the first production machine appeared in February 1940. In October the US Navy officially adopted the name 'Wildcat' for the new aircraft by which time the new carrier fighter was attracting foreign interest, with both France and the UK placing orders for F4Fs during the first half of 1940.

France ordered 81 examples of a variant similar to the F4F-3 under the export designation G-36A for use by the Aeronavale. This was to be powered by the Wright R-1820 Cyclone, fitted with Darne 7.5mm (0.29in) machine guns, and French radios and gunsights but by the time the first example flew at Grumman's Bethpage factory on 11 May 1940, France was on the cusp of capitulation and none of the G-36As was delivered. Instead, the order was transferred to Britain, adding to the order of 100 Pratt & Whitney S3C4 powered G-36B aircraft already placed

Grumman Martlet Mk II

Weight (maximum take-off): 3821kg (8423lb)

Dimensions: Length 9.09m (29ft 10in), Wingspan 11.59m (38ft), Height 3.44m (11ft 4in)

Powerplant: One 895kW (1200hp) Pratt & Whitney R-1830-S3C4-G Twin Wasp 14-cylinder air-cooled radial piston engine

Maximum speed: 472km/h (293mph)

Range: 1432km (890 miles)

Ceiling: 8840m (29,000ft)

Crew: 1

Armament: Six 12.7mm (0.5in) AN/M2 Browning machine guns fixed forward-firing in wings

Grumman Martlet II

Another of the more successful Martlet pilots, Sub-Lt BJ Waller of No. 881 Sqn shared in three victories (over a Vichy French Potez 63 and a pair of MS.406s) off Madagascar in May 1942. His squadron was based aboard HMS *Illustrious*.

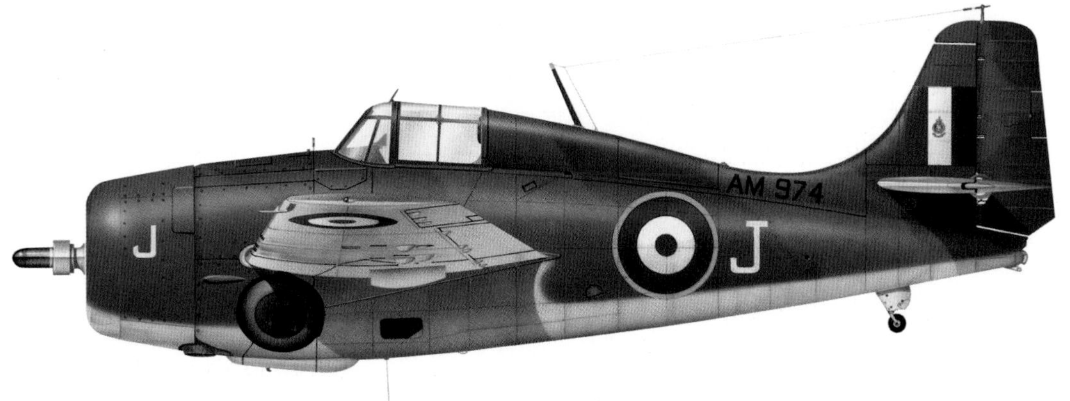

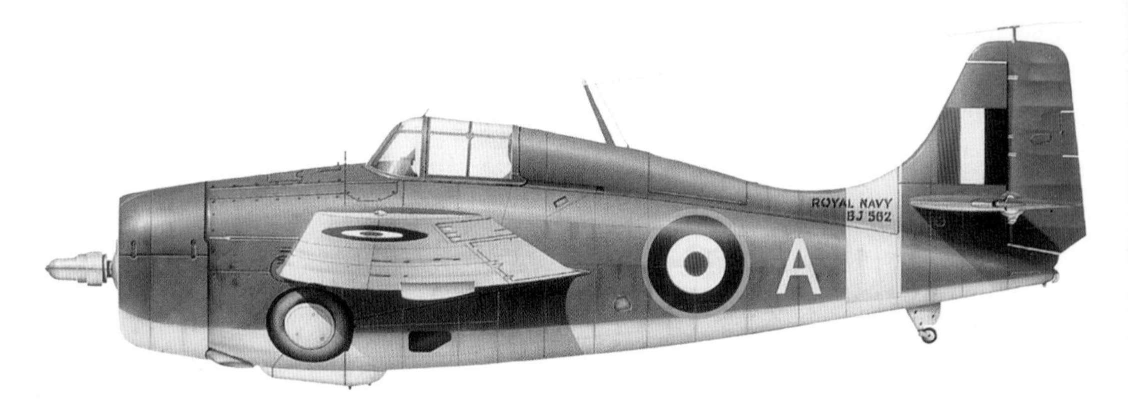

by the British Purchasing Commission, the first of which was flown in October 1940. However, when it became known that Grumman were developing a folding-wing version of the aircraft, the British decided that this feature was of sufficient utility to accept a delay in deliveries of the British order (though to expedite service entry the first 10 were accepted with fixed wings). As a result, the ex-French G-36As became the first examples of the Grumman fighter to arrive in the UK, entering service as the Martlet Mk I. Subsequent aircraft built on the British order became the Martlet Mk II.

Grumman Martlet Mk I

Shown as it appeared when serving with No. 804 Naval Air Squadron based at RNAS Skaebrae in the Orkney Isles, BJ562 was one of the two Martlets that shared in the type's first victory on 25 December 1940.

Grumman Martlet Mk I

The first Martlets were finished in 'equivalent' paints that were the closest Grumman could obtain to official Royal Naval shades. As a result some Martlet Mk Is appear in some quite unusual colours. One such was BJ569 with sky blue undersides, black port wing and two odd shades of green on the upper surfaces.

Grumman Martlet Mk I

Weight (maximum take-off): 3367kg (7423lb)
Dimensions: Length: 8.76m (28ft 9in), Wingspan: 11.59m (38ft), Height: 3.44m (11ft 4in)
Powerplant: One 895kw (1200hp) Wright R-1820-G205A Cyclone nine cylinder air-cooled radial piston engine
Speed: 491km/h (305mph)
Range: 1884km (1170 miles)
Ceiling: 12,000m (39,500ft)
Crew: 1
Armament: Four 12.7mm (0.5in) AN/M2 Browning machine guns fixed forward-firing in wings

First combat

The first unit to receive the Martlet was No. 804 Squadron and two Mk Is of this unit shot down a Junkers Ju 88 over the Orkney Islands on Christmas day 1940, the first instance of a US built aircraft in British service claiming a combat victory. As well as the ex-French aircraft, Britain also received 30 examples of the F4F-3A intended for Greece that were in the process of being delivered when Greece capitulated. The Greek F4Fs were then taken on by the UK and designated the Martlet Mk III(B). This variant did not possess folding wings and was subsequently used at shore bases in the Western Desert, Egypt. The first folding wing Mk IIs were delivered in August 1941 and were initially used aboard small escort carriers, the first embarking on HMS *Audacity* in September 1941 to escort a convoy to Gibraltar, the Martlets claiming a Fw 200 Condor shot down on 20th September 1941. A further four of these patrol bombers were claimed during Audacity's second voyage in November 1941.

The lend-lease act of March 1941 paved the way for greater numbers of F4Fs to be supplied to the UK and the first were 220 Martlet Mk IVs, virtually identical to the USN F4F-4 but powered by the Wright R-1820-40B engine with single-stage, two-speed supercharger. These were followed by 312 FM-1s built by General Motors' Eastern Aircraft Division which differed from the F4F-4 only in being fitted with four rather than six guns and were designated the Martlet Mk V. During 1943, with Martlet V deliveries in full swing and Grumman concentrating on Hellcat development and production, General Motors undertook total responsibility for production of the Wildcat and eventually delivered over 4,400 examples (over half of the 7,860 Wildcats produced in total) of the final F4F-8 variant, developed by Grumman but designated FM-2 when produced by General Motors. Easily recognisable by its taller vertical tail the FM-2 was produced specifically to serve on escort carriers, which were thought too small

Grumman Wildcat Mk V

In early 1945 Sub Lieutenant RA Fleischmann Allen was flying this Wildcat V from the escort carrier HMS *Vindex* when he shot down a Junkers Ju 88 and shared in the destruction of a Fw 200 Condor.

Grumman Wildcat Mk V

Weight (maximum take-off): 3978kg (8762lb)

Dimensions: Length: 8.85m (29ft), Wingspan: 11.59m (38ft), Height: 3.44m (11ft 4in)

Powerplant: One 895kw (1200hp) Pratt & Whitney R-1830-86 Twin Wasp 14-cylinder air-cooled radial piston engine

Speed: 515km/h (320mph)

Range (with external tanks): 2051km (1275 miles)

Ceiling: 10,370m (34,000ft)

Crew: 1

Armament: Four 12.7mm (0.5in) AN/M2 Browning machine guns fixed forward-firing in wings; up to 90kg (200lb) bombload under wings

This trio of early Martlet Mk Is were pictured on a training flight in October 1941. They are on the strength of No. 804 Squadron based in the Orkney Isles, the first RN Martlet unit and the first to score a victory with the Grumman fighter.

to handle the larger, more modern fighters that had superseded the F4F on fleet carriers. The impeccable deck manners of the FM-1 and FM-2, combined with their ability to fly off a short flightdeck without catapult assistance – essential as no such equipment was fitted to escort carriers – saw the Wildcat widely employed on these vessels by both the US and UK.

Wildcat Mk VI

The FM-2 was designated the Wildcat Mk VI by the RN, the Martlet name having been dropped in March 1944 in order to standardise with the US and all preceding marks were retrospectively renamed. In British service, Wildcat Mks IV, V, and VI were primarily, though not exclusively, used on escort carriers. The standard practice on these vessels was to embark a single mixed squadron comprising four to six Wildcats as well as up to 12 anti-submarine aircraft, either Swordfish, Barracudas or Avengers. Over 15 RN units flew Wildcats on these duties, in which the aircraft was employed until the end of the conflict, and another six squadrons primarily flew the Grumman fighter aboard larger carriers, notably on HMS *Illustrious* at the Salerno landings and HMS *Victorious* in the South West Pacific. Additionally a single Royal Canadian Navy (RCN) unit flew Wildcats, under RN control, aboard the RCN-crewed HMS *Puncher*.

Notwithstanding the fact that its performance had largely been surpassed by early 1945, the Wildcat Mk VI was responsible for the last RN victories in Europe when, on 26 March 1945, eight Messerschmitt Bf 109Gs attacked a squadron of Avengers and Wildcats flying off HMS *Searcher* near the Norwegian coast. The Wildcats shot down three Bf 109s and seriously damaged a fourth for no loss.

Vought Corsair

An outstanding performer in the air, the Corsair was a capricious aircraft to operate from a carrier. Despite its somewhat poor deck-landing reputation, the Corsair nonetheless formed an important part of the Fleet Air Arm (FAA) as well as becoming New Zealand's standard land-based fighter.

First flown on 29 May 1939, the prototype XF4U-1 possessed the largest and most powerful engine, largest propeller and largest wing of any Naval fighter yet built but its most striking design feature was its inverted gull wing, adopted to allow clearance for the huge propeller without requiring prohibitively long undercarriage legs. The XF4U-1 became the first US fighter to exceed 650km/h (400mph) in level flight and it also demonstrated an excellent rate of climb. Unfortunately the aircraft was also prone to some problematic handling characteristics, not least a tendency to drop a wing when it approached touchdown speed.

Nonetheless, the terrific performance of the aircraft resulted in an order for 584 F4U-1s being placed in March 1941 as the XF4U-1 was being put through service testing. This was a huge order for the period and reflected the increasing expectation that the US would be involved in imminent war. By this time, combat reports of air-to-air combat over Europe suggested the design should be altered, most significantly by increasing the armament. The wing was therefore redesigned to accept three 12.7mm (0.5in) machine guns on each side, but this used up space in the wings that contained fuel and a new fuel tank had to be incorporated into the fuselage.

For centre of gravity reasons, the tank could only be placed above the aircraft's wing, requiring the cockpit to be moved 92cm (36in) rearwards. This made for a poor view forward, especially when combined with the nose-high attitude necessary for deck-landing.

Although the first USN F4U unit passed its carrier qualification trials as early as April 1943, the fact that there were still doubts about the ability of the average pilot to land the Corsair on a carrier without special training combined with the availability of the F6F, a superior deck-landing aircraft, saw the Navy take the decision to restrict the F4U to shore-based use, mostly, though not exclusively, with US

Vought Corsair Mk I

Weight (maximum take-off): 6350kg (14,000lb)
Dimensions: Length 10.16m (33ft 4in), Wingspan 12.5m (41ft), Height 5.13m (16ft 10in)
Powerplant: One 1492kW (2000hp) Pratt & Whitney R-2800-8 Double Wasp 18-cylinder air-cooled radial piston engine
Maximum speed: 671km/h (417mph)
Range: 1633km (1015 miles)
Ceiling: 11247m (36,900ft)
Crew: 1
Armament: Six 12.7mm (0.5in) Browning M2 machine guns fixed firing forward in wings

Vought Corsair Mk I

Featuring the distinctive, heavily framed 'birdcage' canopy of early Corsairs, this Mk I was based at Brunswick Air Station in Maine, USA, while No. 1835 Squadron worked up and undertook deck landing training.

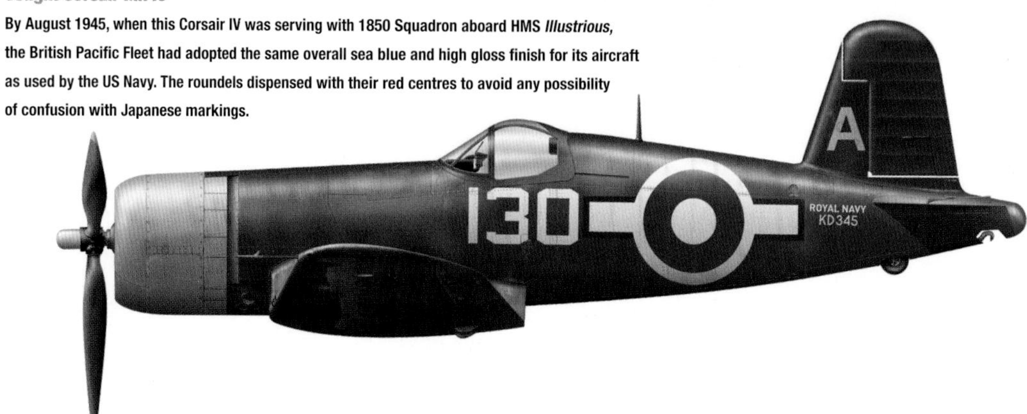

Vought Corsair Mk IV

By August 1945, when this Corsair IV was serving with 1850 Squadron aboard HMS *Illustrious*, the British Pacific Fleet had adopted the same overall sea blue and high gloss finish for its aircraft as used by the US Navy. The roundels dispensed with their red centres to avoid any possibility of confusion with Japanese markings.

Marine Corps (USMC) units. This meant that only one type of fighter, the Hellcat, was serving on US carriers, simplifying the logistics of supplying spare parts at sea and it therefore fell to the Royal Navy (RN) to introduce carrier-based Corsairs to regular combat operations. The first Corsairs for British use were 95 F4U-1s, designated the Corsair F Mk I by the FAA, fitted with the early heavily framed 'birdcage' cockpit canopy, which began to be delivered in early 1943, these being followed by 510 Corsair F Mk IIs with the raised cockpit canopy.

Corsair units worked up at bases in North America and then transferred with their aircraft on escort carriers to the UK, the first unit to do so being No. 1830 Squadron, commissioned on 1 June 1943 and subsequently embarked in HMS *Illustrious*. Further Corsair units followed rapidly and eventually 19 FAA units would be equipped with the Corsair, the final squadron forming in April 1945. In British service the Corsair received several modifications, the most obvious being the 22cm (8in) clipped from each wingtip to allow the aircraft to fit in the hangar decks of RN carriers. This modification also resulted in the side effect of improving the stall characteristics of the fighter and partially eradicating its tendency to float on landing. Additionally, the top two cowling cooling gills were wired shut to improve view during deck landing, a modification subsequently taken up by Vought on later production aircraft. Britain received 430 F3A Corsairs built by Brewster Aeronautical Corporation, though this variant was used for training only, along with 977 Goodyear FG-1s, these types being referred to as the Corsair Mk III and Mk IV respectively.

The operational debut of the Corsair in British hands occurred during April 1944 in both Europe and the Pacific with No. 1834 Squadron supplying fighter cover for Fairey Barracudas dive bombing the *Tirpitz* in Norway. Aircraft from HMS *Illustrious* escorted Barracudas and Grumman Avengers attacking the oil refineries on Sabang, Sumatra, and subsequently engaged in combat operations with the British Pacific Fleet (BPF) all the way to Japanese home waters. The only other wartime user was New Zealand, with early delivery of Corsairs to the Royal New Zealand Air Force (RNZAF) being authorised by the US following the impressive showing of New Zealand squadrons flying the P-40 in the South Pacific, particularly in air-to-air combat.

Vought Corsair Mk IV

Weight (maximum take-off): 6350kg (14,000lbs)

Dimensions Length: 10.16m (33ft 4in), Wingspan: 12.09m (39ft 8in), Height: 5.13m (16ft 10in)

Powerplant: One 1492kW (2000hp) Pratt & Whitney R-2800-8W Double Wasp 14-cylinder air-cooled radial piston engine

Speed: 671km/h (417mph)

Range: 1633km (1015 miles)

Ceiling: 11,247m (36,900ft)

Crew: 1

Armament: Six 12.7mm (0.50in) M2 Browning machine guns fixed forward-firing in wings; up to 907kg (2000lb) bombload or six 127mm (5in) rockets under wings

Eventually 424 Corsairs equipped 13 RNZAF squadrons with the first 30 being delivered in March 1944. The RNZAF Corsairs operated mainly in the close support role, though some patrol, escort and tactical bombing missions were also flown as the need arose. Although most of the Corsairs were withdrawn from use at the end of the war, No. 14 Squadron RNZAF formed part of the British Commonwealth Air Group stationed in Japan directly after the war's end and would become the last RNZAF unit to fly Corsairs, only retiring the aircraft at the end of 1947 when the squadron returned to New Zealand.

Grumman Hellcat

The most successful US carrier fighter of World War II, the Hellcat was also supplied in large numbers to the Royal Navy (RN). Although not as numerous in British service as the Corsair, the Hellcat delivered dependable service in RN use for the last two years of the conflict.

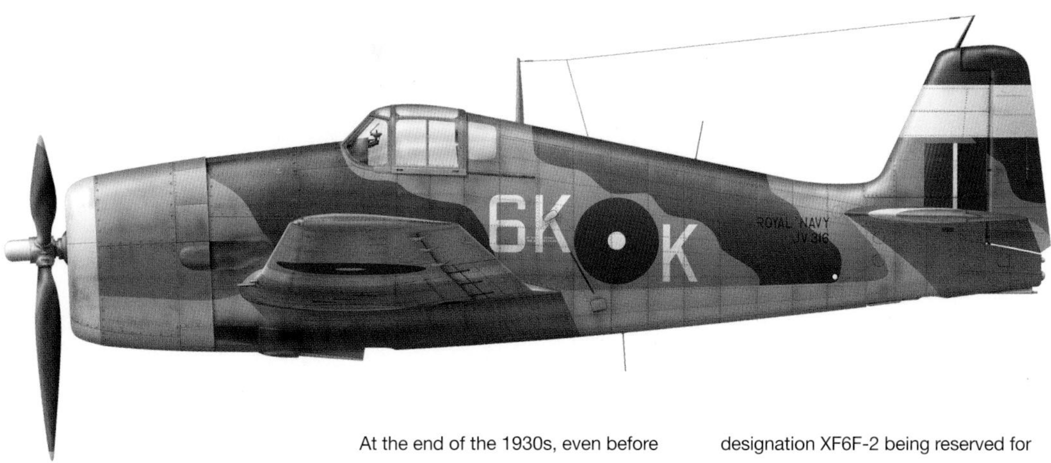

Grumman Hellcat Mk I

JV316 was on the strength of 804 Naval Air Squadron aboard HMS *Ameer* for operations in Sumatra and Malaya with the British East Indies Fleet towards the end of the war.

Grumman Hellcat Mk I
Weight (maximum take-off): 6000kg (13,217lb)
Dimensions: Length 10.17m (33ft 4in), Wingspan 13.08m (42ft 10in), Height 4.4m (14ft 5in)
Powerplant: One 1490kW (2000hp) Pratt & Whitney R-2800-10 Double Wasp 18-cylinder air cooled radial piston engine
Maximum speed: 600km/h (373mph)
Range: 1755km (1090 miles)
Ceiling: 11,438m (37,500ft)
Crew: 1
Armament: Six 12.7mm (0.5in) Browning M2 machine guns fixed firing forward in wings; up to 907kg (2000lb) bombload under wings

At the end of the 1930s, even before it had entered service, the US Navy sought a better fighter than the F4F Wildcat. The F4U Corsair had begun flight testing by 1940 but progress was slow and it was considered prudent to obtain a back-up fighter to the Vought aircraft. In 1941 therefore, an 'improved F4F' was ordered, consisting of an F4F airframe fitted with the Wright R-2600 Cyclone. Grumman argued that a new design would be greatly superior and despite the risk of significant delay that the development of an entirely new aircraft carried, the Navy agreed and Grumman prepared a new design, the F6F, in a remarkably short period of time.

Considerably larger than the Wildcat, the F6F possessed a loaded weight around 60 per cent greater than that of the earlier aircraft and before long, the wisdom of powering the F6F with the Cyclone was being questioned as the Pratt & Whitney R-2800 Double Wasp appeared to offer greater development potential. Grumman obtained Navy approval to fit the R-2800 to the second prototype F6F, designated XF6F-3, (the designation XF6F-2 being reserved for an experimental turbo-supercharged variant). The Cyclone-powered prototype XF6F-1 flew for the first time on 26 June 1942, and it was followed into the air by the Double Wasp-powered XF6F-3 a little over a month later. Flight trials were highly satisfactory, which was fortunate as large-scale production had already been ordered by the Navy as the F6F-3 Hellcat on 23 May 1942, before either prototype had even flown.

First combat

Less immediately successful were the carrier acceptance trials which saw the arrestor hook torn completely out of an early production F6F and a second landing incident resulted in the failure of the entire rear fuselage. Localised structural strengthening was applied and no further trouble of this kind was encountered. Initial deliveries to US units began in January 1943, and on 31 August VF-5 operating from the USS *Yorktown* took the F6F-3 into combat for the first time as part of a force attacking Japanese positions on

Marcus Island. During early 1943 the RN began to receive the first of 252 F6F-3s, designated Hellcat Mk I, as part of lend-lease arrangements, the name 'Gannet' having been initially chosen but discarded in favour of the US name before the aircraft entered service. The first Hellcats entered service with No. 800 Squadron on 1 July 1943, replacing the Sea Hurricane, and the Hellcat began its RN service with anti-shipping missions along the Norwegian coast. Later that year Hellcats escorted Fairey Barracudas attacking the battleship *Tirpitz*, an operation which resulted in three Hellcats shooting down a German fighter each and No. 800 Squadron provided part of the fighter cover supplied for the August 1944 landings in the south of France. Like their American counterparts however, the majority of British Hellcat operations would take place in the Far East.

Hellcat Mk II

The only other major production variant of the Hellcat was the F6F-5 which appeared in April 1944 and featured a new closer-fitting engine cowling, the deletion of the windows behind the cockpit canopy and the removal of the curved front windscreen as fitted to the F6F-3. Provision was made on the F6F-5 for the first time for the aircraft to carry underwing stores, enhancing the aircraft's versatility, and the new variant was in widespread service by the late summer of 1944. A total of 930 F6F-5s were supplied to Britain, where it was designated the Hellcat Mk II. By August 1945 Hellcats equipped 10 RN squadrons, most of which were operating off escort carriers, with HMS *Indomitable* becoming the only fleet carrier to carry the type. Both Nos 1839 and 1844 Squadrons served aboard *Indomitable*, combining to form No. 5 Fighter Wing, which served in the first major attack by the Fleet Air Arm (FAA) against Japanese targets, the January 1945 attack on oil refineries in Sumatra, Indonesia. Subsequently RN Hellcats operating from escort carriers flew in action off the Malayan coast and over Burma (modern-day Myanmar).

In addition to the basic fighter version flown by most British Hellcat squadrons, one unit, No. 888, operated the camera equipped Hellcat FR Mk II, similar to the US F6F-5P, in the reconnaissance role. In addition, 80 examples of the F6F-5N, which featured an AN/APS-6 radar pod mounted on the starboard wing, were supplied to the RN and flown in the night fighting role by No. 891 squadrons. In total Britain received 1,182 Hellcats in the last two years of the war, though the end of hostilities saw the type swiftly disappear from RN service. Nos 892 and 888 Squadron became the last British units to fly the Hellcat and both were disbanded by August 1946.

Grumman Hellcat Mk I

Weight (maximum take-off): 6000kg (13,217lb)
Dimensions: Length 10.17m (33ft 4in), Wingspan 13.08m (42ft 10in), Height 4.4m (14ft 5in)
Powerplant: One 1490kW (2000hp) Pratt & Whitney R-2800-10 Double Wasp 18-cylinder air cooled radial piston engine
Maximum speed: 600km/h (373mph)
Range: 1755km (1090 miles)
Ceiling: 11,438m (37,500ft)
Crew: 1
Armament: Six 12.7mm (0.5in) Browning M2 machine guns fixed firing forward in wings; up to 907kg (2000lb) bombload under wings

Grumman Hellcat Mk I

Few F6Fs received D-Day invasion stripes, as the vast majority of Fleet Air Arm Hellcats served exclusively against the Japanese. An exception to the rule was 800 Naval Air Squadron, which flew the Hellcat Mk I from HMS *Emperor* to cover the landings in southern France in August 1944.

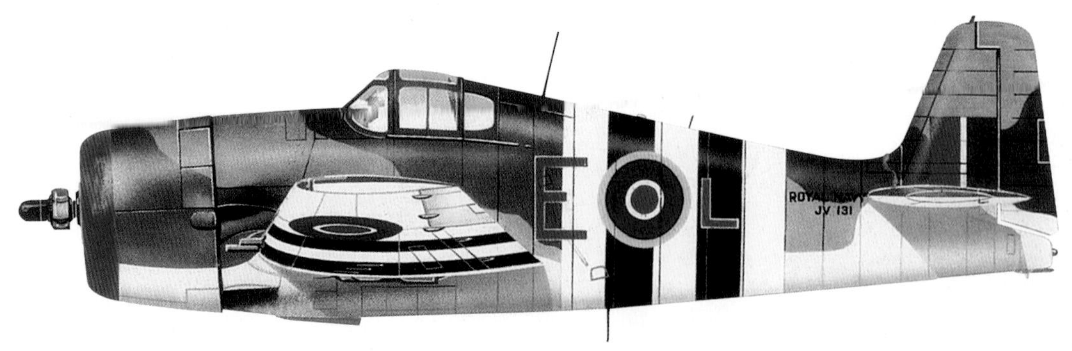

Supermarine Seafire

A naval derivative of the famous Spitfire, the Seafire proved ill-suited to carrier operations, yet despite this impediment it became the most-produced British carrier fighter of World War II, and saw widespread use over its long career.

Supermarine Seafire Mk IIC

MB270 was built at the Supermarine satellite factory at Chattis Hill in Hampshire in December 1942. Its career ended a little under two years later when it was written off following a barrier strike on HMS *Attacker* during operations near Crete.

The Royal Navy (RN) had been keen to adapt the Spitfire for naval use almost as soon as it appeared. As early as 1938 the Admiralty approached Fairey about the possibility of producing a licence-built naval Spitfire but the following year Naval representatives began working with Vickers-Supermarine on the design of an arrestor hook and folding wings for the Spitfire. After the war had begun, the Navy's initial requests to develop a navalised Spitfire were rejected by the Air Ministry, mainly for financial reasons. However, by mid-1941 the Sea Hurricane was considered obsolete and the Grumman Martlet, though proving an excellent fighter in Fleet Air Arm (FAA) service, could not be obtained in sufficient quantity from the US.

The situation changed markedly following a visit by Winston Churchill (1874–1965) to the carrier HMS *Indomitable* in September 1941 revealed how much their fighter component lagged behind contemporary standards. The following month in October 1941, Churchill gave his personal support to Admiralty requests for Spitfires, resulting in work on a carrier-capable Spitfire proceeding rapidly. Indeed, such was the rush to get the Seafire into service that by the time the formal specification and contract for production had been issued in August 1942, most of the initial batch of 48 Seafires had already been delivered.

The name 'Sea Spitfire' was officially adopted but this was immediately, and near universally, shortened to 'Seafire', this subsequently became the official name of the aircraft. The (FAA) also made use of many 'hooked Spitfires' which were standard ex-Royal Air Force (RAF) Spitfires fitted with an arrestor hook but lacking any other naval equipment. These were used for training only and the aircraft were never referred to as Seafires.

Seafire Mk IB

The first Seafire Mk IBs were minimal conversions of RAF Mk VB Spitfires, the most obvious external change being the addition of an A-frame arrestor hook under the rear fuselage, with the weight of the hook balanced by two 12kg (26.5lb) lead weights in the nose, mounted either side of the

---

Supermarine Seafire Mk IIC

Weight (maximum take-off): 3240kg (7145lb)
Dimensions: Length 9.12m (29ft 11in), Wingspan 11.23m (36ft 10in), Height 3.02m (9ft 10in)
Powerplant: One 1055kW (1415hp) Rolls-Royce Merlin 46 V-12 liquid-cooled piston engine
Maximum speed: 555km/h (345mph)
Range: 793km (493 miles)
Ceiling: 9755m (32,000ft)
Crew: 1
Armament: Two 20mm (0.79in) Hispano cannon and four 7.7mm (0.303in) Browning machine guns fixed firing forward in wings; up to 115kg (250lb) bombload under wings

---

Supermarine Seafire F Mk III

The most successful Seafire pilot was Sub Lieutenant Richard Reynolds of 894 Naval Air Squadron. Operating from HMS *Indefatigable*, Reynolds shot down two Mitsubishi A6M Zeroes in PR256 on 31 March 1945.

Supermarine Seafire F Mk III
Weight (maximum take-off): 3280kg (7232lb)
Dimensions: Length 9.2m (30ft 3in), Wingspan 11.23m (36ft 10in), Height 3.49m (11ft 6in)
Powerplant: One 1182kW (1585hp) Rolls-Royce Merlin 55 V-12 liquid-cooled piston engine
Maximum speed: 578km/h (359mph)
Range: 748km (465 miles)
Ceiling: 11,000m (36,000ft)
Crew: 1
Armament: Two 20mm (0.79in) Hispano cannon and four 12.7mm (0.5in) Browning machine guns fixed firing forward in wings; up to 226kg (500lb) bombload or eight 27kg (60llb) rockets under wings

engine. Internal changes included fitting a naval radio and an airspeed indicator calibrated in knots rather than miles per hour. An initial assessment of the Seafire's deck landing characteristics during 1942 rated the aircraft as satisfactory, though concern was raised about the long nose adversely affecting visibility on approach.

As the trials were progressing, work was going ahead on the development of the Seafire Mk II, a slightly more thoroughly navalised aircraft fitted with catapult spools to allow for catapult launch if necessary. These were new build airframes rather than conversions but still very much a derivative of the Spitfire V, featuring 20mm (0.79in) cannon in the 'universal' wing and production aircraft were designated Seafire Mk IIC, the 'C' denoting the cannon armament.

Deck problems

The first unit to convert to Seafires, No. 807 Squadron, embarked on HMS *Furious* during August 1942 and other units converted swiftly. By the end of September 1942 a further four units had re-equipped. The Seafire made its combat debut during the Operation Torch landings, where it scored its initial aerial victories, the first on 8 November 1942 when a Vichy French Martin 167 was shot down. The Seafire had inherited the Spitfire's excellent handling in the air but quickly gained an unfortunate reputation during operational use for fragility on deck. The aircraft had a tendency to 'float' on landing before touching down, which was of little concern on an airfield but meant that the Seafire regularly floated over all the arrestor wires on a carrier to crash into the crash barrier.

Even when an arrestor wire was caught, the position of the hook under the fuselage resulted in a sharp nose down pitch as the aircraft decelerated, and this combined with the Spitfire's minimal airscrew clearance often caused propeller blades to strike the deck and render the aircraft unserviceable.

To make matters worse, the undercarriage was relatively weak and prone to collapse. During the Salerno landings, low wind over the deck, poor visibility and inexperience with the type combined to exacerbate the

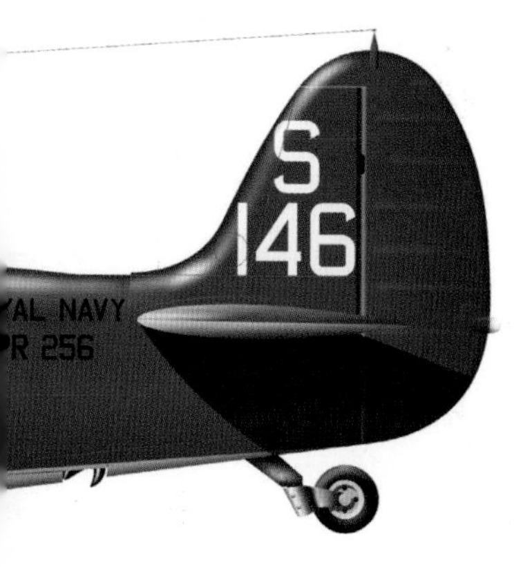

Seafire's problematic deck landing ability. This resulted in the horrific total of 73 aircraft from the original force of 105 lost or seriously damaged to non-combat causes over the course of only three days, nearly all due to deck landing incidents. Despite this, the Seafire's combat performance whilst airborne was superior to any other available naval fighter and work continued to mitigate the worst of its deck landing issues.

Seafire Mk III

Meanwhile, collaborative work by Supermarine and the Ministry of Aircraft Production resulted in the appearance of a folding wing for the Seafire. The wings folded vertically upwards but to allow clearance within the limited height of standard British carrier hangars, the wingtips folded separately resulting in a 'Z' shape when folded and viewed from the front. The first production Mk IIC was rebuilt with folding wings in December 1942 with flight trials beginning in the following month and the aircraft was quickly ordered into production as the Seafire Mk III. The first aircraft began to be delivered in April 1943 consisting of three subtypes, the standard F Mk III, fighter-reconnaissance FR Mk III which featured provision for cameras in the rear fuselage, both powered by the Rolls-Royce Merlin 55, and the L Mk III, intended for low-altitude operations, utilised the Merlin 55M driving a four-blade propeller. By now deck landing issues had improved somewhat but the Seafire was still more susceptible to accidents than contemporary US-built carrier fighters.

Pacific War

The majority of the Seafire III's service took place fighting the Japanese with the British Pacific Fleet (BPF) where the aircraft's short range began to prove a liability, though the adaptation at unit level of 90 gallon Kittyhawk drop tanks, fitted under the fuselage, improved the situation.

With the decline of enemy air activity, the Seafire was increasingly used for ground attack but it proved effective against Japanese aircraft when they did make an appearance and the last confirmed air-to-air victory of the war was achieved by a Seafire L Mk III flown by Sub Lieutenant JG Murphy on the morning of 15 August 1945.

Late-war Seafire development had concentrated on adapting the Rolls-Royce Griffon-powered Spitfire into a carrier aircraft and this work resulted in the Seafire Mk XV which just failed to enter service before Victory over Japan (VJ) day.

Supermarine Seafire F Mk III

An unusual variant, the Mk III (Hybrid) utilised the Merlin 55 engine and four-blade airscrew of the Mk III mated to the non-folding wing of the Mk IIC. Only around 30 were built and LR792 (picture here) served aboard HMS *Battler* in the Indian Ocean during June 1944.

A folding wing revolutionized the Seafire's practicality at sea, allowing more aircraft to be carried in the confined space of a carrier. The low height of British carrier hangars required the wingtips to fold as well, demonstrated here by a Griffon powered Seafire Mk XV.

Unfortunately the Seafire XV displayed handling problems in the air and, more seriously, very poor behaviour on deck, being prone to a potentially uncontrollable swing on take-off and fitted with an inadequate undercarriage, inherited from the Seafire III despite the much greater weight of the new aircraft, which regularly collapsed. Despite this it served with the RN, Royal Canadian Navy (RCN) and French Navy.

To counter these issues, the much improved Mk XVII (later F Mk 17) was developed, which was fitted with a bubble canopy, before the definitive FR Mk 47 entered service in 1948. This variant saw combat over Malaya (modern-day Malaysia) and Korea before its retirement in the mid-1950s.

Fairey Firefly

The Fairey Firefly was a much more formidable aircraft than the Fulmar that it replaced and was heavily committed to operations during the last two years of the war, subsequently remaining in service well into the Cold War.

The specification that led to the Firefly was issued shortly before the war calling for an aircraft of the seemingly outmoded two-seat concept. Using the Fulmar as a basis, designer HE 'Charlie' Chaplin drew up a design based around the new Rolls-Royce Griffon engine, and although the original specification stipulated the fitting of a power operated gun turret, this requirement was dropped following the underwhelming combat performance of the Blackburn Roc.

A new specification, N.5/40, was written around Fairey's proposed design and the Ministry of Aircraft Production ordered 200 off the drawing board after Fairey had presented a mock-up of the aircraft during June 1940 with the first three production machines intended to be used as prototypes. The first Firefly made its maiden flight on 22 December 1941.

Test flights

Testing proved remarkably trouble free, and though the Firefly needed significant physical effort to perform aerobatics, especially to a pilot used to the beautifully light controls of the Seafire, the aircraft was considered agile. The patented Fairey-Youngman flaps allowed for excellent low-speed handling and during tests in the US during 1944 the Firefly I was demonstrated to be able to out-turn the F6F Hellcat. However, with a top speed of 509km/h (316mph), the Firefly was undeniably slow, mainly as a result of the weight penalty imposed by the requirement to carry a second crew member and associated equipment. The chin-mounted radiator also imposed a considerable drag penalty and the radiators were moved to a more aerodynamic position on the wing leading edge in the next major production version, the postwar F Mk 4. Deck landing trials took place during the summer of 1943 and in October the first frontline Navy unit, No. 1770 Squadron, formed on the type. The Firefly's first major combat mission took place on 17 July 1944 when the squadron took part in an attack on the German battleship Tirpitz anchored at Kåfjord in Norway.

Pacific action

The bulk of the Firefly's wartime career took place in the Pacific, however, beginning when No. 1770 Squadron

Fairey Firefly Mk I
Weight (maximum take-off): 6375kg (14,054lb)
Dimensions: Length 11.45m (37ft 7in), Wingspan 13.6m (44ft 6in), Height 4.15m (13ft 7in)
Powerplant: One 970kW (1735hp) Rolls-Royce Griffon IIB V-12 liquid-cooled piston engine
Maximum speed: 509km/h (316mph)
Range: 2100km (1305 miles)
Ceiling: 8535m (28,000ft)
Crew: 2
Armament: Four 20mm Hispano cannon fixed firing forward in wings; up to 907kg (2000lb) bombload or eight 27kg (60lb) rockets under wings

Fairey Firefly Mk I
The first production Fireflies such as Z2035 featured a low profile canopy, but the restricted headroom this provided led to the introduction of a taller canopy that was fitted to the majority of Fireflies.

embarked on HMS *Indefatigable* in December 1944. Less than a month later the Fireflies would lead Operation Meridian, a series of successful strikes against oil refineries on Sumatra, Indonesia. During the course of these operations the Firefly scored its first aerial victories, when two Nakajima Ki-43s were destroyed by Fireflies. The aircraft subsequently undertook an intense period of operations with the British Pacific Fleet (BPF), culminating in strikes on the Japanese mainland, during the course of which the Firefly became the first British aircraft to fly over Tokyo. Encounters with Japanese aircraft were relatively rare during the late war period but one pilot, Sub Lt Phil Stott, managed to become an 'ace' on the type by scoring five victories.

Although successful by day, development of a night fighter variant of the Firefly proved difficult. The purpose-built NF II utilised British AI Mk X radar, which required a radome on each wing and an extended fuselage, suffered from stability issues. None of the 37 built entered service, nearly all subsequently being converted to standard Mk Is. A better solution was utilised in the NF Mk I, which used an American AN/APS-4 radar mounted in a fibreglass pod on a ventral rack and this variant saw service over Europe before the end of the war though no successful interceptions were made. Eventually sufficient AN/APS-4 units became available for the radar to be fitted to day fighters as well, being designated the FR I. The first unit, No. 816 Squadron, received FR Is as a replacement for the Barracuda in July 1945 but saw no action before Victory over Japan (VJ) day.

Post-war the aircraft was widely used in its original role as well as a trainer, anti-submarine aircraft, target tug and drone controller. Fireflies operated for the duration of the Korean War and were still flying attack operations as late as 1962 in the Royal Netherlands Navy (RNN) service against Indonesian forces.

The Firefly served long after the end of World War II with several air arms. These Australian Firefly AS.6s were pictured during the catapult launch procedure on HMAS *Sydney*.

Hawker Sea Fury

Although it failed to enter service during World War II, the Fury represented the zenith of the line of fighters directly developed from the Typhoon of 1939. In naval form as the Sea Fury, it became the final piston engine fighter design to enter British service.

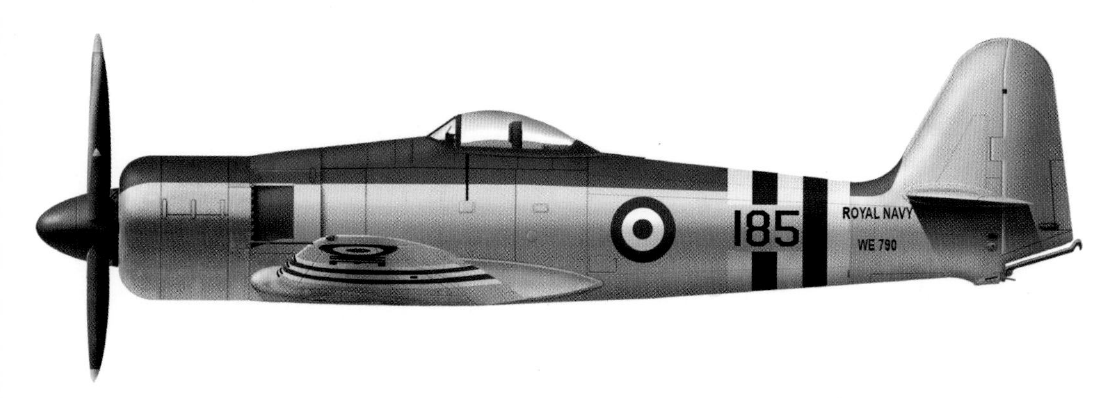

Hawker Sea Fury FB Mk 11

Despite the Royal Navy markings on the rear fuselage, WE790 was actually on the strength of the Royal Australian Navy, operating from the carrier HMAS *Sydney* during the Korean War.

Hawker Sea Fury FB Mk 11

Weight (maximum take-off): 6645kg (14,650lb)
Dimensions: Length 10.57m (34ft 8in), Wingspan 11.7m (38ft 5in), Height 4.84m (15ft 11in)
Powerplant: One 1850kW (2480hp) Bristol Centaurus 18-cylinder air-cooled radial piston engine
Maximum speed: 740km/h (470mph)
Range: 1260km (780 miles)
Ceiling: 10,900m (35,800ft)
Crew: 1
Armament: Four 20mm (0.79in) Hispano cannon fixed firing forward in wings; up to 907kg (2000lb) bombload or 16 7.62mm (3in) rockets under wings

---

The Fury was developed as a lightened version of the Hawker Tempest, influenced in part by the Focke Wulf Fw 190, an example of which was captured in mid-1942, and seeking to stem the weight growth of the sturdy Typhoon and Tempest. The Fury featured wings attached directly to the fuselage, discarding the centre section as fitted to the Tempest thus reducing weight and shortening the span and the fuselage now featured a slightly humped profile to improve pilot view over the nose. The Fury was tested with the Rolls-Royce Griffon and Napier Sabre, but first flew powered by the Bristol Centaurus on 1 September 1944.

Successful flight testing led to an order for 200 land-based aircraft as well as a further 200 navalised Sea Furies to be developed by Boulton Paul Aircraft. The Sea Fury was flown for the first time on 21 February 1945, though the definitive second prototype with five-bladed propeller and folding wings only flew in October 1945. Just before the end of the war a Fury prototype powered by the Napier Sabre VII attained 777km/h (483mph), the fastest speed ever achieved by a Hawker piston-engined fighter. However, the end of hostilities saw development cease and Royal Air Force (RAF) production orders cancelled, as well as Boulton Paul Aircraft's involvement with the Sea Fury.

Meanwhile, Hawker continued development of the naval variant and the initial production version, the F Mk X, entered service in February 1947. The Sea Fury would ultimately equip 30 British squadrons – 615 of the total 864 built served with the Royal Navy (RN), most being the FB Mk 11 version tailored for fighter bomber operations. Sea Furies saw action during the Korean War, managing to record a 'kill' against a MiG-15 jet fighter and the type eventually retired from units of the Royal Naval Volunteer Reserve (RNVR) in 1955. Export Sea Furies served with 10 other air arms worldwide and became one of only a few aircraft to have scored victories on both sides of the Cold War, when in 1961 Cuban Sea Furies shot down two Central Intelligence Agency (CIA) operated B-26s during the Bay of Pigs invasion.

JET FIGHTERS

The gas turbine engine had been developed secretly and in parallel by both Germany and the United Kingdom, with the first jet fighters of both nations entering service within weeks of each other. The German-built Messerschmitt Me 262 entered service first and was initially built in much larger numbers, but the Meteor and Vampire became arguably the most successful of the first generation jet fighters.

The following aircraft are featured in this chapter:

- Gloster Meteor
- de Havilland Vampire

The first British jet fighter and the Allies' only jet aircraft to undertake combat operations during World War II, the Gloster Meteor entered service with No. 616 Squadron in July 1944. Photographed in January 1945 at Manston, Kent, this aircraft EE227 was later re-engined with Rolls-Royce Trent turboprops, becoming the world's first turboprop-powered aircraft to fly on 20 September 1945.

Gloster Meteor

The only Allied jet to be used in combat during World War II, the Meteor was, by its very nature, a groundbreaking machine. A more conservative design than its German Me 262 counterpart, it proved an excellent basis for future development.

Gloster Aircraft Company was contracted to build the first two British research aircraft powered by jet engines and as a result had forged close links with the Power Jets company that had been formed to develop and build Frank Whittle's (1907–96) revolutionary gas turbine engine. The Gloster E.28/39 became the first British jet aircraft to fly on 15 May 1941, and although it was destined to remain a research aircraft, George Carter (1889–1969), chief designer at Gloster had by that time been working for several months on the design of a single-seat jet-propelled fighter. Due to the low power output of early jet engines, a twin-jet layout was decided upon, as it had been with the Me 262 in Germany and P-59 in the US.

Plans for the fighter were submitted to the Air Ministry in August 1940 and Specification F.9/40 was issued based on Carter's design. No fewer than 12 prototypes were ordered, though this was later reduced to eight, and the aircraft was to be named 'Thunderbolt', soon changed to 'Meteor' after the initial name was adopted for the Republic P-47. Such was the Ministry's enthusiasm for the design that 300 production aircraft were ordered in August 1941, nearly two years before the aircraft would make its first flight.

Engine development

Apart from its powerplant, the Meteor was a fairly conventional fighter (although it was the first British fighter to be fitted with a tricycle undercarriage) and it was engine delays that dictated the slow pace of the programme. The engine intended for the Meteor, the Power Jets W.2B, was to be built by the Rover Car company but relations between the two companies were strained and progress was slow until development was transferred to Rolls-Royce which eventually produced the design as the 'Welland'.

Before a production W.2B was cleared for flight however, other companies had built their own gas turbine designs and the design of the Meteor, with its separate engine nacelles, lent itself to fitting alternative engines with relative simplicity. The first Meteor to fly was the fifth prototype powered by the Halford H.1, which became the de Havilland Goblin, making its first flight on 5 March 1943. The first aircraft powered by Rover-built

Gloster Meteor F Mk III

Weight (maximum take-off): 6559kg (14,460lb)
Dimensions: Length 12.57m (41ft 3in), Wingspan 13.11m (43ft), Height 3.96 m (13ft)
Powerplant: Two Rolls-Royce Derwent I centrifugal flow turbojet engines, each rated at 8.9kN (2000lb) thrust
Maximum speed: 837km/h (515mph)
Range: 2160km (1350 miles)
Ceiling: 13,400m (43,950ft)
Crew: 1
Armament: Four 20mm (0.79in) Hispano cannon fixed, firing forward in nose

Gloster Meteor F Mk III

No. 616 Squadron was the first RAF jet unit and by December 1944 was beginning to receive the improved F Mk III. EE246 features the original short engine nacelles – the lengthened nacelles of later Mk IIIs were found to improve the top speed at altitude by 120km/h (75mph).

Gloster Meteor F Mk IV

The Mk IV had flown as early as May 1945, but did not enter service until after the end of the war. Serving with No. 600 Squadron of the Royal Auxiliary Air Force in 1951, RA381 displays the return to colourful 1930s style squadron markings of the postwar RAF.

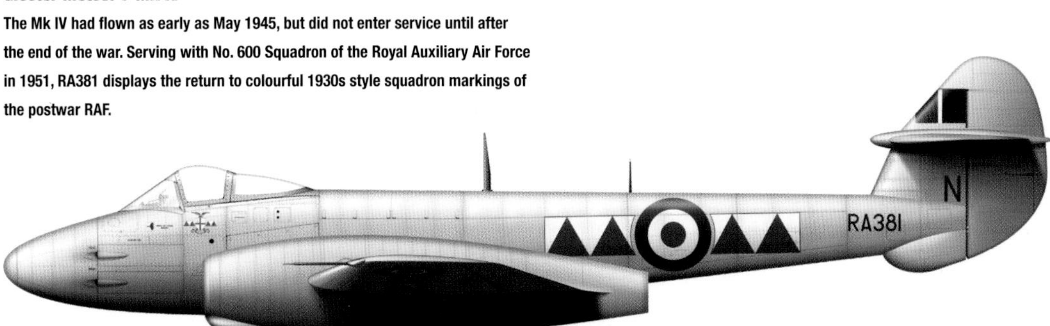

W.2Bs flew in July 1943, and a third engine type, the axial flow Metrovick F.2, flew in November 1943. The first batch of 20 Meteor F Mk Is were however powered by the Rolls-Royce Welland and the first production aircraft flew on 12 January 1944. The Meteor F Mk II was to be powered by the more powerful Halford H.1, though the de Havilland Vampire programme subsequently received precedence for this engine. No Meteor IIs were produced, meaning the next Meteor variant would be the F Mk III which featured a sliding bubble canopy, greater fuel capacity and Rolls-Royce Derwent engines, a much improved and more powerful derivative of the Welland, though delays to this power unit meant the first 15 Meteor IIIs were fitted with the earlier engine.

First jet squadron

On 12 July 1944 the first Meteor was delivered to an operational unit, No. 616 Squadron, which was fully equipped with the fighter by the end of August to become the Royal Air Force's first jet squadron. By this time the V-1 flying bomb campaign had been launched against Britain and the Meteor, capable of high speed at low level, was well suited to intercept the missiles. The first V-1 to fall victim to a Meteor was destroyed on 4 August 1944, when Flying Officer T.D. Dean used his wing to 'topple' the V-1 after his guns jammed. By early 1945, No. 616 Squadron was based in Belgium as part of the RAF's Second Tactical Air Force (2TAF) and a second unit, No. 504 Squadron, equipped with the Derwent-powered Meteor III, also began flying operations in Europe before the end of the war. The Meteors were used almost entirely for ground attack during this period and the aircraft were painted in an overall white scheme for easy identification by ground troops, who generally assumed any jet-propelled aircraft were German.

On 17 May 1945 the first Meteor Mk IV took to the air which, although it was destined not to enter operational service before the end of the conflict, featured a pair of Derwent V engines, which finally provided sufficient thrust for the Meteor to demonstrate its true potential. This and subsequent marks saw operational service for the next two decades or so in a wide variety of roles including night fighting, training, and reconnaissance, and with 3,947 built, the Meteor eventually became the UK's most produced jet aircraft. The last RAF examples were used as target tugs and served until 1982.

Gloster Meteor F Mk IV

Weight (maximum take-off): 6598kg (14,545lb)
Dimensions: Length 12.6m (41ft), Wingspan 11.33m (37ft 2in), Height 3.96m (13ft)
Powerplant: Two Rolls-Royce Derwent V centrifugal flow turbojet engines, each rated at 15.57kN (3500lb) thrust
Maximum speed: 950km/h (590mph)
Range (with external tanks): 980km (713 miles)
Ceiling: 13,564m (44,500ft)
Crew: 1
Armament: Four 20mm (0.79in) Hispano cannon fixed, firing forward in nose; up to 907kg (2000lb) bombload

de Havilland Vampire

On the cusp of entering service at the end of the war, the Vampire was Britain's second jet fighter design and made history as the first pure jet aircraft to land and take off from an aircraft carrier.

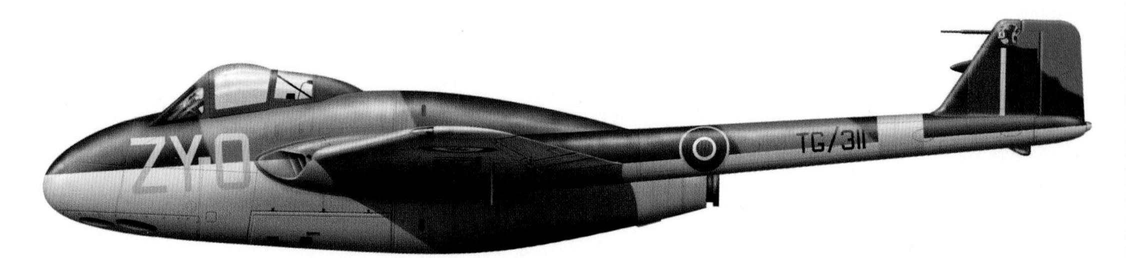

In April 1942, the H.1 turbojet designed by engineering consultant Frank Halford (1894–1955) ran for the first time. A simpler design than the Whittle designed W.2B, the potential of the engine was recognised by the de Havilland Engine Company which began to scheme a fighter design around it, subsequently purchasing Halford's company, making him chairman of the de Havilland Engine Company, and changing the name of the engine from H-1 to 'Goblin'. The D.H.100 fighter design crystallised as a twin boom aircraft largely constructed of moulded plywood, as pioneered in the Mosquito, with the engine and cockpit in a central pod, allowing the jet-pipe to be as short as possible and avoid thrust losses as a result.

First flown on 26 September 1943, the aircraft was originally known as the 'Spider Crab' but was renamed the 'Vampire' by the time an order for 120 aircraft was placed in May 1944. Production was to be handled by the English Electric company as the de Havilland Engine Company was completely committed to Mosquito production. The first production Vampire F Mk I flew on 20 April 1945 powered by a Goblin I and with an unpressurised cockpit, though later Mk Is featured a Goblin III engine and cockpit pressurisation. Tested against a Spitfire Mk XIV, one of the most formidable of late war piston-engined fighters, the Vampire I proved not only to be 145km/h (90mph) faster, but also able to out-turn and outperform the Spitfire in all parameters except rate of roll, thanks to its light weight and low wing loading.

Sadly for the Royal Air Force (RAF), sufficient quantities of the Vampire did not appear in time to allow the aircraft to enter service before the end of the war but the aircraft went on to serve in 32 air arms worldwide. In total 3268 were built in the UK, Australia, France, India and Italy, a large proportion of which were two-seat trainers.

Naval interest in the aircraft led to the development of a carrier variant with an arrestor hook contained in a fairing above the jet pipe. Converted from one of the early production F Is, test pilot Eric Brown (1920–2016) landed this Sea Vampire aboard HMS *Ocean* on 3 December 1945, the first deck landing by a jet-propelled aircraft; later the same day Brown made the first jet take-off from a carrier in the same aircraft.

de Havilland Vampire F Mk I

In March 1946, No. 247 Sqn relinquished its Hawker Tempests to become the first unit to operate the Vampire F Mk I. The squadron operated successive marks of the Vampire, until re-equipping with the Hawker Hunter. TG311 was later transferred to the French air force.

---

de Havilland Vampire F Mk I

Weight (maximum take-off): 4758kg (10,480lb)

Dimensions: Length 9.37m (30ft 9in), Wingspan 12.19m (40ft), Height 2.69m (8ft 10in)

Powerplant: One de Havilland Goblin 2 centrifugal flow turbojet engine rated at 13.8kN (3100lb) thrust

Maximum speed: 869km/h (540mph)

Range: 1175km (730 miles)

Ceiling: 12,192m (40,000ft)

Crew: 1

Armament: Four 20mm (0.79in) Hispano cannon, fixed firing forward in underside of nose

---

de Havilland Vampire F Mk III

Detached to Malta in 1952, this Mk III of No. 601 Squadron is painted in the standard high-speed silver finish adopted for day fighters. The postwar Mk III introduced the provision for external underwing fuel tanks, as well as reshaped vertical tails and square-cut wingtips.

de Havilland Vampire F Mk III

Weight (maximum take-off): 5429kg (11,970lb)
Dimensions: Length 9.37m (30ft 9in),Wingspan 12.19m (40ft), Height 2.69m (8ft 10in)
Powerplant: One de Havilland Goblin 2 centrifugal flow turbojet engine rated at 13.8kN (3100lb) thrust
Maximum speed: 855km/h (531mph)
Range: 1690km (1050 miles)
Ceiling: 13,259m (43,500ft)
Crew: 1
Armament: Four 20mm (0.79in) Hispano cannon, fixed firing forward in underside of nose

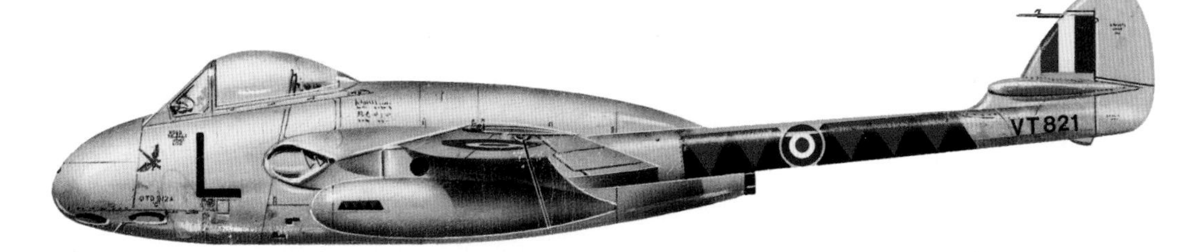

de Havilland Vampire FB Mk 5

Developed as a fighter bomber, the Mk 5 featured further clipped wings for improved handling at low altitude and hardpoints for stores. WA235 served with 112 Sqn in 1953 and wears the Squadron's shark mouth marking, first used on the Tomahawk over a decade earlier.

de Havilland Vampire FB Mk 5

Weight (maximum take-off): 5606kg (12,360lb)
Dimensions: four 20mm (0.79in) Hispano cannon, fixed firing forward in underside of nose; up to 907kg (2000lb) bombload or eight RP-3 rockets
Powerplant: One de Havilland Goblin 2 centrifugal flow turbojet engine rated at 13.8kN (3100lb) thrust
Maximum speed: 861km/h (535mph)
Range (with external tanks): 1843km (1145 miles)
Ceiling: 12,192m (40,000ft)
Crew: 1
Armament: Four 20mm (0.79in) Hispano cannon, fixed firing forward in underside of nose; up to 907kg (2000lb) bombload or eight RP-3 rockets

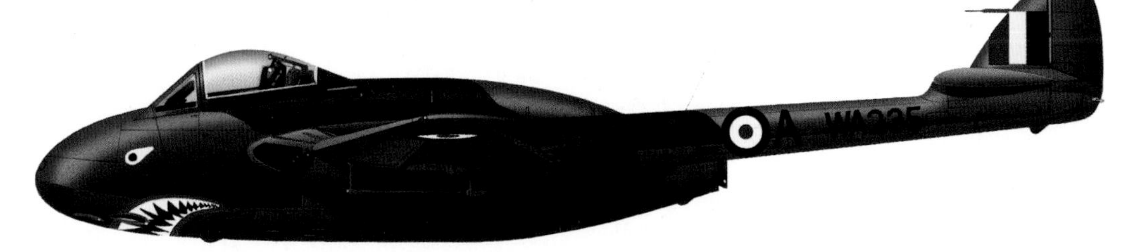

Index

Picture Credits

PHOTOGRAPHS:

AirSeaLand Images: 42, 48, 88, 91, 94, 100, 106, 114, 116

Alamy: 97 (Chronicle)

Amber Books: 6, 7, 8, 20, 36, 39, 53, 64, 67, 76

Public Domain: 43, 118

ARTWORKS:

Amber Books: 11–13 all, 21 all, 24–28 all, 33 all, 35 all, 37 all, 40 all, 44 both, 47, 49 both, 51, 54–56 all, 60/61, 68–70 all, 74–75 all, 80 top, 82–86 all, 89, 90, 92, 96, 98, 99, 103–105 all, 107, 110, 115, 123 both

Ronny Bar: 29, 31, 32

Teasel Studios: 10, 30, 34, 38, 41, 45, 46, 52, 62, 71 bottom, 73 bottom, 78, 79, 80 bottom, 81, 111–113 all, 117, 121

Rolando Ugolini: 5, 14–19 all, 22, 23 both, 50, 57–59 all, 63–66 all, 71 top, 72, 73 top, 101–102 all, 108, 109, 120, 122